Praise for Innocent Spouse

"Life isn't what it appears to be in *Innocent Spouse*. . . . Husband's sudden death, learning of his secrets, put [the] author on [a] path to self-sufficiency."

—*TODAY*

"Not only was her castle built on sand, it was made of smoke and mirrors."

—JACQUELYN MITCHARD, *New York Times* bestselling author of *Deep End of the Ocean*

"A page-turning, name-dropping memoir."

—*INSTYLE*

"A searing personal journey where the pages fall away from one's hand like meat from a bone."

—DAVID BALDACCI, *New York Times* bestselling author of *Simple Genius*

"A moving story of posthumous betrayal, and of survival."

—CHRISTOPHER BUCKLEY, national bestselling author of *Thank You for Smoking*

"A dishy new memoir."

—*WOWOWOW*

"Inspiring."

—*BOOKLIST*

"An honest telling of a woman betrayed by her husband whom she had loved and her determination to protect herself and her son."

—*PUBLISHERS WEEKLY*

"Excellent recounting of the author's lost decade, during which she rebuilt her life, became self-sufficient, and found peace following her husband's deceit."

—*KIRKUS REVIEWS*

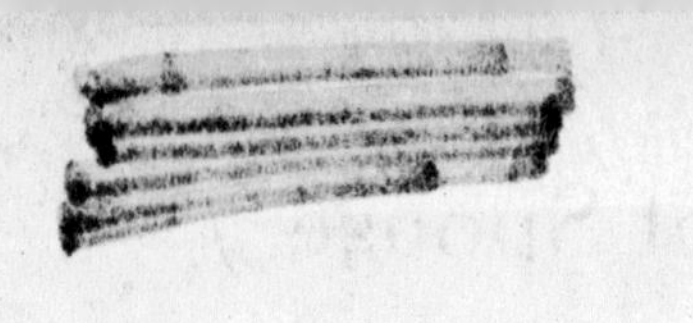

Innocent Spouse

[*A Memoir*]

Carol Ross Joynt

Broadway Paperbacks
New York

Published in the United States by Broadway Paperbacks, an imprint of the Crown Publishing Group, a division of Random House, Inc., New York.
www.crownpublishing.com

Originally published in hardcover in slightly different form by Crown Publishers, an imprint of the Crown Publishing Group, a division of Random House, Inc., New York, in 2011.

Library of Congress Cataloging-in-Publication Data
Joynt, Carol Ross.
Innocent spouse: a memoir / Carol Ross Joynt.
p. cm.
1. Joynt, Carol Ross. 2. Women journalists—United States—Biography. 3. Journalists—United States—Biography. 4. Businesswomen—Washington (D.C.)—Biography. 5. Nathans (Washington, D.C.). 6. Joynt, Carol Ross—Marriage. 7. Joynt, Howard, III. 8. Husbands—Death—Case studies. 9. Husband and wife—Taxation—United States—Case studies. 10. Washington (D.C.)—Biography. I. Title.
CT275.J926A3 2011
975.3092—dc22
[B] 2010045602

ISBN: 978-0-307-59211-8
eISBN: 978-0-307-59212-5

Printed in the United States of America

Book design by Lauren Dong
Cover design by Erin Schell
Cover photography: courtesy of the author (wedding photograph);
Broken Flower *by Diane Wesson © Special Photographers Archive/Bridgeman Art Library; Bridgeman Art Library (background)*

10 9 8 7 6 5 4 3 2 1

First Paperback Edition

For Spencer

I thought I was your guide, but as it turned out,

you were my guide, too.

ONE

Chapter 1

We were stuck in heavy Friday afternoon rush-hour traffic on M Street, the main thoroughfare in Georgetown. It was January. Everyone was headed home at the same time. I slammed the horn at the slowpoke ahead of me every time he cost me another yellow light. I wasn't panicked, but I was frustrated. We needed to go, not sit at a light. From the backseat my husband, Howard, groaned at every stop, start, lane change, and pothole. He was on his back, gasping for breath, and braced himself with his arms.

We did not talk except for my repeated question, "How are you?" And his faint repeated answer, "Every time you hit a pothole it's a stabbing pain." I listened to the all-news radio station to make sure my route was clear. The announcers' voices droned through news updates, commercial breaks, two-minute interviews, and weather. In a way it was so utterly ordinary—the car, the traffic, the potholes, the radio. We might have been on our way to the supermarket. Except we weren't. We were headed to the emergency room at Sibley Hospital, and I was focused like a laser on the road.

When we pulled into the drive I stopped at the door and jumped out. "I'm gonna get a nurse. I'll be right back." My voice was urgent but calm. Calm enough, anyway. I ran inside, through the lobby and to the desk. "I need a nurse! My husband's in the car. He can barely breathe."

The nurse opened the back door, did a quick survey of Howard, and asked, "Can you walk in or do you need a wheelchair?" He said he could walk. We both helped him out of the car. At six foot three he would have towered over us but he was hunched over in pain. His face was pale. His usually slicked-back silver hair was in disarray. His trousers and sweater were loose.

The nurse bolstered Howard with her shoulder under his arm.

Their pace was slow, careful. I left him with her. By the time I parked, gave the admissions clerk the necessary insurance information, and found Howard in the warren of examining rooms, there was an oxygen mask over his face, an IV in his arm, and a young doctor and two nurses hovering over him. His eyes locked with mine. I saw fear. My gut tightened.

"Your husband has bad pneumonia," the doctor said, shoving an X-ray into a wall-mounted light box. His tone was anxious, even a little frazzled. He pointed at the black-and-white picture of my husband's lungs, one quite obviously cloudy and white. "One lung is fully compromised," he said, pointing to the film like a teacher lecturing a class. "We can't let it spread to the other. We're sending him up to the ICU. We have work to do."

I'd brought in a time bomb, but I consoled myself that Howard could talk and his eyes were open. Heck, I thought, people survive pneumonia all the time. Pneumonia is fixable. Maybe he'll be in the hospital a couple of days. He'll learn his lesson about avoiding the doctor until too late.

The medical team disappeared through the drawn white curtain. We were alone. Howard asked for water. "Evian, please."

How sick can he be if he's picky about the water? I stood as close to him as possible, careful not to disturb the tubes and wires. "I'll get some bottled water later. D.C. water will do for now," I said. "This looks like a close call. Thank God I didn't stay longer in New York. Not that it matters now, but I'll never understand why you told me you'd seen Dr. Goldstein." He didn't respond but slowly closed his eyes. He didn't want to hear about it. So I made upbeat small talk. Even though it was loud and crowded in the emergency room, and the curtain was regularly pulled back and closed again by busy nurses and technicians, the moment felt oddly intimate, personal, another experience in our journey together. He was scared and I was there to help take care of him, to calm his fear.

I found a wall phone outside Howard's treatment bay. My first call was to Howard's sister, Martha, in New Castle, Delaware. "I'm at Sibley. Howard has bad pneumonia. That's all I know. They're sending him to the ICU."

She didn't ask any questions. "I'm on my way. It'll probably be three hours."

I called my office at CNN's *Larry King Live,* and talked to the executive producer. "You're not gonna believe this. I'm at Sibley. Howard has bad pneumonia. I found him flat on his back in bed when I got home from New York."

She was alarmed. "What can we do?"

"I don't know," I said. "I'll get back to you."

I made the same call to Nathans, Howard's restaurant in Georgetown. "What can I do?" the manager asked.

"I don't know. Stand by. I'll get back to you."

My last call was the toughest. Home. As we were leaving for the hospital, Howard had paused only long enough to poke his head in on our smiling five-year-old son, playing on the floor of his room with the babysitter. "I'll be back, big guy," he said. I gave the babysitter the update and asked to speak to Spencer.

There was something about that little voice at the other end of the line that underscored my altered reality. Spencer seemed so far removed from the drama involving his parents, but it would soon become his drama, too. Blessedly, I suppose, he was too young to understand where I was, what had happened, and what it meant, and therefore at this point it could not scare him. "I'm at the hospital with Daddy," I said. "There are lots of nice doctors and nurses."

"Mommy, are the doctors going to fix him?" He knew Howard was not well. After all, for the four days I was away Howard had been home in bed.

"Yes, sweetie. The doctors are going to make him all better. You should have your dinner and get ready for bed, and I'll be there as soon as possible."

"Okay, Mommy. Can I talk to Daddy?"

"Soon, but not right now. He's taking a nap. That's how they fix him."

"Okay, Mommy."

Howard was whisked up to the ICU. Bright lights flooded the room. There were two windows, one with the blinds shut, the other facing the nursing station. There was a lot of equipment, most of it hooked up to him. One of the machines beeped constantly, flashing numbers. He had an IV, possibly two. He was in a gown, under white sheets, propped up by pillows. Was I afraid? No, not then. Not yet. Howard was awake, after all. He talked to me through his oxygen mask. I wet washcloths with cold water, squeezed them out, and pressed them against his forehead. There were lots of people fussing with him. Something was being done. I said to myself, "This is bad for him but routine for them. He'll be here a couple nights and then home."

What did I know?

We had gotten to the hospital at five in the afternoon. Very quickly it was pushing nine. The nurse called in a new doctor, who arrived in shirtsleeves and tie but no jacket or white coat. He was friendly but instantly serious when he looked at Howard's charts and machines. His one good lung was not absorbing enough oxygen. In a whisper, out of Howard's range, I asked the nurse, "Is this serious?"

She nodded. "We've got to get his blood oxygen up." She pointed to an "85" on the monitor.

"So he's in serious condition?"

Her voice went flat. "No, he's critical."

I turned to the sink and splashed water on my face. It was the only way to hide the rush of tears. The fear arrived with a jolt and made me queasy, woozy, unsteady. My breath stopped somewhere near my breastbone. My mouth was dry. But I couldn't let myself become unhinged in front of Howard. Composure was essential. I inhaled as deeply as I could, wiped my face, wet another washcloth, turned, and went to him, pressing it against his cheeks and brow. I looked him in the eyes, the beautiful brown eyes I'd known and loved for twenty years. I could see the same fear. "This is no way to spend Friday night," he said.

"It's going to be okay," I said. "You're in good hands and Martha is on her way. She'll be here so I can go check on Spencer. You won't be alone."

The doctor called me outside. His hands were on his hips, head tilted down toward me, expression engaged but grim. "We have to sedate him. We have to get a tube down into his good lung to get more oxygen into him. I don't know if it will work but we've got to give it a try." He didn't call it life support, but that's what it was. I behaved calmly, but by then I was functioning on pure adrenaline.

Back at Howard's bedside, the doctor explained the procedure to him while the nurses prepared to put him under. No one offered us a moment alone, nor did we ask for one. It didn't seem necessary. This was still so simple. They would sedate him, do their work, fix him, and he'd be better. I kissed him awkwardly on the arm or shoulder—whatever part of him it was I could reach—and asked if there was anything I could bring him from home, anything he wanted me to do. His look was woeful. "I want to be back in the Caribbean."

"Yes," I said. "Me, too." I blew him another kiss, grabbed my coat, and headed out the door.

Chapter 2

A MONTH EARLIER WE had been sailing in the Caribbean on a sixty-three-foot sloop. Her sails were up and full. She yawed softly. The air smelled salty sweet. During a night sail the water splashed the hull and spilled away in twinkling phosphorescence. As I lay on the deck, the rich indigo of the sky mesmerized me. Howard was beside me, his hand in mine. Spencer slept in his bunk below. Stars crowded the sky, brilliant and wondrous. The breeze, a steady twelve to fifteen knots, filled the big jib. The boat was following a northerly course, away from the sandbar island of Barbuda toward the more volcanic and mountainous St. Bart's. We could see the shadowed hulk of St. Kitts on the western horizon.

I knew that sky and I knew those waters. I'd lived in the Caribbean for a while before I met Howard, and after we married we returned together many times. This was our first trip with our son. To our delight he took to the surf and sand and steel drums like an island native. He responded to the motion of the boat, the pitch and roll and heel, like a seasoned deckhand. I sighed and squeezed Howard's hand. We shared so much happiness—our love for each other, our son, that night, that place, and those lovely, soothing sounds. My head found its familiar spot on his shoulder.

Howard was the embodiment of the irresistible rogue. He wore money well—with the distinguished good looks, grace, and style of a rakish prince, underscored by just enough pirate to seem slightly dangerous. That was what had initially attracted me, but I loved him for so much more. I was drawn to his dash, of course, but there was intelligence shielded behind that glossy veneer. He had a remarkable BS detector, which was useful in the bar business and impressive to me. Over the years I watched as he unerringly called out various posers and charlatans. He had a keen business sense and the math skills of an accountant. Some would say he was too smart to own a bar, but maybe that was the point.

Away from work, Howard knew and loved history and art and had a well-read appreciation for design. He could stand in an art gallery and zero in on the one true gem. A frustrated landscape architect—what he would have studied in college had his father not rejected the pursuit as "sissy"—he loved to research, plant, and tend gardens. He could recite virtually every variety of daffodil, his favorite flower. He was also a handyman who could get down on his hands and knees to fix the kitchen sink. He was sincerely thoughtful toward others, though he was not a schmoozer. He had a sense of duty—to his parents, his sister, and to my family—which awed me because my family was not that way. When I had a bad day he made it his project to lift my spirits. He made me feel safe and secure and adored. I was serenely happy to be his wife. I believed that without him I could not exist.

On the other hand, he was catnip to women and he knew it; he had lived a life of so much privilege that the rules of law were a gray area; he too often confused material luxury with love, and his personal motto was "Anything worth doing is worth overdoing."

Still, he was my knight in shining armor.

"I am the happiest I have ever been in my whole life," I said to him. Right there, right then, I had everything I wanted in the world.

HOWARD AND I had met two decades earlier at an after-hours party at Clyde's, a Georgetown bar a block away from Nathans, its chief competitor. Nathans and Clyde's were founded a few years apart in the 1960s. Both were legends in the Washington, D.C. bar business—just like their owners. Stuart Davidson, who owned Clyde's, and Howard, who owned Nathans, were gentlemen saloon owners, which meant they didn't need the work or the money. Howard's father was a successful patent lawyer who had secured rights for windfall American staples such as the parking meter and stainless steel, and his wife was a rare-books expert and had a famed collection of eighteenth-century American furniture and art. A Washington native, Howard preferred

New York, especially the bars on the Upper East Side along Second and Third avenues. He'd been a denizen of that scene after a year or so of college. When Howard returned to Washington, his father wanted him to find a job.

"You seem to like to spend a lot of time in bars," his father had said to Howard, "so you might as well own one." With that, Mr. Joynt paid off two partners and bought Nathans for Howard, who made it a rumpus room for trust-fund prepster types, celebrities, the social, the powerful, and anybody else who wanted to join the party. He styled Nathans as a homage to his two favorite New York haunts, P. J. Clarke's and the 21 Club. The logo was a jockey on a racehorse. The cover of the matchboxes showed a bottle of Dom Pérignon beside a rubrum lily.

The restaurant business provided the perfect stage for Howard's larger-than-life character: tall, lean, with a natural virility, his hair slicked back and curling at the collar, his brown eyes and serious eyebrows, the strong and purposeful chin, the tailored suits, the perfectly knotted Hermès ties, the polished Gucci slip-ons. Any room picked up when he walked in. A few glasses of vintage wine or cognac only heightened his effect. He could be a lover and friend to women, but men, too, heartily enjoyed his company. He had the gift for making any conversation about the other person, not himself. He could charm anybody, and usually did.

He smoked cigarettes, Kents, with the panache of an uptown gangster in a '40s-era film noir. He could talk like one, too. With his deep gravel and sandpaper voice, he was fresh off the pages of Damon Runyon. If the engine on his vintage twelve-cylinder Jaguar XKE didn't turn over, it was "deader than Kelso's nuts." When he wanted something fast, it had to happen "in a New York minute." He comfortably talked the talk with Madison Avenue antiques dealers and always impressed them with his seasoned eye for what was good; handled appointments with his tailor as a necessity not an indulgence; and fit in as well with the bookies at the bar (after all, he got Nathans in part due to a bookie's gambling debt) as he did with the café society types with whom he sometimes jetted about. He cussed a blue streak, but not in front of women or children. It was second nature for him to offer a woman a seat, pull out her chair, open her door, or send her flowers and thoughtful gifts. He combined a salty swagger with refined good manners at a time when manners like his were becoming as rare as his parents' antiques.

Howard liked the good life and he introduced me to it. I'd never before experienced anyone quite like him—he swept me off my feet. He was a character from the movies: the legendary New York restaurateur Toots Shor as played by a combination of Cary Grant and Jack Nicholson. At the party where we met, the jaunty way he arrived—in his tuxedo, tie hanging loose—turned my head. No way was this man a lawyer or government worker or lobbyist. He had a devilish gleam in his eye as he scanned the room. He set his bemused smile on me and walked over. "Where's the champagne?" he asked. I gestured behind me. "Can I get you a glass?" he offered. I nodded.

Howard had come to Clyde's from a formal dinner party at the home of a rich young socialite. I had arrived straight from eight hours under the fluorescent lights at the NBC News Washington Bureau, where I worked the late shift as the night assignment editor. It was 1977, and in the spirit of the times I was dressed in the androgynous style of Mick Jagger—chic Soho thrift-shop trousers and a bomber jacket, my dark brown hair in a chin-length bob. I'd been in Washington only a few months. I'd spent four years in New York as Walter Cronkite's writer at CBS News, covering Watergate, the Nixon resignation, and the end of the Vietnam War. I loved it, but after those nonstop New York years, when I turned twenty-five I checked out for a year to pursue another passion: crewing on sailboats in the West Indies and France. I was freshly back and ambitious to succeed in my news career. I was proud of what I'd accomplished with my life. I wasn't sheltered or unsophisticated about the world, or at least I didn't think so. I'd been on my own since high school. I thought I was fairly savvy. But Howard, at thirty-eight, was savvier.

At his invitation we left the party together. He helped me into his shiny black Jaguar sedan and we sped off into the balmy spring night. On the car stereo the Eagles sang "Life in the Fast Lane." I fastened my seat belt.

"You're a strange one," he said. "Why haven't I met you before?"

"I just moved back here. I work the late shift and don't get out much."

In 1977 I owned nothing but an assortment of eccentric but trendy clothing, a suitcase, a black-and-white TV, and a one-LP record player. I camped in a studio apartment. Literally. My home décor was L.L.Bean, my "end tables" cardboard boxes. I slept in a sleeping bag on a cot. The refrigerator held a few bottles of Korbel sparkling wine and that was it. I was a vegetarian and swam for a half hour every day, but would party till dawn if the party was good enough. My network TV salary was good. I easily paid rent, bought stuff, took trips, went out with friends. I had one credit card, a checking account, and no savings. I had no one to support but me. I had no responsibilities, no strings. Howard played in a different league.

From the party in Georgetown we headed to another restaurant he owned, Nathans II. It was downtown and, with dinner service over, closed for the night. He unlocked the door and turned on a light switch that brought the spacious, elegant room to life. He walked me over to the black lacquered bar, opened a bottle of Dom Pérignon, and poured two glasses. He stood behind the bar, hitched his foot up on the beer cooler, and cocked his glass toward me.

"To the strange one," he said.

Strange? Maybe. I didn't see myself that way, but I knew I didn't fit the mold for Washington, which tilted strongly toward buttoned-up and conservative. Professionally, in an important job at a network news bureau, I played by the rules of the town's mainstream. But after life in New York, and time in the Caribbean and Europe, I was easily seduced by what was outside the box. Howard Joynt was outside the box. With his elegant suits and distinguished good looks he may have looked like he was on the conventional Washington team, but I sensed his subversive soul from the start.

From his smart tuxedo jacket Howard pulled out the fattest joint I'd ever seen, lit it, and offered me a hit. Weed wasn't my particular habit but I wasn't averse to it. Most of what I smoked was my brother's homegrown, which was the 3.2 beer of marijuana. Howard's grass, on the other hand, was fully loaded. "It's Thai stick," he said. "You sure you can handle it?"

"Oh sure," I said. "Of course." I inhaled deeply. When it hit me I almost took a header off the barstool.

On that first evening we talked all night, and we continued to talk for the next two weeks. When I got off work at eleven, he would be waiting in his Jaguar outside NBC's front doors to whisk us off to what was then the chicest restaurant in town, the Jockey Club, which looked and felt like the 21 Club and was open late. I felt sophisticated, out among the grown-ups. At every other table were Washington movers and shakers I recognized from the news I'd covered that day or from the gossip columns. We talked through dinner. Then, after hours at his bar, alone or with a ragtag group of bookies and well-funded drunks, or in his car driving until dawn with no particular destination, we continued to talk. I was not involved with anyone at the time. He told me he was in the midst of a divorce from his second wife, with two young sons. I didn't like that he wasn't yet divorced, but he assured me that he would be soon. The coast was clear, or so I thought.

We were alone at Nathans II in the wee hours of the morning on one of these early occasions when he came up behind me, put his hands on my shoulders, and whispered in my ear, "I think I'm falling in love with you." The words wrapped me in a soft, warm blanket. I fell back into his strong arms and savored the most profound feeling of belonging. For my heart he felt like home. Nothing else mattered.

Two weeks after we met, we made love for the first time. The next day he moved into the Madison Hotel, the most exclusive in Washington at the time. To celebrate his first night there, he took me to the hotel's dining room, the Montpelier Room, where the waiters treated him—as did the waiters at the Jockey Club—as if he were James Bond. He ordered Dom Pérignon and a tin of Iranian Beluga Malossol caviar, which he spread on toast points, spritzed with lemon, and fed to me. He didn't do this as a phony playing a role. It was as natural to him as breathing air. If that was our first date, and surely glamorous, our second date showed me more of the man I would come to love so dearly. He took me to Colonial Williamsburg—yes, a touristy museum town—to share with me his affection for all things eighteenth-century American, particularly the architecture and gardens. We walked leafy historic streets hand in hand, watched the Fifes and Drums perform at day's end, and drank cider with our crab and ham.

A few days later I gave up my studio apartment, packed my things, discarded the camping gear, and moved in with Howard at the Madison Hotel. I was a kid in the candy store of love. He'd send flowers, champagne, even caviar (with toast) to NBC. He'd call one, two, three times when I still had hours to go before my workday ended. "How many minutes until you get off work? I can't wait for you to get here. I'll send a car to pick you up. Just come in the room, don't say a word, let me make love to you." Sure enough, as I walked out the door at eleven, there would be a driver holding open the door to a black sedan. I was swept away by this unending cornucopia of affection.

At the hotel, Howard was always as good as his word. With very few exceptions, we shared the same bed every night for two decades.

After we had settled in, he told me that his divorce hadn't actually begun until the week after we met. He brushed it away with a wave of his hand. "It was coming, regardless. Strange One, you aren't to blame. You're just the catalyst for what I already wanted to do."

I didn't like it, but I had no clear idea what to do about the situation. I could have walked out the door, but I didn't. Howard had lied to me, but I knew from experience that people in the first flush of love say all kinds of things they'd like to be true but, in fact, are not. It was his marriage and his divorce and he'd been down that road before. None of my business. I was madly in love, and as everybody knows, love is blind—and sometimes a bit dumb. With little regard for judgment or common sense, I signed myself over to him. His divorce was granted within the year, and we eventually married. I quit my job at NBC News and our love nest became the manor house of a five-hundred-acre farm an hour from the city in Upperville, Virginia, the heart of the hunt country. I had visions of foxes and hounds and hunt breakfasts and witty repartee with the landed gentry. The reality was different. We spent most of our time together, whole days and weeks, which was fine, but it narrowed our landscape. Even wrapped head to toe in Ralph Lauren, I didn't fit in with the horse-farm trust-fund crowd, nor did I want to. I was a middle-class girl with a work ethic. With a few exceptions, no one we knew did anything. I was interested in the world. They were interested in horses, land, and one another. Some were flat-out bigots. The countryside was beautiful, our home was a dream, but my brain was slowly dying.

Howard wasn't happy, either, and he succumbed easily to disturbingly dark moods. Nathans II failed and closed, leaving only the original in Georgetown. Too much weed, too much alcohol, too little to do, and he would transform from Dr. Jekyll into Mr. Hyde. For every lark that was a "high"—good living, good times, good travel—there would be the inevitable "down." Benders happened. Rage happened, too. He'd have sudden meltdowns. He became abusive and cruel. On occasion, out of the blue, he hit me. More often he was plain out of control. He locked me out of the house. He pushed me out of the car one night in a rainstorm, miles from home, without money or identification. A stranger who saw me crying at a pay telephone drove me home, forty minutes away. My problem was I never saw the meltdowns coming. He could go to dinner five times, have wine, and remain charming, loving, and completely normal. And then there would be that sixth time, where mid-dinner or mid-party he'd suddenly turn an invisible corner, cross an unseen line, and change: not able to stop drinking, aggressive, and crazy, as if invaded by an alien—an alien who hated himself and anyone in proximity, chiefly me.

Howard would recover from the episodes and return to his other wonderful self, not remembering any of the gory details, while I'd remember all of them. He'd make up for it with affectionate words of contrition and gifts. A handful of Anna Weatherley dresses would arrive, boxes of beautiful silk chiffon as delicate as cotton candy, a ring from Tiffany, a necklace from Cartier, and I, reluctant to say "No, thank you" and happy to have the storm over, would accept the gifts and his apology. I would invent one story or another to explain away a black eye. My seemingly confident exterior fooled so many. I told no one what was really happening, not even my closest friends. Who would believe me? I could hear them: "Not Howard! That's not possible." Besides, where would I go? I had no one but him, or so I thought, and I'd brought this on myself. I was becoming the classic abused wife.

Howard was my entire world, and when his mood was dark, my world was dark. I was stranded in bizarre splendor in a grand house at the end of a long dirt road surrounded by fields and foxhunters. It was a million miles from the world I had left. Eventually I fell apart, what they used to call a "nervous breakdown." I had disappeared as a person. I was invisible. I was Mrs. John Howard Joynt III, but Carol Ross had left the planet. My self-esteem was zero. At one point I curled up in a closet—not a walk-in—wanting everything just to go away. The outside world appeared not to notice—I was always good at maintaining a façade—but I did. I knew it. I was living it. I was hating it.

I confided to my physician one day in a routine exam and he sent me to a psychiatrist. Through weekly therapy, I gradually worked my way back to solid ground. Howard followed me into therapy with the same doctor. We saw him at different times on different days. It may seem strange that we shared the same shrink, but it worked. Chronic depression was fueling his manic ups and downs. The doctor put him on Prozac and, just like that, he was transformed. The dark side of Howard retreated, and the bright, happy, charming side—the side I had fallen in love with—became the constant. It was an astonishing turn and convinced me ours was a marriage worth saving.

"We've got to get back to the world," I told Howard in the den of our house in Upperville. We'd lived there for seven years in what was more a hideout than a home. "I have to go back to work. You have to go back to work, too." He agreed. He'd neglected Nathans, leaving it in the hands of managers and bartenders. No one was minding the store. He hired Pinkerton detectives, whose investigation revealed that the staff was stuffing dollars in their pockets—tens of thousands of dollars—selling cocaine across the bar, and walking out the back door with whatever they wanted. It was time for both of us to go back to work.

My career was built on curiosity, instinct, and asking questions, and yet I never once questioned our life of quiet luxury. I'd grown up in an emotionally chaotic household where I'd rarely felt like I was on firm footing. I loved my parents dearly but I had moved out of their home the moment I could, at age eighteen, and embarked on a good career. But when I met Howard, and even though I had living parents, brothers, and a sister, I felt somehow like an orphan. Howard adopted me, took me in, and put a secure roof over my head, and in spite of the fighting made me feel safe, protected, secure, and loved. I traded in my self-respect to preserve that fragile deception. Not his. My own. If my house was a house of cards, I didn't want to know about it.

The second decade of our marriage was better, and it kept getting better with each passing year. I had begun to assert myself. I became again the master of my own life. We packed up and moved to the Chesapeake Bay while keeping a small apartment in Georgetown. We were water people. We liked to sail. Howard jumped back into the day-to-day management of Nathans, and I returned to television as a producer for the CBS News overnight broadcast, *Nightwatch,* hosted by Charlie Rose. I loved being back at work, sharing my days with people like me who were involved in the world, excited by it.

Who wouldn't be? In the first years of my career, at United Press International, I had stood mere yards from President Johnson soon after he announced he would not seek reelection. Helen Thomas included me on a visit to President Nixon's "hideaway" office in the Old Executive Office Building where he sat at his desk and talked about the bombing of Cambodia. In my next job, with *Time* magazine, I asked Elvis Presley what he was doing after his show. "I don't know, baby," he said. "If ya tell me where you'll be, I'll tell ya what I'll be doin'." Also at *Time,* I went to my first presidential conventions and on the road with Jane Fonda and Tom Hayden at the height of their antiwar activism. In various jobs I met all the presidents of my time: Gerald Ford, Jimmy Carter, Ronald Reagan, Bill Clinton, and both of the presidents Bush. With Larry King, I met Elizabeth Taylor, Princess Diana, and John F. Kennedy, Jr., who did a live interview while I kept company with Carolyn Bessette.

The New York socialite C. Z. Guest, one of Truman Capote's favored "swans," agreed to do an interview with Larry about the Duke and Duchess of Windsor for the auction of their possessions. Sotheby's invited me to bring C.Z. to their warehouse to go over the items. She met me looking like a glass of lemonade, all sparkling and fresh and blond. Not for nothing was she on the best-dressed list year after year. The warehouse held vast rooms of furniture, racks of clothing, boxes filled with bed linens. While the staff was coding and tagging, C.Z. and I wandered unattended, fingering suits, jackets, dresses, the Windsors' stuffed Pug dolls, their silver. There was the duke's "abdication desk," and his much-photographed greatcoat. C.Z. pulled it on, smiled, and twirled. It looked made for her.

This was fun, some of it was fascinating, and all of it sure beat living the idle life. The one interview I didn't want to touch was Charles Manson, the truly sick mastermind behind the grisly 1969 murders of Sharon Tate, the actress and Roman Polanski's wife, along with four others in Polanski's Los Angeles home. John Huddy, executive producer at CBS News *Nightwatch,* pushed me into it. I balked, but he called me his "star" producer and told me this was a professional step I needed to take, so I made a call to the warden of San Quentin. He said Manson was permitted to do one interview per quarter. "It's up to him. You have to write him directly." He gave me a prison address.

For the next year, Manson and I exchanged letters. Mine were typed and antiseptic. I was careful not to fall into the usual fawning that went with pursuing a big "get." Manson's letters to me, on the other hand, were wild and required several readings to decipher. They went on for pages and pages, written with a pencil in longhand on yellow legal paper. One day the warden phoned. "Manson has agreed to an interview."

In February 1987, Charlie Rose and I—and Howard—flew to San Francisco. I gave Charlie the "prep packet" of all my notes from interviews with prosecutors, forensic psychiatrists, and others. I'd also asked him to read Vincent Bugliosi's *Helter Skelter.* When we arrived at San Quentin no two people were more read up on Charles Manson. There was no way not to be anxious as we went through three gates and listened to a recitation of the prison's "no hostage" policy ("We will not negotiate your safety for the freedom of an inmate. . . ."). Gulp. I had purposely dressed down. White shirt, gray pants, no jewelry, no makeup. Charlie Rose wore a suit. The two of us and the two-man crew were taken to the large parole hearing room, with a big wooden conference table and windows with a stunning view of San Francisco Bay.

Guards led Manson in, shackled at the wrists and ankles. He was slight, weighed down by the chains that wrapped around his waist. His skin had the pallor of milk—skin that never sees sunlight. He was kept in solitary; he wouldn't have lasted long in the general population. I asked the guards to remove the shackles, thinking that might make him more comfortable and easier to interview. We introduced ourselves. I didn't know whether to shake his hand, and then I did. "We'll start in a few minutes," I said, "if you'd like some time to relax." He walked over to the window and stood stock still, staring out at the world he had left forever, the sparkling blue bay drenched in sunlight and dotted with sailboats.

Once the interview began, we stopped only for Skip Brown, the cameraman, to make quick tape changes. Manson began calmly, but as time was running out he got more animated and explosive, eventually becoming barely coherent. And then it was over. He was shackled again and the guards led him away, his chains clanking. The program aired within days of the interview. Later that year Charlie Rose and I stepped up to the stage at New York's Waldorf Astoria to accept Emmy Awards for best network interview. Not even a year spent pursuing Elizabeth Taylor could top that.

From CBS News I went to the start-up of the television version of *USA Today,* where I was Washington bureau chief; the show failed but I learned a lot. Then it was on to producer roles at *This Week with David Brinkley,* and *Nightline* at ABC News. Working with Ted Koppel was the closest I'd come to an experience that matched the excellence of Walter Cronkite. These were great jobs and my career blossomed. But I was forty years old and eager to get pregnant, which is tough when you work for a show like *Nightline,* where the workday ended at midnight and began with an early morning conference call. A sensible interlude followed at the National Gallery of Art, where I was brought in by director J. Carter Brown to make documentary films. The hours were essentially nine to five.

Meanwhile, business was booming at Nathans. Howard and I focused on making our house on the Chesapeake into the home of our dreams. When I didn't think life could get any sweeter, I became pregnant and it did. Spencer was born in November 1991, when I was forty-one and Howard was fifty-three. It was the right time. We were ready. After Spencer's birth, our life together became a succession of quiet but very happy rewards. Like so many baby boomers, we replaced the all-nighters and nightclubbing and madcap adventure with the simple pleasures of home and hearth. Howard quit smoking. He grew a slight paunch. His hair turned silver. We woke up early and went to bed early. We were a family, and as we sailed through the Caribbean islands that December we seemed as solid and happy as we had ever been.

Chapter 3

I'd left the hospital for home late Friday night. Now it was the wee hours of Saturday morning. The phone on the bedside table jolted me from a sleep as deep as the sea. It took me a moment to realize where I was. My own bed. The clock said four a.m. No husband beside me. Oh, damn. That. This is real, not a nightmare. The sinking feeling returned. Half of my brain told me a predawn phone call is never good news. The other half instinctively guided my hand to the receiver.

"Carol, it's Martha. I'm at the hospital. They say Howard's condition is grave. They're not sure he'll make it through to dawn. Get here."

In one urgent continuous motion I dressed, kissed Spencer, woke the live-in babysitter, and rushed into the elevator and to a waiting car. I didn't dare try driving. Again my breath couldn't get below my breastbone. My mouth was sand. I'd begun to exist in two worlds: one where I knew what I had to do and did it; another in which I was spiraling out of control. In the bitter cold of that early Saturday morning in January, Washington was still tucked in. The streets were empty, houses were dark, and I thought of the people inside, sleeping undisturbed in the safety of their beds, and I envied them.

The scene at the ICU was much more frightening than what I'd left six hours earlier. My husband was hooked up to an elaborate life-support system, surrounded by men and women in white coats whose demeanor was too urgent, too serious, and too focused to give me any reassurance. "We can't get his oxygen absorption up," an anxious nurse told me. There was nothing for me to do but stand on the sidelines and stare. I knew only that under that tangle of tubes and monitors and wires and IVs that make up the armamentarium of modern medicine beat the heart of the husband I loved, and he was dying.

When either Martha or I weren't at his bedside, we sat quietly stunned in the small, dim waiting room, trying to keep our courage up. Every chat with a doctor was dire. Dawn became morning, which turned into midday and then afternoon. Good friends arrived from Maryland's Eastern Shore. Wendy Walker, the executive producer of *Larry King Live,* came with her husband. My younger brother, Robert, arrived from rural Virginia. I phoned home to check on Spencer. "He's fine," the babysitter said, "playing with his Legos. Don't worry, Carol. Things are under control here." They may have been under control there, but my life was slipping off the rails.

Spencer and I had not been together since Friday afternoon. There was the quick hug and kiss before I rushed Howard to the hospital, and he was asleep when I was briefly home that night. Our time together over the past week had been fractured as well, which was unusual, because I had taken a business trip without the family. I hadn't wanted to make the trip to New York, but I had made a personal New Year's resolution to do more for *Larry King Live* on my own. Typically, when I had CNN business in New York, we all went, including Spencer, the babysitter, and the dog. We would check into the Carlyle hotel, where we always had the same rooms that felt as comfortable and familiar as home. I would work during the day, Howard and Spencer would enjoy the city, and in the evening Howard and I would try a favorite old restaurant or a hot new one.

We'd been there only a week ago for New Year's. It was a continuation of the good times we shared in the Caribbean. Except Howard had a cough. Not a bad cough but a nagging cough. "I feel like shit," he'd say.

"Have the hotel call a doctor," I advised. But no, too much fuss.

"I'll see Goldstein when we get home," he promised. Kenneth Goldstein was his hematologist. Howard had been diagnosed with chronic lymphocytic leukemia several years earlier. There was no cure for CLL, though many people live long normal lives with the disease. Howard's was stage zero. Though I had a meltdown when he was first diagnosed, he was stoic, and we both learned it was just something that had to be minded.

Howard's cough persisted and was not better when I had to turn around and head back to New York with Larry King immediately after the holiday. Howard assured me he would see his doctor. I phoned Dr. Goldstein from Washington's Union Station and left a message for him to call Howard. The rest of the week I called home often. The conversation that haunts me still was from one of the wooden phone booths at the 21 Club, where Larry, the executive producer Wendy, and I had lunch with the publisher of John F. Kennedy, Jr.'s magazine, *George*. We were in the center of the front room at the A-est of A-list tables with every boldface name in the place doing a drop-by to greet Larry. But my mind was on Howard. I slipped away to the phone.

The anger in his voice was shocking and confusing. "I feel horrible. I can't believe you're there and not here taking care of me."

"C'mon, Howard, we discussed this trip. You said I should do it, that you would go to the doctor. I asked Dr. Goldstein to call you. Can't you get yourself to the doctor?"

"That's not the point. You don't care about me. You just want to be in New York."

"Howard, seriously. I'll come home right now if that's what it takes, but please go to the doctor."

He didn't back down. "I can't believe you are doing this to me," he said. "You should be here taking care of me." When we hung up I was gutted.

That evening I called from the hotel. His spirits were much brighter. "I went to see Goldstein," he said. "He put me on antibiotics, an IV in my arm just like when I had Lyme disease."

"Thank God. Do you want me to come back in the morning?"

"No, no. Stay up there. Do your work. I'll be fine. Much better already. The drugs are working. I can feel it."

After a pretape of the show, Larry and I were on familiar ground, the back of a town car on our way to a movie premiere, this one a new Woody Allen movie. "How ya doin'?" he asked. "We've had quite a week. Dinner with Al Pacino, now a party with Woody Allen. Are you having fun?" I loved my work, but I was not having fun. I was guilt-ridden about not being with my husband.

Friday morning my work was done and I was on an early train back to Washington. I would pick up some groceries on the way home and take care of my husband all weekend.

Dismay is not a strong enough word to describe how I felt when I walked into our bedroom. Howard was flat on his back, gasping for air, and very pale. I called Dr. Goldstein's office and lit into the receptionist. "How could you let Howard leave your office like this?"

"What do you mean?" she said.

"He's sick as a dog. The antibiotics obviously aren't working."

"What antibiotics?"

"The ones Dr. Goldstein gave him. The IV."

"You better talk to the doctor," she said.

"I haven't seen your husband since November," Dr. Goldstein said. "I got your message and called him but he never called back."

So there it was. No doctor. No IV. No antibiotics. At that point, I was more angry than anything else.

I looked across the bed at Howard. "Howard! You didn't go to the doctor. Why did you tell me that?" He looked back in resignation.

Goldstein said, "Please put him on the phone." I held the receiver to Howard's ear. He said only a few words and gestured for me to get back on.

"His breathing sounds terrible," Dr. Goldstein said. "Get him to the Sibley emergency room immediately. I'll call them."

So now the wee hours of Saturday morning had turned from afternoon to evening, Howard had been in Sibley's intensive care unit for more than twenty-five hours, and his condition was "grave." The ICU doctors had run out of tricks. They'd shopped him around to a few hospitals and the only one that would take him was the Washington Hospital Center. "It's your best hope," a doctor said. "They have a breathing device there that can feed oxygen to both lungs, giving him what he needs. We don't have one here."

"Let's do it. What's the holdup?" I asked.

"They can take him, but it's Saturday night and no one is on duty who can authorize a medevac helicopter and we don't want to send him by ambulance."

I played the only power card I had and called Larry King. Earlier he'd said, "If there's anything I can do, just let me know." Now there was something he could do. "Will you please call the Washington Hospital Center and get us a helicopter for Howard?"

Ten minutes later he called back. "I reached the head of the hospital. A helicopter should be on its way." Sure enough, in fifteen minutes we could hear the *whup whup whup* of the chopper blades outside the ICU windows.

A team of faceless people in helmets and jumpsuits rushed in with a gurney. They lifted Howard's seemingly lifeless body onto it, hooked up the life-support system, the IVs, and the myriad other tubes and bags, and—sweetly—covered him with a blanket and tucked him in. He was under there somewhere but I couldn't see him apart from a little tuft of his hair. He'd hate that. He'd want me to smooth it down. They rolled him out with military precision. My brother Robert, Martha, and I stood side by side, our backs against the wall. In the time it takes to stop, take a breath, and move on, one of the crew, a woman, lifted the visor of her helmet, looked me square in the eyes, and said, "Don't worry. We'll take good care of him." And they were gone.

Now it was midnight on Saturday. I'd been awake since four o'clock that morning. Martha hadn't slept at all. It didn't matter. The hours were a blur. All of us were functioning on adrenaline. Robert and I headed to his car, stepping carefully over the small piles of freshly plowed snow and ice in the mostly empty parking lot. The air was frigid; we could see our breath. The night sky was clear and sharp, with little stars twinkling above. We shivered inside the car and silently looked through the windshield across the lot to the brightly lit MedSTAR helicopter preparing to lift off, its blades a blur. Up, up it went, its beacon lights flashing in the dark clear night, then heeling a little, speeding up, and heading across the city.

This will work out, I told myself. It will get better now. My brother nodded, turned the ignition, and said only, "So like Howard to be in grave condition but still traveling in style."

At the Washington Hospital Center a vigil began. My other brother, David, arrived from Seattle. Martha, Robert, David, and assorted friends camped with me in a small waiting room with a pay phone on the wall outside the hospital's second-floor medical intensive care unit, steps away from the cramped, cluttered high-tech bay where Howard continued to struggle on life support. We lived there with pillows, blankets, food, and a TV from home. I taped family photos on the wall of Howard's bay. I wanted his dedicated medical team to see the healthy, handsome, happy Howard.

One week stretched into two, then three. Day turned to night turned to day turned to night. Time lost all boundaries. I returned home only to hug Spencer, clean up, change clothes, and occasionally sleep—or, more correctly, pass out. In a bizarre contrast, as I drove through the city, I passed the preparations for Bill Clinton's upcoming second inauguration, an event in which as a network news producer I would ordinarily have been deeply engaged. Instead I existed in another universe of grief and pain, good news, bad news, good news, bad news. Up, down, up, down. My language was medical jargon. My most intimate conversations were with doctors. My husband was as still and silent as a stone, his body animated only by a respirator. Sometimes I would walk to the end of the hall to a large picture window with a view of the city. Hope ebbing, I would press my cheek against the glass and sob.

On day nineteen, Howard's good, kind, and hard-working doctors, Michael Hockstein and Peter Levit, closed the door of the small waiting room and sat down with Martha and me. It was empty but for us. They could only be honest. "He's not going to make it. We can keep him on life support, but that won't change anything." Martha and I had more or less expected the news. We didn't break down. We didn't fall apart. Instead, we dealt with the moment. "No, no," I said, about continuing life support. "He wouldn't want it that way. We have to let him go."

Dr. Levit said, "I'll sign the order."

Spencer returned from preschool that day in his usual bubbly mood. He was such a happy little boy. Three weeks without his daddy and he was still in high spirits, though aware that our routine was jarringly different. Now I had to rob him of his joy, let him know that something irreversible and terribly, terribly sad was about to happen.

"Let's take a walk," I said, "out along the canal."

He was instantly agreeable. I bundled him up—puffy jacket, hat, mittens, scarf. We leashed up the dog, too. I didn't know how I could inflict such incomprehensible pain upon him—almost an act of violence. But he had to know. I wanted him to understand as best he could what was happening to his father, that he didn't just disappear into thin air. Even a five-year-old needs to say good-bye.

The grass along the towpath was covered with patches of snow; the sun was breaking through the mottled gray clouds. We stopped at a pretty spot where we were alone. "I need to talk to you about Daddy," I said, holding his hand in mine.

His head was down, and I heard the little voice. "I know. He's going to die, isn't he?"

"Yes," I said, my heart sinking.

Spencer grimaced and held his eyes shut. He plowed his head into my stomach and grabbed onto me with both arms and stayed like that, his head buried in my winter coat, his fists and arms tight on my hips. He tried to stop the tears. He wiped them away with his mittens as they spilled from his eyes. I kneeled, stroked his head and his back, and wrapped my arms around him as tightly as I could. His heartbreak tore through me.

"Do you want to say good-bye to him?" I asked.

His head was pressed against me but I could feel his nod.

"I think it would be a good idea," I said, holding him, "and I will be there with you."

The next morning Spencer got dressed in his blue blazer and gray trousers, looking every bit his father's son. But he was not our happy little boy of the morning before. He didn't cry. Something that had been there yesterday was not there today.

"Daddy will be sleeping," I told him as we drove to the hospital. "But even so, he'll be able to hear you."

Spencer and I walked into the ICU holding hands. The staff stood practically at attention. It was as quiet as it had ever been. We made small talk with the nurses. They pulled a chair up to Howard's bed and hoisted Spencer onto it so he could see his father. The nurse had given Howard a shave and combed his hair and cleaned him up, and tried to make the room look as normal as possible.

"Can I be alone with Daddy?" he asked.

"Of course, angel," I said, and walked out of the bay with the others. A nurse pulled the curtains.

From inside we heard Spencer's young, tentative voice begin to sing:

You are my sunshine, my only sunshine . . .
Please don't take my sunshine away.

Typically, at school or at home, when anyone sang that song Spencer ran from the room in tears. "The song is too sad," he said, "because it's about the sun going away."

Now, as it came softly from his lips, I cried. The nurses cried, too. And then the singing stopped.

Spencer pulled back the curtains and walked out of Howard's room with red, bruised eyes. "I said good-bye," he said, taking my hand. "Can we go home?" We walked down the long empty corridor in silence.

Through that long night, at Howard's bedside, I said my own good-byes. The next day, at ten-sixteen on the morning of Saturday, February 1, 1997, three weeks and a day after I had driven him to the hospital, with Martha and my brothers and our medical team at his side and his hand in mine, Howard Joynt died. He was fifty-seven years old.

Chapter 4

THIS IS THE thing about grief: If you allow it to, it will protect you. It's an organic drug for the broken soul. Mine was an all-encompassing fog, and I welcomed it. This doesn't mean I didn't ache or feel shattered, but each time I reached the breaking point, the fog would roll in and I could function. With a grieving little boy, I had to function. But here's the other thing about grief: There's no road map.

In the first hours after Howard's death we escaped to our house on the Chesapeake Bay. Even though it was primarily a weekend retreat, it felt like home and was where we as a family had been our happiest. Now with Howard gone, it echoed with memories like an empty shell echoes the sea.

Spencer knew something momentous and irreversible had happened. He knew his father was gone and not coming back. By his logic, Daddy was in heaven, whatever *that* was. Distractions worked for only a little while. Spencer couldn't understand why his toys didn't keep him happy. He'd go from playing with Legos to playing with toy tools to playing outside. He'd be into it for a while and then quickly lose interest. He'd retreat to his room to fondle his cuddle toy, "Baby," and suck his thumb. Or, he'd veer to the other extreme. One day as I was toweling him dry after a bath he cried and begged, "Please stab me, Mommy, kill me. I want to be with Daddy in heaven."

On another afternoon, as I washed dishes by the kitchen window, Spencer walked down to the water's edge and looked out. I dried my hands and joined him. I gave him a squeeze and a kiss and plopped down on the grass beside him, on my back, resting on my elbows, looking out to where his gaze was fixed. "What are you thinking?" I asked.

"I'm just missing Daddy and wishing he was out there in his boat." At bedtime, between tears, he had more questions.

"Why did God take Daddy? Why did he *do* that?"

Some parents might respond with an affirmation of faith and explain how the ways of God are beyond our understanding, but we have to believe that God does everything for a reason even if the reason is a mystery to us.

That's not what I did. I said, "I don't know."

Not much help for a little boy.

"Nobody will ever love me again," he cried.

"I love you," I said. "I need you. I know how you feel. That's the way I felt yesterday in the car, when you got so mad at me for crying. I felt like I would never fit in again, never be part of the world again, like there was no reason for going on. But the feeling passed. The way you feel hurts now, but it will pass, too."

I was strong through his dinner, his bath, and his bedtime, but not for long after. In those early days, when grief was a shot of Novocain to my nervous system, I got through most of the daylight hours in my protective fog. But after Spencer was asleep, after dark when I was alone in the rooms I had shared with Howard, the numbness wore off and I was saturated in sadness. I puttered and searched, or sat on the edge of our bed and stared into space. Inside my head was a chorus of "He's gone, he's gone, he's gone." I was a "widow" now, the way some people become an "amputee" or a "cancer survivor" or "blind." It was a designation I'd never considered, and it couldn't be altered or washed away. There's no way to become an ex-widow. I was branded for life.

I was drawn to Howard's closet, to the fragrant nest of his suits and sport jackets, where my nose inhaled the familiar scent of him, where I pressed a cheek against the cloth and imagined him there. I fingered his sweaters and his shirts and his ties. His shoes were still neatly lined up in a row, as he'd left them. I crumpled to the floor, tears streaming, holding a shoe to my breast as if it were the dearest thing in the world. I slept in his boxer shorts. They made me feel womanly, but they comforted me, too.

I looked up the word *widow* in the dictionary. One definition was "a woman whose husband has died." Another was "an additional hand dealt to the table," and the third, "an incomplete line of type." Each worked for me, but especially the last.

I felt incomplete in every possible way. My bed was empty, my home was empty, the other end of the kitchen table was empty, the driver's seat, his desk chair, the chair where he read and watched TV—all were empty. The other half of my conversations was no longer there. The memories we had shared were only my memories now. I picked up the phone but had no one to call. In the shower before bed I slumped to the floor and let the water wash away my tears.

The public rituals of death played out. The obituaries glowed. One said the Georgetown community was "robbed of a touch of class." Another said, "If ever there was [an] establishment which bore the taste, the vision, the touch and personal image of its owner, then it was Nathans. It was Howard Joynt's place, and there was no mistaking that. . . . With his graying, slicked-back hair, the sweater thrown over the shoulders, he often looked like he just came back from the country and was on his way to the bank, with a good glass of wine waiting for lunch." They noted he was a generous tipper, too, and the son of Howard and May Joynt, "collectors of 18th century American furniture and art." They mentioned his schools: St. Stephen's, Choate, the University of Pennsylvania, and Georgetown University. I filled the biggest reception suite of Gawler's funeral home with bouquets of his beloved daffodils—every last one that could be found in Washington in February. His mahogany urn rested on a table, a photo of his eighteen-foot sailboat, the *Carol Ann,* beside it. The room was packed with people, a crush to the walls, with the hum and verve of a festive cocktail party.

Back at home it was a different story. On Howard's desk was the six-inch stack of bills that had arrived during the three weeks of the hospital vigil. All things financial—bills, banking, bookkeeping—were his department. I had my own checking account and paid my own credit cards, but Howard paid all the big stuff: electric, gas, phones, condo, cable, grocery, laundry, school, kennel, department stores, housekeeper, live-in babysitter. I ripped open the envelopes, threw away the promotions, placed the bills in a neat pile, and began to sort through them. The amounts of money staggered me. Moreover, there were two bills from a mortgage company, each for about $1,200. Curious, I called the 800 number on the mortgage invoice. I patiently worked my way through the automated prompts until I reached a human being.

"Mortgages?" I asked. "What mortgages?"

"You took out two mortgages about eighteen months ago," he replied brusquely.

What? Why did Howard boast about owning all our property "free and clear" when we had two mortgages? And why didn't I know about them? I turned on Howard's adding machine—practically an appendage to him—and added up the bills. I ripped off the tally and looked at the number: $15,000. My God, I thought, that's a boatload of money! And that was only for a month. How do I get that kind of money? What am I going to do *next* month? My heart sank.

I had no idea what income came from the restaurant or whether Howard even got a paycheck. He never told me his income, but I assumed that we lived off Nathans, the Joynt family trust, and his stock portfolio. We certainly didn't want for anything. The money for the occasional Cartier bauble had to have come from somewhere. Certainly we didn't live on my $50,000 a year from CNN. That might have gotten Howard through a month. He always tamped down my occasional money questions with "You don't need to worry." So I didn't. Big mistake.

Looking at the bills made my head hurt. I stacked them back in a pile, clicked off the light, pushed back from the desk, put the chair neatly back in place, and walked out of the den. On the sofa in the living room I lay down and stared at the ceiling, tears welling.

"If anything ever happens to me," Howard had said, "sell Nathans immediately. Don't take a partner because they'll rob you. Don't try to run it yourself, because it will kill you. Just sell it. Get a good broker, put it on the market, and sell it." What would I get, I asked. "On a good day you'd clear $2 million."

Although publicly I insisted that I would keep Nathans—it was, after all, a family business—privately I planned to heed Howard's advice and sell it as fast as possible. I was no more qualified to run a restaurant and bar than to wield a scalpel if Howard had been a heart surgeon and left me his medical practice. In my mind I was a widow and a mother, and I wanted to get back to my work as a producer for *Larry King Live.* I wanted to run our household, not a twenty-eight-year-old bar with fifty-five employees. My only interest in Nathans was the financial security it could provide for my son and me.

In the first few weeks I tried to get us back to some kind of routine. In the morning, I got up, woke Spencer, and welcomed the babysitter, who lived down the hall in a small apartment we owned. I'd get in a good run, make breakfast, drop Spencer at nursery school, make a quick stop at Nathans, drive across town to the CNN building, and work at *Larry King Live* until mid-afternoon when I drove back to Georgetown to pick up Spencer from school. Rather than work from home in the afternoons, as I did before, I left Spencer with the babysitter and returned to Nathans until Spencer's dinnertime. I found comfort in order and routine. If I could get through one day I could maybe get through the next.

I dreamed about Howard. In one dream I was in the car, speeding haphazardly from one end of town to the other, all the while trying to reach him on the phone. I was lost and I needed directions. Do I turn left? Do I turn right? Howard would know what to do. I had to reach Howard. But Howard was not there.

Chapter 5

LOOKING BACK, I'VE always called it "The Morning of the Lawyers." Like so many twists and turns in my life after Howard died, everything seemed benign at the outset. His accountant said, "You need to call Howard's lawyers," and I took that as just another bureaucratic hurdle I had to jump in settling my dead husband's estate. My entire focus was on shoring up whatever was needed to protect my son and myself, and to get Nathans sold as quickly as possible. I wanted all the loose ends tied up, some money in the bank, and then a period of time to grieve, settle our hearts, and figure out the rest of our lives.

I'd grown up solidly middle class in a military/academic family with little money to spare. From age eighteen until I met Howard I'd earned my own way, modestly but comfortably. Life with Howard was a big step up, and it taught me that having money was better. Money bought good schools, good doctors, restful vacations, beautiful homes, excellent services, and a world of agreeable people who more often than not enjoyed similarly comfortable lives. I might be a widow now, but at least Spencer and I would have enough money. We would survive, but there were steps I had to take, like visiting his lawyers, to get it locked down.

That morning, like all the other mornings since Howard died, I moved from sleep to the wakeful haze of grief with my attitude fixed somewhere between dread and the need to persevere. I got up, ran, made breakfast, got Spencer off to school, and prepared to face the day.

I dressed for my meeting with the lawyers like an actress preparing for a new role, the role of Howard's widow. I did it more for Howard's sake than for my own. He was always particular, and I wanted him to approve of my appearance. I wore my best black suit and shoes and my most discreet jewelry, and carried a plain but fashionable black leather handbag. The only thing missing was a black veil.

The offices of Caplin and Drysdale are in an impressive building that hugs Thomas Circle, off Fourteenth Street about a half mile from the White House. It's the edge of what's known as "the new downtown." The firm specializes in tax law and is named for heavy hitters Mortimer Caplin, a former commissioner of the IRS, and Douglas Drysdale, a tax lawyer with more than four decades of experience. The firm employs dozens of lawyers.

I stepped off the elevator into the reception area. There was a wash of plush, cool gray in the walls, the carpet, the furniture, and the mood. The receptionist invited me to take a seat. "I'll let them know you're here, Mrs. Joynt," she said. I sat on a gray sofa, handbag in lap, hands on handbag, and stared into the middle distance. I waited for my cue. The experience was new to me, and a little bit unsettling. The truth is, I felt completely out of place. Lawyers, contracts, business matters—these were all things Howard loved and handled completely on his own. I never felt any curiosity when it came to what went down between Howard and his lawyers. I was happy to stay out of it. My meeting today, I assumed, would be a mere formality. The lawyers would offer their condolences, maybe have me sign some documents, wish me well, and send me on my way. Done.

Not quite. Howard's accountant, Martin Gray, said it was urgent that I attend the meeting. That seemed strange. And then there was something Howard had said over dinner awhile back. He casually mentioned a tax audit. "I won't bother you with the details, and I'm not really supposed to talk about it. But you don't need to worry. It's bad, but I have a plan." The statement was unremarkable because whenever Howard mentioned audits—not uncommon with small businesses—they were nothing more than twenty-four-hour storm clouds that always passed. When Howard told me not to worry about something, that he had a plan, I didn't think anything more about it. He always worked it out. That was the magic of the man, and why I ceded the business side of our lives to him. He took care of things, just as he took care of me.

"Hello, Carol." An attractive woman walked toward me smartly dressed, wearing a silk blouse with a bow at the neck and a straight skirt. She was of a certain age, and confident. She introduced herself as Julie Davis, one of Howard's lawyers. She ushered me down a short hall and into a conference room. When I walked into that room all I saw was the large, dark conference table. It reminded me of the first time I walked into a bedroom with a man, and all I saw was the bed. My heart started to race and I took a deep breath to relax.

Several men stood around the table. Only one of them wore a tie, and that was Martin, the accountant. I wondered why he was there, and why he had arrived before me. But I didn't have time to dwell on such things. One by one the men introduced themselves. There was a moment of almost Japanese politeness as we nodded toward one another. The men offered their condolences, hoped Spencer and I were doing well, and said they knew this was a hard time for us. "We don't always dress this way," one of them added. He seemed self-conscious as he went on to explain that it was "casual Friday" at the firm. His tone was familiar but somehow condescending. I had expected warmth and something more—I don't know what exactly—maybe intimacy?

Because I was meeting with Howard's lawyers I let myself believe they would be acting toward me on his behalf so, although I had approached this meeting with anxiety, I also expected it would be like visiting friends. The lawyers, as Howard's surrogates, would wrap their arms around me and make me feel safe.

That wasn't how it happened. Each man, and the woman, squared their shoulders, adjusted the papers in front of them, and fixed their eyes on me. The needle on my fight-or-flight instinct quite suddenly moved to flight. Cono Namarato, the lead lawyer, spoke first. He carefully explained that when Howard died he was under investigation for federal criminal tax fraud and that the case against him covered both our personal taxes and the taxes of the business. As Mr. Namarato detailed Howard's legal transgressions, I nodded as if I understood what he was talking about. Here was this respected criminal tax lawyer with a sculpted face and crisp manner telling me that my husband was under investigation for tax fraud. What happened to the simple audit Howard had mentioned? What happened to the warm arms of lawyerly love? And why was it taking so long to get to the part where I sign whatever documents I had to sign so I could just leave?

"Of course, as his will is written, with you as the sole heir, the case is now your responsibility," Mr. Namarato said. "You are the defendant."

I froze. It was difficult enough to comprehend the trouble Howard was in, but almost impossible to absorb the shock of being told that his mess, whatever it was, was now my mess. I felt like I was in a slow-motion car crash. This was crazy. I hadn't done anything wrong. How could I be the defendant in anything?

"At one point we were afraid Howard would be indicted," Mr. Namarato said. He'd been a criminal tax enforcement official at the Justice Department. "But we were able to clear that up. They didn't have a strong enough case for a criminal indictment."

The blood rushed from my face. My throat went dry. I kept hoping that Howard would walk through the door and tell me everything would be okay.

"Did Howard know that?" I asked.

"Yes." Mr. Namarato folded his hands on the papers in front of him. "That was decided before the end of the year."

"Then does that mean the case is closed?"

"No," he said. "We got rid of the criminal charges but we've got a long way to go. There's still the debt and the penalties. This case is attractive to the IRS because it's a big number."

My composure cracked. My voice was thin and barely audible. "Big number? What does that mean?"

"We don't know the final number, but it's large."

"How large?"

"In the millions," Mr. Namarato said. "We don't yet know how many."

I couldn't swallow. I had the same sinking feeling I'd had in the intensive care unit at Sibley Hospital. There I learned I could lose my husband. Here I was being told that I could now lose everything else. My fear very nearly flared into panic. I had nowhere to turn. I was on my own, and the other lawyers and the accountant all chimed in to tell me what to do, as I felt the panic rising.

"Sell everything," one of them said with such mindless gusto that I wanted to grab a tire iron and whack him. I didn't have that option at hand, but the anger helped quell the panic. "Pay the debt and get this behind you."

"If I sold every last thing—and I mean everything—home, apartment, the boat, the cars, books, clothes, art, toys, knickknacks, and my wedding ring—I wouldn't be able to come up with millions of dollars," I said.

"Where's the money?" Mr. Casual Friday asked me, as if I'd robbed a bank and stashed the goods.

"What do you mean, where's the money?" The needle on my fight-or-flight gauge was now moving sharply toward fight.

"There must be money somewhere," he said. "He had to do something with the money. Is it in offshore accounts?"

Offshore accounts? These people were his lawyers, for God's sake! Wouldn't they have known if there were offshore accounts? Wasn't that their job? Obviously they didn't know Howard.

"Howard didn't hide money," I said. "He spent it. He liked to spread it around. He didn't want his money stashed on an island somewhere. He wanted it close, and available." The room was suddenly quiet.

I finally worked up the courage to ask the question I wanted most not to think about: "What happens if I can't pay?"

That certainly got everyone's attention. It was clear they'd never considered that possibility. I looked at them. They looked at one another and then back at me. I could hear the hum of the ventilating system. Martin Gray tapped his pen on the table. Someone cleared his throat. Finally, Julie, the only woman there from the firm, broke the silence. "Well, you could go for 'innocent spouse.'"

"What's 'innocent spouse'?" I asked.

"It's a code in the tax law that's designed for cases where a spouse who has committed, say, fraud, dies, but the surviving spouse doesn't know anything about the fraud. The surviving spouse can be declared innocent. When that status is awarded, the surviving spouse is absolved of responsibility for the debt."

That's it! Thank God. That's the solution! Before I could open my mouth, Julie added, "But you wouldn't qualify."

"What? Why not? I *am* innocent."

"Because . . ." She paused, gathered her breath, then poured it out in a rush: "You had to know. How could you not know? Look at you!"

Look at me? *Look* at me? I wrapped my arms around myself. I could feel the cloth of my expensive black suit but I felt naked and exposed.

I felt like I was a criminal in the dock, charged with a crime I knew nothing about.

"But I *didn't* know," I said. "The only thing Howard told me was he was being audited and that the lawyers told him not to talk to me about it. So he didn't. You were his lawyers. You must have told him that."

They nodded but offered nothing else. I felt that in their eyes I was as guilty as my husband. Mr. Namarato said they would have better information in a couple of weeks, when we would reconvene. In the meantime I should start to get my house in order.

I walked out of the office building back onto the same street and into the same daylight that was there when I arrived, but everything was different. The numbing fog of widow's grief that had been present when I got up and dressed that morning was gone, replaced by blunt fear. I was hollow inside except for dread. My hands shook. Before starting the car I had to take a few deep breaths to calm down, to focus. For the first time in my life I felt trapped. And Howard, the very person I always went to, who would listen and understand and give me good advice and protect me, he was gone, too, leaving me to fight his tax fraud case. He left me in a minefield of his making. The irony that the very man responsible for this mess was the same man I yearned to run to didn't hit me then, but it did soon enough.

The IRS agent on the case was a woman named Deborah Martin. "She's a junior agent," Mr. Namarato explained. "That's why she's so eager to get a big dollar amount. This is huge for her."

Deborah Martin submitted her report on April 16, 1997, the day I returned to the lawyers' office. I knew the damage done by my earlier appearance—the widow in the Chanel suit—couldn't be undone and only emphasized the image of me as a coconspirator in a tax fraud, the client who "had to know." This time I was the one who dressed casually.

Deborah Martin, I was surprised to discover, was not present. When I asked about meeting her, Cono Namarato's response was swift. "No. We'll keep you away from her. No contact. That's what we're here for."

It was becoming clear that my lawyers viewed me as precisely the person Deborah Martin described in the opening of her report. I was a woman living a "lavish" and "luxe" lifestyle. Almost all the elements of my life she took to be incriminating. When she cited her damning evidence, it didn't matter that I didn't know we couldn't afford the life we lived. I drove a Range Rover, for instance. Yes, I drove it. Still did. In fact, it was parked outside. I also had a weekday live-in babysitter and a weekend babysitter who doubled as a housekeeper. I had a demanding job, for God's sake! And when we had a big dinner party I hired a cook who worked for a catering company. I thought we could afford it. It made sense to me.

And so it went. Deborah Martin's report read like the tumescent tabloid profile of a frivolous, spendthrift airhead. That was not me. Everything she wrote was technically true, although highly embellished. It documented every dime Howard had spent in the past five years. All his credit card charges, all the checks, money he'd deposited, all his investments. She made our very comfortable but comparatively low-wattage life sound like high-rolling pornography costarring me and my son. According to Martin's report, when I wasn't off on a luxurious holiday, aboard a private jet or yacht, I sunbathed by the pool at my "estate" on the Chesapeake Bay while relying on my domestic staff to attend to my needs. That wasn't how I saw my life but it was how a young IRS agent looking to make her first big haul chose to describe it. I thought we were living within our means. I didn't pay the bills. I didn't know that Howard couldn't pay for the life we were living. My protests either didn't register with my lawyers or simply sounded lame to them. They painted me with the same brush they'd used for coloring the guilty party, Howard.

Deborah Martin's report explained how Howard ran his expenses through Nathans and thus operated the business at a loss. Essentially the only annual income reported was mine, which created a discrepancy of at least several hundred thousand dollars. While Howard withheld about two hundred thousand dollars in federal taxes from his employees' paychecks, he didn't send that money to the government. He kept it for himself, for Nathans, and for some favored employees. There was a section of the report that listed which employees got money "off the books," with their names and the amounts documented because Howard had given them the money in checks, pink checks.

As I continued reading, each page of the report felt heavier than the last. When I got to the part where it detailed that my husband wrote off the live-in babysitter's wages as "trash collection" and some of my Christmas presents as "uniforms," I stopped reading. I had reached my threshold of humiliation, embarrassment, shame, and guilt—and before an audience, too. Deborah Martin caught a man who had broken the law, who'd committed tax fraud against the U.S. government. It was as simple as that. The crook was my husband. It didn't matter that he was ashes; the investigation stood on its merits and she had a case. The government wanted its money and since dead people don't write checks, I would be the one to pay. I was the defendant.

Mr. Namarato slid a single sheet of paper across the polished table. It broke down what was owed. The debt to the feds came to almost $2.5 million, and the meter on interest and penalties was still running. The total was a breath shy of $3 million, an amount of money that was incomprehensible to me. Amounts owed to the District of Columbia and the state of Maryland hadn't yet been calculated. I stared at the numbers, speechless, as the lawyers and accountant talked about my options. My inner voice begged: Don't cry, don't cry, not here, please don't cry, not here, don't cry, don't cry.

"Well, she still has the issue of the promissory note."

"We're going to have to comb through that, but I don't think it will fly."

"The withholding is the big issue, and that's where most of the debt is."

"But we can try to flip that one issue with another. . . ."

"No, it won't work."

"I think we go back to Deborah and ask for some backup on a few of these numbers."

"At least Carol has her job at CNN. That looks good."

"You can't take this into a courtroom. It's a slam dunk against her."

They debated while I sat there, invisible. No one asked my opinion. As the shock of the numbers wore off and I began to tune into the words of the lawyers, something inside me clicked, some little gear shifted from frozen to boiling.

"Wait!" I fumed. "Stop! Listen to me." All eyes shifted in my direction. "I don't understand any of this." I gestured at the documents on the table, the pages of evidence, and the numbers that toted up the debt. "And I don't understand half of what you're saying."

They were silent.

I looked from one lawyer to the next. "Doesn't anybody understand that I didn't do this? They've got the wrong person. The person who did this is dead! This is all news to me. I found out only two weeks ago that we even *have* mortgages! There wasn't anything about our lives that struck me as inappropriate. Yes, we lived well, but it wasn't outrageous, it wasn't ridiculous, it wasn't gross and over the top. My husband had a successful business. He had an inheritance. It all made sense to me. There were no bags of money lying around the house, piles of cash stacked in the closets. There weren't trips to Vegas. There weren't shady characters. I'm to be condemned because I had live-in help for my son? I work! I'm allowed to have a babysitter. I can pay her. Is that criminal?"

I continued to fight back the tears. The last thing I wanted was to let these people see me crumble.

"I don't know what Howard did," I said, calmer now. "I hope that whatever it was, he didn't do it on purpose, that it was a mistake. But I can't ask him. He's not here. But I do know this: I didn't do it and my son didn't do it. I'm innocent!"

There was silence. Finally, Mr. Namarato spoke up. "But you signed the tax returns."

"I know, but they were filled out by an accountant." I looked at the accountant, who looked away. "Why *wouldn't* I sign them?" I asked. "I assumed they were properly put together. I didn't feel I needed to pore over them."

Martin Gray shifted in his seat and cleared his throat. "I was working with the numbers Howard provided me," he said.

"So was I!"

"We've got a long way to go," Mr. Namarato said, obviously trying to calm me down.

"What happens now?" I asked.

"We'll talk to Deborah Martin," Julie said. "They can put liens on your accounts. We'll try to stop that. You should find out how much you can come up with. What if you sell your house? What will you get for that? And the art? You have a lot of antiques, right? What would that add up to?"

"My house? Just sell it?"

"That's one way of paying this off," someone added.

"I want to keep my house." It was our safe harbor. It was my little boy's home.

"What about the life insurance?" one of the lawyers asked.

"There is no life insurance," I said.

"What? How can that be?"

"Howard didn't believe in life insurance," I said. "Look, I only got him to sign a will a year ago. He didn't want to do it because he thought it would jinx him, that he would die. . . ." I smiled weakly at the irony. "It looks like he was right."

That was that. The meeting ended with a refrain of "We'll make some calls and get back to you. We'll meet again next week."

Mr. Namarato casually wrapped his arm around my shoulder and walked me to the elevator. "Now, Carol," he said, "don't leave here depressed."

Was he mad? All my worst fears had come true. Spencer and I were going to lose everything. Our lives would be ruined. I was beyond depressed.

That night I had a fitful sleep, but that I slept at all was probably the bigger surprise. What kept me awake was not simply the perplexing bad deeds my beloved husband had done, but the sheer magnitude of what had landed on us. There was my frightening ignorance of this dangerous new world of cash flows and taxes, criminal fraud and lawyers. I had to get sophisticated fast. Grief, I knew, would have to wait. Tears could come later. First, I had to save us.

TWO

Chapter 6

His full name was John Howard Joynt III. He was many things I was not: a child of money and privilege, casual about work but serious about living well. If there was anything we had in common it was that we were both shy. It wasn't obvious. After all, his game was the restaurant business and I worked in broadcasting, neither of them known as a refuge for the timid. But for both of us work provided protection. Howard's poise and the alcohol-infused bonhomie of his bar masked his shyness. Hard-charging television journalism masked mine. I was a different person at work. I don't think anyone would have described that person as shy. When we first met I was dazzled by Howard's star quality but fell in love with the sensitive man I saw within. I know, that's what every woman says. That doesn't make it a lie. Despite everything I learned about Howard after his death and my fury at what he had done to us and the frightening mess he had left me to clean up, when Howard and I were in each other's company I was most myself and he had seemed most himself. I felt we were transparent to each other. There were the little fibs that happen in any relationship, but never lies. I didn't lie to him and I didn't believe he lied to me, though after the lawyers, I knew there was one huge and hugely important exception: where the money came from to support the way we lived. The answer was simple and disturbing: Much of it wasn't ours.

I thought I had good instincts, but my radar didn't extend far beyond the heart. I knew Howard loved me—but transparent? No. I may have been transparent to him, but clearly there was a part of Howard, the larcenous part, that he kept opaque. Looking back now I realize that his deception was in plain sight. He had a good BS detector for a reason. My eyes were dazzled by Howard's brightness, blinding me to the whole man.

The day my beautiful Romanian mother met Howard, he drove up in a white Jaguar XKE convertible like a character out of *The Great Gatsby,* wearing white pleated flannels and a blue and white striped shirt, with a tennis sweater tied casually around his shoulders, a Kent hanging out of the corner of his mouth, and a chilled bottle of Dom Pérignon in his hand. Howard was a master of the grand gesture, and my mother ate it up. She had an instant crush.

"Let's have some champagne, Olga," Howard said, the bottle still in his hand—he cocked his head in my direction—"and ignore her."

My parents lived in Warrenton, Virginia, a small country town an hour outside Washington where my father, Richard Ross, after time in the military and a stint as a dean at George Washington University, ran the Airlie Foundation, a think tank used by the federal government, Washington-based corporations, and academia. The job came with a lovely yellow stucco four-bedroom house, a pool, a pond, gardens, and bucolic views. From almost the moment we met, Howard and I would spend weekends there with my family. It wasn't unusual for me to go to bed, only to wake in the wee hours to find Howard and my mother still at the kitchen table, drinking, smoking, debating politics, discussing history, and gossiping about movie stars. My mother had moved to Hollywood as a girl; her role models were movie stars.

Before the move to rural Virginia, the Ross family's usually happy suburban home life had become increasingly emotionally chaotic. My parents fought a lot over money—the lack of it—and over my older sister, who had had too many run-ins with the law because of drugs and other misbehavior. The chaos was the main reason I moved out at age eighteen. But with the job at Airlie, which was a virtual fresh start, my parents and younger brothers regained a sense of calm, and the spirit of fun and affection prevailed. When I was growing up, my father, a native of Minnesota, was a Barry Goldwater Republican, an Episcopalian, and traditional to the core; my mother, the immigrant, was a Eugene McCarthy Democrat, raised a strict Catholic but with the soul of a gypsy. She had few boundaries and didn't care about possessions except, perhaps, animals. I think she was happiest when Dad had new assignments and we camped in hotels or some kind of temporary housing. She taught us how to travel with very little baggage.

She was wedded to the notion of ghosts and we routinely had to visit houses thought to be haunted. We were raised on goulash and chicken paprikash. Her philosophy of raising my sister, brothers, and me was "Water you and you will grow."

My parents met on a Friday in Los Angeles, when my father, an Army Air Force pilot who dropped paratroopers over Normandy on D-day, had exactly one week's leave in the United States. They married at the end of that week. In the early years of their marriage, and while my brothers, sister, and I were little, my dad continued his air force career, ending up a full-bird colonel. We lived part of the time in the United States and part of the time in Europe, chiefly Wiesbaden, Germany, where he worked on the postwar cleanup. Our assigned housing in a nineteenth-century hotel had been Hermann Göring's personal quarters when he was in Wiesbaden. The rooms went on forever, with high ceilings, gilded moldings, and beautiful crystal chandeliers. I loved to twirl on the parquet floors in the ballroom. Still, Mother made our spaghetti dinners on a hot plate. Hotels felt like home. We would bounce on the beds, go to the lounge and get fruit drinks with paper parasols, and generally charm or terrorize the staff. We traveled to Berlin a lot, which was among the more exciting aspects of living abroad. It was before the Wall went up, and my father would take us by car to tour reconstructed sections of East Berlin. It seemed like a movie set—a row of restored buildings and behind them acres of rubble.

Back in the States we moved a lot—Ohio, Maryland, Virginia—and that was before I turned fourteen. Furniture came and went, nothing stayed the same. We were always in debt, about to fly off the rails. Money management was not a particularly important part of my parents' style. It was the postwar boom. Let the good times roll. Borrowing money was just what you did. I was too young to know what debt was, but I knew it followed us wherever we went. The money ups and downs, the travel, and the fluid living arrangements combined to make me, as a teenager, an expert at arriving in new neighborhoods and schools and quickly finding friends. Even when we moved to a home of our own near Mount Vernon and stayed for all four years of my high school, I didn't entirely buy into the seeming stability. It always felt elusive. There was a lesson here, but I didn't learn it.

I was fortunate to have had my parents much of my adult life. Olga died from lung cancer when I was thirty-seven, exactly ten years before Howard's death. Hers was a quick and terrible decline, as so many cancer deaths are, especially with the adverse effects of radiation and other treatments. The family was at her bedside in the last days, and she died peacefully at home.

HOWARD APPEARED TO have had stability, money, and comfort from the start. He was born March 21, 1939, and came home to a historic house in Alexandria, Virginia, where he lived until he moved out as an adult. It was the Benjamin Dulany House, one of the finest in Old Town. The record shows that George Washington dined there. (He ate out a lot in that part of Virginia.) Howard's parents, Howard and May, bought the house in 1932 and lived there until Mr. Joynt died in July 1989. May Joynt died less than a decade later, after a long struggle with Alzheimer's. But through much of Howard's life he had the apparent security of one home, with successful and cultured parents.

Life in the elegant Joynt household was lived as close to the 1750s model as one could reasonably get. Modern amenities, such as televisions, were tucked away out of sight. The silver was made by Paul Revere, William Hollingshead, and Jacob Hurd. The furniture was Chippendale, Queen Anne, and Federal from Philadelphia and Massachusetts. The paintings that hung on the drawing room and library walls were by Gilbert Stuart and John Singleton Copley, the prints by Audubon. The porcelain was Chinese export, Sèvres, or Delft, and the rugs were Aubusson. The floors, moldings, windows, and doors were original to the house. The boxwood garden was designed by a famed expert in eighteenth-century landscaping. Mr. Joynt made one concession to the early twentieth century. He ate his morning cereal from Supreme Court justice Oliver Wendell Holmes's breakfast bowl. It was all very lovely but, frankly, like living in a museum. For Howard, it was stifling.

I went from public high school straight to work. Howard went from school to freshman year at the University of Pennsylvania. I eventually learned that he embellished the stories of his past. Howard was a bit of what the French call a *mythomane.* He told wonderful tales about himself and others whose faithfulness to the facts could fairly be described as problematic.

Odd that I point this out, given what happened, but I was more into facts. I really *liked* digging up details about things that had happened, and I was rigid about telling the truth. There'd been a lot of lying in my household growing up—about my parents' debts, their drinking, their fights, and my sister. No doubt my veracity was at the root of my fondness for journalism. After high school I went from hometown newspaper to the Washington bureau of United Press International, where I started with an entry-level job that led to reporting on the antiwar movement. That got me front-page bylines all over the world as the protests rose in volume and intensity. It was a heady experience. I loved my work—and it seemed like only an incidental bonus that they were paying me to do it.

From UPI to *Time* magazine in New York, and then at twenty-two I landed the big prize—writing the *CBS Evening News with Walter Cronkite.* Walter hired me personally. Naturally the gaggle at the water coolers speculated about whether there was something more to my being hired—like that I'd slept with him. Why else would he bring on board a twenty-two-year-old woman whose only real qualification was that she had what they called a nose for news?

Walter was the one who told me about the rumors. I'd been writing for him for almost a year when he leaned over his table at Copenhagen, where he'd invited me to lunch, and said in that inimitable voice, "You know, there are rumors around the office that we're having an affair."

I was mortified, shocked, embarrassed. Walter was the same age as my father! I didn't know what to say. I was stammering out some response, when he laughed and said, "Do me a favor, will you? Please don't deny it."

Actually, Walter and his wife, Betsy, became my friends. Over the years they became friends to Howard, too. We would meet for a meal or to go sailing. After Howard died, Walter kept in close touch and faithfully phoned every Christmas morning—wherever he was, wherever we were—to make sure Spencer and I were doing okay. We would see him if we were in New York, and a year before he died we visited him on Martha's Vineyard. He took us sailing and, in a moment I'll never forget, showed sixteen-year-old Spencer how to handle the helm.

MY TIME ON the *CBS Evening News* spanned an era that included the death of President Johnson, Watergate, Nixon's resignation, the kidnapping of Patty Hearst, and the fall of Saigon. When Walter offered me the job he told me there were many candidates, all of them older, more experienced, and male. But he wanted someone with wire-service experience. "Also," he added, "there's pressure on me to hire a woman. You qualify on both counts."

The two other writers, the editor, and I sat beside Walter just off camera every weeknight. Together we did the news and all other specials he anchored. I was sitting beside Walter in our Washington bureau at the moment Nixon announced his resignation. I ripped the "flash" off the AP wire and ran it to him. For me, the job was always that exciting.

I rented a small house in New York's West Village. I was loose in the big city, young, unencumbered, and well-paid, but my work always came first and I approached it with dedication and passion. The matter of college came up from time to time, and it was something I was always going to do at some point, but campuses were erupting with protests and turmoil, none of my employers demanded a college degree, and my jobs felt like an education. At the *CBS Evening News* I was proud of what we did, how we did it, and why. My parents were proud, too, especially because each time the show went to commercial there was a "bumper," or wide shot, that showed me sitting beside Walter. My brother David said, "They bought a big new TV just to watch you on the *Evening News.*"

In 1972, CBS paid me $38,000, double what I earned at *Time,* and, my father pointed out again and again, just about what he earned running a foundation. I put my paychecks in the bank, paid my rent and utilities, and felt financially secure. I knew where my money came from, how much money I had, and where it was going. I managed my money well, in the sense that I lived within my means, but I was not sophisticated about money. I would have been happy to let someone else take over all that. For a few years my father had done my taxes, but now that I was twenty-two and earning real money at CBS, I hired my own accountant. It seemed the grown-up thing to do.

Watergate was over and the Vietnam War had come to an inglorious end, when I decided to check out of the *CBS Evening News.* It felt like the right time to use my savings and take a break. A random invite lead me to the West Indies, where I got a job crewing on *Spartan,* a seventy-three-foot wooden Herreshoff yawl that was built in 1918. My sole qualification was that I'd fallen in love with the captain, a tan, ripped, and sun-bleached California surfer dude named Lewis Starkey. With him as my teacher I became a sailor quickly. After seven months in the Caribbean and falling out of love with Lewis, I spent four months enjoying the south of France.

That was enough. I loved the vagabond life, but I missed my work. On the day before the 1976 bicentennial, almost a year after leaving the Cronkite show, I flew home to New York, breezed into CBS News, and got hired on the spot as a writer for the upcoming Republican National Convention in Kansas City. After that I relocated to Washington, and was over the moon when an old friend, the new chief of the NBC News bureau there, hired me to run the night assignment desk, essentially a flight controller's job. It was exactly what I wanted, an ideal perch back in network news. I didn't intend to stay in Washington; I wanted the world. Then I met Howard.

Chapter 7

AFTER MEETING WITH Howard's lawyers, panic hit. Twenty-four hours earlier I had thought Howard's death was the worst that could happen to us, and now I was a federal tax fraud defendant who owed the government almost $3 million I did not have. The lawyers—now *my* lawyers—didn't believe I was an innocent spouse. They believed I was guilty.

The first stage of grief is shock, whether the loss is a person or everything you believed was solid in your life. I went into shock. I went off the deep end. With Spencer tucked in, I attacked Howard's large mahogany partners desk. There were four drawers on either side and one drawer in the middle. One was mine, the others were his. I never went into them. Barefoot, in jeans and a T-shirt, I crouched on my knees and pulled out every drawer. My goal was to dig through everything. He was so amazingly organized. One drawer held only canceled checks going back years, but I didn't know what to make of them. I slit open envelopes, pored over documents, fingered through manila folders—all without a clue as to what I was looking for.

I did find one seemingly relevant file that held a page from a yellow legal pad. In Howard's precise prep school scrawl was a list of things we owned. Beside each item he'd jotted an amount of money, a value. At the bottom of the column was a total. It looked like he was calculating how much money he could come up with if we sold everything. And he listed every last thing: our Chesapeake Bay home, the two modest apartments in Georgetown, cars, art, antiques, boats, stuff. The total was $1.2 million. Distraught, I tossed the list across the room. "This is hopeless," I said out loud. "Not even close."

But who was I kidding? Whatever Howard had done wasn't going to be found in a lockbox with a secret code attached explaining everything for me. I sat in the middle of the floor, haggard, hands covered in grime, with all this crap around me, absolutely paranoid about what the IRS could rain down on me. The later the hour, the darker the fears. Would jackbooted IRS muscle kick down the door to drag me away in handcuffs, my sobbing child clinging to my ankles? I knew it had happened because at CBS News we reported on that very thing—IRS agents, minus the jackboots, coming in the night, carting people off to the slammer. That story made a lasting impression. It didn't matter at that moment that perhaps my case didn't qualify for prison (yet); I was in a panic.

It lasted through the night. The clock hands moved from midnight to two, then three. The dog looked at me, head cocked, wondering if we would ever go to bed. I took paintings off the walls and carted them to the basement storage bin. I took my few pieces of real jewelry and hid them in socks. Socks! It didn't occur to me that this was a waste of time. Either the IRS wouldn't care or they'd look first in the storage bin and sock drawer.

I didn't understand what had happened to me, I didn't understand how it had happened, and I certainly couldn't ask Howard why it had happened. I had an emotional twofer—hopeless *and* helpless. The level of despair outweighed the fear I had felt at the hospital, where at least the doctors and nurses answered my questions and were on my side. Who was I going to call? Who could I tell? Why would I want to reveal this awful turn of events? And it's three in the morning. Not a good time to call anyone. The normal emotion might be anger. But no, I wasn't there yet. I was still in the stages of shock and denial.

At Nathans, once the floodgates were open, bad news began to cascade. A man arrived in the basement office who said he was the bookkeeper and there to take care of the quarterly tax payments for unemployment and other city and federal obligations. I welcomed him to do whatever it was he was there to do. When he was done, he asked to talk to me. Privately.

Upstairs in the bar, for the better part of an hour, we talked about what people had started to call my "situation." The bar business, I discovered, is as gossipy as the news business, and word had begun to spread about Howard's fraud and the mess he had left behind. None of the gossips knew details, but that didn't stop the grapevine from growing and expanding like kudzu. The bookkeeper had factual knowledge of the business, though, and talked about the different ways Howard wrote checks out of Nathans and what he wrote off or didn't. He added that essentially Howard had run the business "in his head."

I told him I had found a binder with daily numbers in it and comparisons to the year before. "It looks like a daily account of money earned or spent or both. To me, mostly a lot of numbers."

"That's your book," he said. "I'm sure there are two sets of books. If you can find the other, try to figure out which one is real."

Figure out which one is real? How was I going to do that? I knew the bookkeeper wanted to help, but the more he explained the more my mind began to slide into the fear zone. I wished I could dig deep into the crisis and hit the bottom, but there was no bottom. Digging deep meant only having to dig deeper.

"Well, I'm going to bill you, but Howard always gave me a periodic $5,000." That snapped me back to attention. I'm sure my jaw dropped.

"Can I afford that?" I asked.

"I don't know if you can," he said, adding, "He also let me run a tab." All I could do was mumble, "Let me talk to the manager and get back to you."

I didn't immediately find the Nathans "book" but I found Howard's personal checkbook. In all our twenty years together I'd never looked in his checkbook. He had his, I had mine. He balanced both. He liked doing that. The book was big, brown, and covered in leather. I took a deep breath before lifting the cover. I flipped through the pages going back a year or so. Most of the entries were conventional, normal. But there were also entries for a few men I knew to be, well, characters around town. I didn't know them personally, but Howard would mention them—with a salty anecdote and a groan—from time to time. One or the other was always down on his luck, in need of a loan. "But are you actually going to give him money?" I would ask, incredulous. "No fucking way," he'd say. But now I noticed he'd written them checks. Not one, not two, but several. Five thousand here, three thousand there. I was certain they were loans rather than gifts. I wondered if they would offer to repay me, but they never did.

I welcomed the company of friends and took advantage of every opportunity to be with them. In the early months after Howard's death they were my core support. They included Howard's only sibling, his sister, Martha, a presidency scholar, who had the advantage of being available almost on the spot. Her husband, Vijay Kumar, lived full-time at their home in New Castle, Delaware. Martha, who was camped at the White House and taught one night a week, commuted home on weekends. My other girlfriends lived up or down the street or around the corner, but they had husbands and children to tend to and were not available on demand. I would see them for lunch or at children's parties and the occasional weekend gathering of all the married folks. I didn't feel it then, but I was already becoming the odd one out: the widow, the business owner, the defendant in a tax fraud case. Most of all the defendant.

I liked these men and women who were almost all a decade younger than me. Many of the women had come to the hospital and had helped out in the immediate aftermath of Howard's death, bringing food and flowers to our apartment, inviting Spencer for extra playdates with their children. Their husbands were business owners, developers, lawyers. At one particular dinner party in the suburbs, I sought business advice from some of the men. They spoke the new language I was trying to learn, and I had to learn it fast.

"Well, Carol, now you know why they called Nathans 'the Bank of Howard,'" said the fellow who owned the linen company that provided Nathans' napkins, tablecloths, and kitchen uniforms. The men laughed. I didn't. "Howard did it so smoothly, everybody figured he would get away with it forever."

One of the businessmen told me, "Just remember, your lawyers work for you, you don't work for them. If they aren't serving you, fire 'em." He was talking about firing the lawyers and I hadn't even hired them. I was in so far over my head.

A chilling encounter with a complete stranger made me fully grasp my vulnerability and see that there was a bull's-eye on my back. It was at a small neighborhood cocktail party for Anthony Williams, the expected next mayor of Washington. I was invited not as a journalist but as the owner of a prominent small business. Knowing only the hosts, I was a wallflower, but was rescued by an attractive man with European deportment and a distinct appealing accent. "Can we sit somewhere quiet?" he asked, leading me to a sofa in a far corner.

It was Anthony Lanier, a native of Austria, and a Washington developer who even I knew was managing impressive makeovers of old buildings in Georgetown's commercial area, buildings just like mine. The word was he had $800 million investor dollars to play with and that a large chunk came from George Soros, the Hungarian-American businessman and financier worth many millions, even billions.

Our conversation was all business. He knew more about my building and my landlords than I myself knew, and a fair amount about my predicament, and he made clear that he wanted my building because it was the jewel in the crown, "on the best corner of the most powerful city in the world." I was intimidated but listened closely.

"Everybody wants your space," he said. "They will come at you from every direction. No one thinks you can survive. You are not in a position to trust anyone—your staff, your landlords, your lawyers. The landlords are worried about you, they live entirely off that building, and they will go in another direction if they can, but they don't move fast, which is in your favor."

I sighed. "So, what are you going to do to me?" I asked.

"I could steamroll you, but I'm not going to," he said. "Your husband left you in a mess. I want your building but I will try to work with you rather than against you."

Anthony was a man of his word and became an invaluable ally. His insider information often scared me out of my wits but it made me stronger and braver as I struggled to get that bull's-eye off my back.

THE YACHT YARD near us on the Chesapeake Bay sent out a periodic newsletter. It was not something I usually read, but when the new issue arrived it got my attention. On the cover was a tribute to Howard. It saluted his sailing skills and commended his attention to detail when he refurbished a boat. At the end it said: "We will always remember his lovely Hinckley Pilot 35, *Penguin,* and how beautifully he spruced her up."

Penguin? A Hinckley Pilot 35? We didn't own a Hinckley, and the sailboat we did own, a little eighteen-foot day sailer, was named the *Carol Ann.* There had been a Hinckley Pilot 35 at the yard a year or so earlier. Howard took me out on her one beautiful sunny day, put her enthusiastically through her paces, even brought a picnic lunch, and when I was happily relaxing he announced she was for sale. "Should we buy her?" he asked. She was a lovely black-hulled gem, and I knew he considered Hinckley to be the ultimate in boatbuilding, but we already had a sailboat.

"No," I said. "Not now. We don't need another boat." And, as far as I knew, that was that.

I dropped the newsletter and called the yacht yard. I thanked the yard manager for the nice tribute to Howard.

"I'm going to ask you a question that may sound dumb, but please answer me honestly." He was silent. "You mentioned the Hinckley Pilot 35, *Penguin,* in your write-up." I paused. "Do we own that boat?"

"Well, yes, you did. Mr. Joynt had her here for a while. He had a lot of work done on her. Made her really sweet. Sold her at a good price, too."

"He sold her?"

"Yeah. Sold her up in Maine. That was earlier last year."

Clearly, when Howard took me sailing on the boat and asked me whether we should buy her, he already had. That's why the fabrics that covered the cushions and bunks down below were from a manufacturer we used for our home. At the time, I considered it an appealing coincidence. What a dunce!

The discovery rattled me. The IRS, a surprise sailboat, big loans from his checkbook, guys who have tabs at the bar, "the Bank of Howard," two sets of books—how much more didn't I know about my husband? One stage of grief is denial, but it's tough to be in denial when there's so much evidence to the contrary.

To ease my pain and confusion, I would lose myself in Spencer. He needed me but I needed him, too. I felt normal when I was alone with him, even if our moments together were anything but. I'd tuck him into bed each night and curl up beside him. "Tell me stories about Daddy," he'd say, and I'd try to pull something up to enchant him. While I talked he would suck his thumb, hug his cuddle toy Baby, and stare into the middle distance. When I stopped he would plead, "More! More! Tell me another story, Mommy. Tell me about Daddy." Sometimes he would cry and I'd hold him until the tears were dry and he was asleep.

Chapter 8

Nothing in my background prepared me for the three-ring circus my life became after Howard's death. Lawyers and the IRS in one ring, Nathans and *Larry King Live* in another, and in the center ring, my son and our home life. The big top was lit up, it was showtime virtually round the clock, and I had to lead the action in each ring simultaneously.

For the moment, the lawyers at Caplin and Drysdale got the most attention. We spoke often over speakerphone. Much of our conversations had to do with their discussions with Deborah Martin at the IRS. The message was clear: I was not gaining ground.

At *Larry King Live,* I tried to keep the productive pace I was known for before Howard's death. In early 1997, I was in the middle of negotiations for several big-ticket projects: Rosie O'Donnell, who'd started a new TV talk show the year before, the notorious Leona Helmsley, who'd been mum since she got out of prison for tax evasion, fashion mogul Calvin Klein, and the Christie's auction of Princess Diana's dresses. These were front-burner gets. I had another dozen or so long-term projects: Mick Jagger, Paul McCartney, John F. Kennedy, Jr., Doris Day, Sting, the Duchess of York, Marv Albert, Kathie Lee and Frank Gifford, the pope, and Queen Elizabeth. My get list, particularly the pope and Queen Elizabeth, made friends laugh, but I assured them that in the talk-show game we were motivated by the fact that, sooner or later, almost every celebrated person would give an interview. The show's hard-charging executive producer, Wendy Walker, was deadly serious about every pursuit, even the most far-fetched.

It was common for me to bag at least one but sometimes as many as two or three household-name guests in a week, and I always had a notorious Triple-A boldfacer in the pipeline. They say that people enjoy diets because it gives them a feeling of control in their lives. After my world turned to chaos that's how I felt about *Larry King Live.* I was in control; everything else was in free fall. But as much as I wanted to shut my new life out of my CNN cubicle, it wasn't possible.

"Carol, you have a call," the office receptionist said, popping her head into Wendy's office where the two of us were having a booking conference. Wendy's eyes lit up, hoping it was a callback from one big target or another. Eager, I dashed out to take the call, but the wind left my sails as soon as I heard the voice at the other end. It was the manager of Nathans. He never had good news. I didn't want to take calls from Nathans but I had to. I couldn't ignore the lawyers, either, who had my life and Spencer's in their hands. If an emergency at Nathans—there were a lot of emergencies at Nathans—demanded an immediate decision, I had to make it. When I returned to Wendy's office she looked up, hoping for news of a hot "get," not of another legal setback or a burst kitchen pipe. These distracting calls became routine. At the beginning she didn't comment on it, but I knew that too much personal drama was seeping into my job.

Howard had made Doug Moran the general manager of Nathans twelve years before. Doug loved Nathans. He'd worked his way up from waiter and floor manager, knew the culture, knew the customers, knew the neighborhood, looked out for the police on the beat with lunch or coffee on the house, and showed up at the tedious Georgetown business association meetings. Howard had relied on Doug to do a lot of the work he found boring. But there was another side to Doug. Maybe twelve years as general manager was beginning to wear on him. Howard had also thought he was lazy, sometimes arrogant. A little too often for Howard's taste Doug would make money, menu, or inventory decisions that Howard found out about only later. There would be an argument—usually over the phone because neither man liked confrontation—and then for a while life at Nathans would return to normal. Howard didn't work out his problems with Doug at the bar; he brought them home. Sometimes our pillow talk was one Doug rant after another.

I came into owning Nathans carrying a lot of baggage as the wife who had listened patiently to her husband's rants, the woman who had waited to begin dinner while listening to her husband yell into the phone. Doug probably assumed that after Howard's death he would be fully in charge, and I would be a shadow owner. That might have happened had Howard's crime not landed on me. But I was caught in the crosshairs of the IRS and I had no options where Nathans was concerned. I was stuck with it and I needed the money it brought in. I needed, as much as it made my hair hurt, to try to understand the place. I also needed Doug—but I didn't need his resentment.

Over dinner a friend who owned another restaurant said, "He's still working for Howard and he clearly doesn't want you there. You better watch out." I respected the warning, but watch out for what? I didn't know enough about the business to recognize my weak spots. Well, they were *all* weak spots. I needed Doug to run the place, like him or not, and any thought of giving him the boot was knocked down by the lawyers, who counseled, "We don't know what he knows. You need to work with him."

A month or so after Howard died, as I started to come to terms with the landscape, I met for a drink with John Laytham, a part owner and the real management force behind Clyde's, which had grown from one 1960s-era Georgetown bar to a corporate family of fifteen or more restaurants throughout the Washington area. Howard and Clyde's founder were friends—but Clyde's had made its owners seriously rich. Nathans was not in their league. As we sat in the bar, warm and fuzzy memories of Howard gave way to a clear-eyed view of Nathans. John displayed an impressive knowledge about my business. "I've never understood why Howard let his general manager work the same hours he did," he said. "It's just a management point, but you should change his hours. He certainly gets a good salary. Howard gave him one percent of the gross, which is very generous. I've heard of general managers getting a percentage of the net but not the gross."

"I didn't know any of that," I said. "I have no idea what he makes." Why didn't I? I asked myself. My entire professional life taught me to ask questions, yet here I was mute, tiptoeing around, perhaps because it was so overwhelming, or because I feared the answers. Would I know what to do with the information? Rare was the question that prompted a reply that made me happy.

John told me Doug's salary and the details of his arrangement with Howard. "He makes top dollar in this town." He paused. "He's okay, though. I think he's honest, and that's rare in this business." That's what Howard had said, too. At the end of a day in which he and Doug were at loggerheads, Howard would say, "He's honest. Full of shit sometimes, but honest."

Sitting with John I couldn't help but recall Howard's philosophy about shenanigans in the saloon business. There was what he called "tolerable theft." Now more than ever I wished I'd probed what that meant. Where was the line and did it apply to management as well as staff, or did it apply only to the owner?

Once the IRS case landed in my lap, I started seeing Doug with new eyes. He had greater value to Howard than simply managing Nathans. As far as the lawyers were concerned, his job was to look the other way. In one of our speakerphone meetings, a disembodied legal voice said, "If Doug knew Howard wasn't paying taxes there was no way he could fire him." Did Doug know? Was that what got him the big salary—a good chunk of it off the books—and his job security? He swore to me he had no idea.

I gave Doug a ride to the office of the accountant, Martin Gray. I expected a routine meeting to bring me up to date on the financial picture at Nathans. Martin's office was cramped. Cardboard boxes were stacked all around, "Nathans" written across most of them. "What are those boxes?" I asked him.

"Nathans checks," he said. "They're being coded for the IRS."

"Oh." There was never an answer that made Howard or the situation he left me in look good.

"Every check that Howard wrote is coded into their report," he said. "They can call up any check they need." So many boxes, so many checks, so much of my life bundled in stacks, wrapped in rubber bands, "coded" for the IRS, and stuffed inside boxes. I sighed.

The meeting had just started when Doug spoke up. "Howard promised he would make me a partner. He said he would give me five percent of the business." That was news to me. I was stunned. "He talked to me about it. I figured it was going to happen soon. I'm prepared for it to happen."

"I don't know, Doug. I'll have to think about it."

Martin, who knew all the players well, seemed equally shocked by

Doug's statement. Later, privately, he said his surprise was "not that Doug would ask for it, but that Howard would have offered. I don't believe that for a minute."

This much I knew: Howard wouldn't have given anybody 5 percent of his business. If he had even been thinking about it, he would have mentioned it to me at the very least. His view of partnerships was "If you have to take a partner, then get out of the business."

A lot got said in the office at Nathans—by Howard, to Howard, with or without Howard in the room. Fabrication and exaggeration weren't uncommon. With Howard suddenly dead there was ample opportunity for people to come to me with their versions of events, their claims of promises he'd made. Employees were scared, especially as rumors spread about an imminent IRS bloodbath. Doug was scared. I was scared.

As much as I wanted to fire him and make a clean start, I finally realized I couldn't run the place without him, at least not at that early stage. We needed each other. We both knew that. What I hoped was that he'd come to me and say, "I'm here for you. Whatever you need, just ask." Instead, he decided to campaign for a piece of the action. I told him "no," and he bristled. He stewed for a few days, and then a letter arrived from his lawyer.

In careful language it made clear that Doug knew private details of the IRS investigation. It mentioned rumors of illegal practices that went on at Nathans about which, the lawyer wrote, "Mr. Moran was completely unaware." The letter cited the pink checks Howard had given "off the books" to Doug and others, and said Howard had promised to cover the taxes Doug owed on that income. The amount was many thousands of dollars. The letter said Doug expected me to honor Howard's promise and pay those taxes. The lawyer made ominous references to what would happen if I did not pay. It was lawyerly and guarded, but the message was clear: Pay up or Doug will talk.

I faxed the letter to Caplin and Drysdale. They took it seriously enough to convene an immediate meeting over speakerphone. "You'd better pay," advised a faceless voice. "We don't know what he knows, but he knows something. It could hurt you."

One of the lawyers spoke up. "It would be a mistake to fire him.

You have too much at risk. Keep him. Find out what he knows. Don't let him wander off the reservation."

Another asked, "Don't the landlords like him and trust him? Aren't they difficult? Doug is someone you need right now."

In a brief exchange with Doug in the cavelike, cluttered basement office, I said I would "lend" him the money for the taxes but that it would have to be paid out in stages, not in a lump sum. And that he would have to pay it back. That demand was folly but it made me feel in charge. Doug's reaction: "If I had died, and Howard was left running the business, it would be closed already."

THE SPRING THAW had arrived. Soon the daffodils would be in flower. I needed sunlight, the outdoors, vitamins, sleep, and a laugh. Every Friday, Spencer and I drove to the house on the Bay. It was good for us to be out there.

"Mommy, come play with me! Mommy! Come on, don't sleep." I was collapsed on a lawn chair, a zombie, as Spencer stood beside me, his adorable little face not more than a foot from mine. It was hard to find the energy to play with him but I dragged myself up and chased him into the woods. They were not deep woods, but deep enough to thrill a five-year-old. He had a little spot among fallen trees he called "Spencer's Lair," where he fancied himself a woodcutter and carpenter, like his heroes Norm and Steve on *This Old House.* I sat on a log nearby as he focused on his "tooling"—banging stick against stick—and talked to me about Howard. I moved leaves around, head down, and listened.

"Do you think Daddy is watching us?"

"I hope so," I said. "I know he's always watching you. He's watching you, loving you, and looking out for you."

Spencer pretended to saw one piece of wood with another, but he was listening closely and thinking hard.

"If he can see me, why can't I see him?"

"Because he doesn't exist as a person anymore. He's a spirit. But that's good. That's how he can be wherever you are. If he was a person your teacher might ask him to leave the classroom or the playground. Because he's a spirit he can always be there and no one else has to know but you."

"I like that," he said. "But I wish he was really here, like a real person." Spencer looked off into the distance. "I miss Daddy," he said.

"Oh, me too," I said. "All the time." My sorrow was part of me, like a second set of internal organs that went where I went, day or night, but it was made twisted and more painful due to what I was learning, on an almost daily basis, about my baffling husband. I couldn't at that stage accept that he'd done this to us on purpose, but I knew it didn't happen by accident.

I took a small sharp rock that was shaped like an arrowhead and carved words into a tree, one below the other:

LOVE
HOME
DEATH
TAXES

Chapter 9

GEORGETOWN AS A business community does not wake up until after the heavy morning rush hour of suburban commuters from Virginia and Maryland who stream through the neighborhood on their way to work downtown. The people who work in Georgetown—at the boutiques, the restaurants and bars, the galleries and delis—don't begin to appear on the brick sidewalks until midmorning. Nathans sat at the convergence of almost all auto and foot traffic. It was impossible to pass through Georgetown's commercial center without passing Nathans.

In its day, the brick and stucco building had looked smart. The top two floors were painted a pale dusky blue and the trim a dark navy, what's called a San Francisco paint job. At ground level the walls were the original red brick with white trim around big windows. It was built in the Civil War era when Georgetown was a seaport and a major thoroughfare for Union soldiers traveling from encampments on the Mall to battlegrounds in Manassas and Leesburg. Legend has it the basement had been a prison, the middle floor a tavern, and the top two floors a brothel. In today's commercial real estate parlance that would be excellent "mixed use." Members of the Halkias family, who owned the building, recalled that when they lived upstairs in the 1940s and '50s they had operated a deli on the ground floor and would pull taffy in the windows. "All the children stood outside to watch," George Halkias had told me.

When Howard died in 1997, both the business and the building were past their prime. The once-smart paint job was faded and cracked, the roof needed repair, the kitchen equipment showed its age. Nonetheless, the brass plaques gleamed on either side of the corner front door; the navy blue awning hung proudly. The plaques and awning each had only one word: NATHANS. No apostrophe. Inside, the wide-beam teak floors got buffed with a fresh coat of polish every morning by the dishwashers, who were the first to arrive at work, followed soon by the cooks. When the day bartender arrived, the five rows of liquor bottles on the back bar were replenished and polished to an inviting shine, the barstools were lined up neatly, and the bar was wiped down and made ready for business.

Howard built the stacked back bar with a group of friends in 1969 when he first got the place. They had been, he had happily reported, "on a colossal bender." His goal was a wall of liquor on both sides of the center cash register. "When a customer walks in a bar he wants only one thing, to know you have what he drinks. I wanted people to walk in and know that, and to see nothing but liquor bottles."

My morning routine became almost as methodical as Georgetown's. Spencer and I would get in the car and I'd drive him the short distance to his pre-K, just up the hill, and then I'd head back down the hill and make a pit stop at Nathans before heading across town to CNN. Typically, outside Nathans, someone would be washing the sidewalk. Like most of the staff, I would enter through the side door. It put me in the kitchen, where the cooks had stockpots brewing and other prep work under way. On my way to the dark basement I dodged deliverymen pushing dollies stacked high with boxes of carrots, lettuce, tomatoes, fish, meat, beer, liquor, aprons, and tablecloths.

The office, far in the back and literally under the floor of the dining room, was a valiant attempt by Howard to create a habitat where he would be comfortable. Like the upstairs bar it looked like a yacht club, with ship prints and other nautical touches. There were three mahogany desks: one for me, one for Doug, and one for the office manager. But however much the office aspired to being livable, it didn't appeal to me. I liked windows, for one thing. This sunless room with its low ceiling made me feel trapped. In fact, I was trapped. I had to be there to learn how the restaurant worked.

Because I could write a script did not mean I could write a menu. Because I could perform under pressure and meet a news deadline did not mean I could convince a belligerent drunk that it was time to pay his tab and go home. Because I could sense which congressional aide was most likely to betray his boss and give me a scoop did not mean I could interview a college student and sense whether he could wait tables, and because I could get Sharon Stone to pop Larry King's suspenders on live television did not mean I could convince Mr. Garcia, whose trucks picked up the trash each morning, that he should wait another day for his overdue check. Nope. None of that computed. My skills here were useless. Mr. Garcia had all the leverage. "Pay me or let the rats pick up the garbage."

The ire of vendors taught me to be afraid of answering Nathans' always jangling telephones. With monthly taxes getting paid, and legal fees, the once fat bank balance—or slush fund—was shrinking fast. But angry suppliers could not always be avoided. Take, for example, the morning of my first plumbing crisis. I saw it as an opportunity to get involved, to be useful. Doug gave me the name and phone number for the plumber, and I jumped on the case. What I didn't know was that we were behind on our account.

"We need you. When can you come?" I asked.

"When I can get there," he said.

"Well, we need you right away."

"I'd like to get paid right away," he said. "When are you going to pay us?"

"We paid you," I said, hoping against hope that we did.

"No, Howard paid us. You don't pay us. Howard always paid his bills. You're a deadbeat."

I wished I had had the moxie to shout, "Yeah, Howard paid his bills all right but he didn't pay the payroll taxes, you asshole!" But I didn't. I kept my trap shut. I needed the plumber on my side. And I wondered why, with all the lawyers and accountants and managers working for me, nobody ever told me we didn't pay the plumber.

Howard's routine was to call the restaurant every night at ten o'clock, no matter where he was. He checked in to get a report from the night manager. How many dinners? What's the take? Who are the customers? Any problems? That's what he wanted to know. I did the same thing, putting up a good front, as if I knew what I was talking about. Most of the time the news was routine. The dining room sat about 65 people comfortably. The barroom, even when 3 or 4 deep at the bar, sat another 20 or so at tables along the big windows. On a good night, when the tables turned twice, that translated to 120–140 dinners, a solid performance. On the other hand, 35–45 dinners meant bring in the body bags. Dead. I learned to roll with it. As with the stock market, a restaurant owner tracks the long-term averages, but when funds are shrinking, what matters is the daily bottom line. It costs a certain amount just to open the door. If that amount of money is met and exceeded, the restaurant turns a profit. If it isn't met, the day is a loser. Even before Howard's death, the restaurant's volume had started to drop. There were many reasons, but chief among them were more competition in a changing Georgetown and customer fatigue. Tastes change, something new comes along, people move on.

Bars attract a motley crowd, that's for sure—some of them behind the bar, some with their belly up to it. A night without an "incident" was rare. A woman claimed her fur coat had been stolen but no one on the staff could remember her arriving in one. A bouncer pummeled a customer for being unruly. The customer claimed he wasn't unruly, just a little frisky. An intoxicated sports star grabbed a woman's breasts "just for fun." The woman didn't get the joke. Two young women vomited all over the ladies' room before passing out in the muck. A waiter wrote in his own tip on a customer's credit card charge. The customer didn't like that. Another waiter tried to get out the back door with a live lobster in his shirt—a risky move, to say the least—but the manager caught him before the lobster did. A regular bar patron, a generally calm fellow, ripped the men's urinal off the wall because he was having a "bad night."

But the standout of my ten o'clock calls came one Saturday night when the floor manager, Bob Walker, told me that the coat-check girl had gone after one of the cooks with a knife in the middle of the busy dinner service. The fight had started in the kitchen and ended up in the basement with Bob, a bartender, and a waiter struggling to pull the women apart. Apparently the white female cook, in a dispute over the staff bathroom, called the African-American coat-check girl a racial epithet, and the fight was on. Fortunately, the patrons remained unaware of it. Half my job, I sometimes thought, was keeping the lid on so diners could enjoy a meal without somebody chasing through the place with knife in hand or lobster at chest.

In all my years in journalism I had seen some tense newsroom arguments but nobody had ever pulled a knife. Bob said the coat-check girl planned to file an equal-opportunity complaint against Nathans.

"You'll probably want to talk to her," he said. "Maybe try to talk her out of it."

This was exactly the kind of mess in which I was loath to get involved. I had no expertise, no training in how to handle staff fights, particularly of a racial nature and potentially involving liability. Professionally I didn't shirk from confrontations, but dodging tear gas covering a story was better than this.

"Please call Doug and ask him to handle it," I said.

"I did call him," Bob replied. "He said that since you're the owner it's your responsibility."

I fell back on my pillow and sighed.

I DEALT WITH the stress by getting away from it. One way was to hop the train to New York, check into a good hotel—on expense account, thank God!—and lose myself in meetings with celebrities or book publicists on behalf of *Larry King Live.* In New York I could pretend life was as it had been. The city bolstered my battered ego. The people I knew there, friends and professional contacts, saw me as a successful TV producer, as a go-getter, a winner. Even with that welcome lift, on the train home, somewhere between Wilmington and Baltimore, the gloom would descend as I went from top of the world back to tax fraud defendant and owner of a very troubled saloon. I liked feeling like a winner. I didn't like feeling like a loser.

The gloom would also bring troubling thoughts about my dear dead husband. I'd left the stage of shock but was still in denial. Howard couldn't be this bad guy, could he? He wasn't the kind of person who would leave his wife and young son holding the bag, would he? If he was this bad guy, how did I not see it? The rolling countryside speeding by the train windows had no answers. No one did.

SOMETIMES NATHANS HAD its perks, though. I would often invite Martha to dinner. She was becoming a close friend. We would sit in my favorite booth, number 26, and try to cheer each other up. From the moment she'd first learned of the mess Howard had left me, she'd been dismayed. She didn't go deep into the subject with me. It was as if she were watching a house on fire, paralyzed, transfixed by the flames, and unable to do anything but stare. She really didn't know what else to do. Years later she would ask, "What was the hurt in Howard that no one could reach?" but in the early days of coming to grips she was, like me, in a state of mystification. When we talked about Howard, every conversation ended with Martha asking the same question: "What was he thinking?"

Thinking? Is that what you call it? Maybe he was thinking about the merits of Iranian versus Russian caviar; he certainly wasn't thinking about the survivors who would have to clean up the mess he left behind.

While some friends with whom I'd shared the dirty laundry were beginning to show anger toward Howard, I wasn't there with them—yet. He had died while we were in love. Love just doesn't turn off, or it didn't in my case, even with the avalanches of dreck that were landing squarely on my head and in my heart. The love had become different, though. As I slogged through one pile of his crap after another, it shifted more to the kind of love a parent has for a child who is self-destructive and always in trouble. It's still love but no longer unconditional. It becomes colored by frustration, regret, and heartache. The way I saw it, there was nothing I could do but pick up the pieces and survive. Making sense of it would have to wait.

Some nights I checked out of my new reality. I would invite Martha and a group of girlfriends for an after-dinner dance party—ten to fifteen women, all mothers, married, near to middle age, usually at least one pregnant, jumping around to Top 40 dance hits spun by a Nathans deejay until midnight. My anthem was the hit "Tubthumping," with the lyrics "I get knocked down, but I get up again, you're never going to keep me down." It was as if Chumbawamba wrote it with me in mind. The dance parties lasted for a year. I wish they'd lasted longer. The whirling, jumping, and sweating cleared my head and boosted my spirits.

The best way to get away from the constant stress of my life was spending time with Spencer. My goal was to wrap my arms around us and our home, to protect us from the government, from problems at Nathans, problems with lawyers—from the horrible way our lives had been upended. I couldn't get enough of Spencer nor give him enough of me. Hand in hand, we'd take walks along the C&O Canal, wander aimlessly (me, not him) through FAO Schwarz, catch an afternoon movie, or go for ice cream. Occasionally I'd pile him and the dog in the car for a drive without any particular destination in mind. From the backseat I'd hear, "Now, remember, I don't like mommies who cry."

The car became a place for us to talk. It would be that way for years. As a little boy, Spencer would begin the same way every time—"Mommy, tell me about Daddy"—and when I did tell him about his father I had to remember that in his eyes, the man was God: not flawed, not fallen. It was that glorious, funny, and—above all—loving father I recalled for him in story after story. Only down the road—well down the road—would I begin to dole out the truth. Sometimes our car talk turned to loopy discussions about life and death. "Can you have a baby and have the baby be Daddy and he can come back that way?" Then, just like that, he'd fall silent and stare out the back window, sucking his thumb and cuddling Baby. I'd stare ahead into traffic, sneaking glances at him in the mirror. When he fell asleep, that's when I'd cry—not about any one thing, just everything. It was a release.

Howard, literally, had left us all alone. He'd brought me into his world, took me to an enchanted place where I'd be safe, and assured me everything would always work out because he had my back. Then he left me there. The reality he left us was not enchanting and not safe, but dangerous and frightening. There was no one who could bail us out and no one to turn to, only lawyers. His parents were dead. My mother was dead and my father was in poor health. My friends and colleagues were supportive, but the IRS was too intimidating. This was bigger than all of us. I had no special talent I could suddenly market for a cool million or two. I knew I'd only blow what little was left if I tried to beat the odds in a Vegas casino. I wasn't a Bonnie and, anyway, there was no Clyde. The burden was on my shoulders. Everybody else—especially the lawyers and Nathans staff—looked to me for answers, solutions.

So I had to come up with some.

I knew this: Howard and I had got Spencer off to a good start and I wanted to keep our lives on course no matter what. We were dedicated to giving him the sound, balanced world neither of us ever had. Howard had screwed it up big time, that's for sure. Maybe he wanted us to have the best of everything? That didn't wash. "The best of everything" was why we were in this mess, why I was a defendant in a federal tax fraud case, why I felt lost, and, day by day, why I was moving from denial toward anger.

Chapter 10

"YOU SHOULD GO to court. You'd be great on the witness stand," Bob Woodward said to me across the table in his Georgetown kitchen. Spencer and I were having pasta with Bob, his wife, Elsa Walsh, and their two-year-old daughter, Diana. Bob and I had met covering the antiwar movement in 1970 when Bob was working for a suburban newspaper and I was with UPI. Not long after that he moved to the *Washington Post* and the rest is history. I met Elsa soon after they married in 1989. Both of them were friends of Howard's and mine.

"A civil court in D.C. will rule against the IRS because the jury'll be with you," Bob said. Elsa nodded.

When he covered Watergate, Bob had had his own moment under the IRS thumb. Both he and his partner, Carl Bernstein, were audited.

"Are you kidding?" I said. "They'd see me the way the IRS sees me, and that's not very flattering."

"How many women in Washington are single parents?" Elsa said. "How many women in Washington are raising boys by themselves? Women jurors would be on your side. You're more sympathetic than you realize."

"I don't know," I said. "I don't know if I have the stomach to have our dirty laundry washed in a courtroom. The government lawyers would turn our world inside out and upside down. Read what the agent on my case wrote about me. That's the approach they'd take. They'd hold me up as the poster child for selfish indulgence."

Bob was the only person I trusted to read Deborah Martin's IRS report. I figured with his experience as an investigative reporter there wasn't anything he'd see that would shock him. He would not make assumptions about Howard or me. He would look at the facts and weigh them. And, above all, he would be discreet.

Bob got back to me quickly. "I'm sending this report over to Sheldon Cohen. He's my tax lawyer. I first went to him during Watergate, when Nixon had the IRS audit me. I've been with him ever since. He's good. He used to be the commissioner of the IRS. You'll like him. Call him in two weeks."

He gave me Sheldon's number and two weeks later, to the day if not the hour, I called him. His voice was calm and assured. His tone was warm. "You're in quite a jam, aren't you? Why don't you come by and see me?" Sheldon was a partner at Morgan, Lewis, and Bockius, where he headed the tax law department. He was one of the sharpest, most respected tax lawyers in the country. I thanked my good fortune that he would see me.

The law firm's offices were about five blocks from the White House. The building was in the hub of the "old" downtown. The meeting was utterly different from my first go-round a few months earlier at Caplin and Drysdale. For one thing, I skipped the elegant suit and the rest of it. Instead I dressed as I usually did, as Spencer's mom. There was one item I added to my plain shift dress: a pasta and bead necklace Spencer had made in art class.

Rather than being led to an austere conference room, I was ushered into Sheldon's corner office. It wasn't grand but it was comfortable. He got up from his desk to greet me, inviting me to sit on the sofa. Sheldon sat in the adjacent chair with the window behind him. "I grew up in Washington," he said. "My father was in the wholesale food business." Sheldon had an accent that is unique to the Washington-Baltimore area—not quite southern and not quite northern, with a dose of the Maryland shore. "I know about the food business," he said, "how restaurants operate. What your husband did goes on in that business sometimes." His tone was warm and sympathetic. I no longer felt that I was already on trial and staring a guilty verdict in the face.

"I don't have a clue what Howard was up to," I said. "He didn't include me in his business affairs."

"Well, that's not unusual. It's not unusual for a wife to be unaware of such things. It happens," he said.

"How did my husband get in this mess?"

"I don't know for sure because I have only the IRS report, but I would imagine he got a little greedy. It seems he ran the books the old-school way—out of his back pocket. That was fine until the tax law changed a couple of years ago. Businessmen couldn't write off all those meals and martinis, and that hit the restaurant business hard. That's when he should have cleaned up his act, because the IRS started looking precisely at small business operators like him." The IRS knew restaurant profits dropped because of the changes in the law; therefore the income of their owners had to drop, too. But restaurant owners, like everybody else, don't enjoy seeing their incomes drop. "All that cash looks so tempting and readily available. In a nutshell, Howard opted to break the law to keep his personal cash flow robust.

"You have a couple of problems here," he continued. "There's the unreported income, that's one thing. But what really gets under their skin is not paying the withholding taxes, especially since he was taking the money from the employees and using it for his own purposes."

A woman charged into the room. "I'm sorry I'm late," she said, coming to a full stop in the middle of the room. She was slight, with short blond hair, modest jewelry, wearing a trim tan pantsuit, and smiling. She was much younger than Sheldon but, like him, all business.

"Let me introduce you to Miriam Fisher," Sheldon said. "She works with me. I asked her to take a look at the report. I wanted her to be in here with us." We shook hands.

"Bob and Elsa think I should go to court and fight," I said. Sheldon smiled.

"There are many things Bob is smart about," Sheldon said, "but he's not a tax lawyer. That's why he has me. It would be wrong for you to go to court. You could lose. This is not an example of the IRS being mean-spirited or wrong. In this case the IRS was doing their job. They got the evidence and they got their man."

Miriam paced back and forth and then perched herself at the edge of Sheldon's desk. "Even with the atmosphere as it is right now on Capitol Hill," she said, "where everyone is down on the IRS, where everyone is crying for reform, this would stand as an example of the IRS behaving properly."

So the IRS was right about Howard. Would they see me the same way? I didn't care about court. What I cared about was survival.

"This is what I'm afraid of," I said. "If I settle with the IRS, if I sell what we have, my son and I will have nothing. If I lose the restaurant, too, we'll be in a very bad way. It supports us. When I went to work at CNN they agreed to let me work part-time and, because I was subsidized by Howard, I accepted a part-timer's salary. I try very hard to be a full-time mother. My savings are nil. I'm getting a salary from Nathans but I'm having to use money from Howard's estate to make ends meet. I know that's money the IRS wants but it's all we have. The situation is spiraling out of control. Every day we have less—and we didn't do the crime."

"I know it looks bad to you," Miriam said, "but I read the report and I see a lot of opportunity."

Miriam resumed pacing. She tossed out ideas that had to do with the ins and outs of tax law and asked me a lot of questions. She wanted to know about my work, my involvement with Nathans, to what extent I'd been involved in the business, if at all. I tried my best to answer, but any tax questions were over my head. I was mesmerized by her, though. Even when she didn't talk she was still in motion. She was younger than me but that wasn't a divide. Miriam and Sheldon traded ideas in the language of the law, but then they'd turn to me and try to explain. They didn't talk down to me. They were struggling to find a solution to my crisis. I watched and listened. Even though I didn't understand all of what they were saying I was overwhelmed. Tears filled my eyes. I couldn't help it. I was so grateful. Sheldon and Miriam were compassionate; they gave me hope, and the more hope they gave me, the more relief I felt, and with the relief came the tears.

Sheldon leaned forward in his chair, resting his arms on his knees, hands clasped in front. "I think you have a colorable argument for innocent spouse," he said. It was the first time he had uttered those words of hope that I was clinging to.

I told them that innocent spouse had come up at Caplin and Drysdale. "That's the first I'd ever heard of it. But they said I didn't stand a chance."

"I disagree," Sheldon said. "I think you do have a chance, and I should know because I wrote the innocent spouse code when I was commissioner." He gave me a brief history of the code, which was written specifically to protect a widow who was unaware of her husband's tax fraud. In that case the woman didn't know her husband had another family and that he was using his income to support them, too, but not paying taxes. When he died, the whole mess landed on her.

"Sheldon, are you sure?" I asked. I was afraid to get my hopes up too high.

"We have to learn a lot more about you. We have to prepare a defense. We're going to have to fight for it. But we will fight."

"When I tell you I knew nothing about this, really nothing, I'm telling you the truth. I had no idea this was going on," I said, looking from Sheldon to Miriam and back to Sheldon. "I know I signed the tax forms. That's my signature and I remember signing them. I just assumed if an accountant prepared them they were okay. It never occurred to me to question them. I don't think I even looked at them."

"It happens all the time," he said. "Wives never read the documents; they just sign them. My wife used to be like that, but I told her she ought to start reading what she signs. You should too, from now on."

"You know," I said, "financially we led separate lives. I wasn't involved in his business. I never saw his books. We had separate checking accounts, separate credit cards. Howard paid almost all the bills, and that was fine with me. I liked it."

"Did you take money from the business?" Miriam asked.

"Not really." I paused. "Well, I guess, sure. Sometimes I would need some cash and Howard would tell me to ask the bartender. I didn't question it."

"Were these large amounts of money?"

"No. A hundred dollars here or there and *very* infrequently, months apart, and this was several years ago, when I wasn't working. I assumed it was our money."

"That's okay. There was no reason for you not to think that," Sheldon said. "What they look for is a pattern of abuse, of regularly taking money, of knowing you are living off ill-gotten gains." On that score I knew I was clean.

I jumped ahead. "Can I switch law firms from Caplin and Drysdale?"

"Yes, you can," Sheldon said.

"I feel like a criminal there."

Sheldon folded his hands. "On their behalf, I would say this: They were used to working with Howard. He'd been with them for months. He was the client. He was the one who did it. And then you walk in the door. Suddenly they have a new client but the same old case. It's not easy to change gears like that."

"Innocent spouse is a tough code," Miriam said, "but it's changing. It's being debated on Capitol Hill at this very moment. There is a move to liberalize the interpretation of innocent spouse and I think it will happen. You could benefit from that. Your timing couldn't be better."

"Innocent spouse has been granted thousands of times," Sheldon said, "but it's not given away. It doesn't work most of the time because the wife knows the income isn't being reported or she participated in the business. She's involved. In that case, no dice."

Sheldon paused then leaned forward in his chair. "If you come to us with the case, this is what we will do," he said. "I will build a wall around you and Spencer and try to save the two of you. The business won't matter. After we save the two of you, then we'll decide whether we want to save the business. But the first fight is to save you and your son."

I had one final question. "How do I pay you?"

Miriam explained the money could legitimately come out of Howard's estate and Nathans. If I won innocent spouse, that arrangement would hold. If I didn't, all bets were off.

The next day I called Sheldon and said, "I want you to represent me." Caplin and Drysdale were understanding about my decision. Now, with Sheldon and Miriam on my side, I was ready to fight.

Chapter 11

In late May, Washington was postcard beautiful. The whole town came alive, and I did, too, because for the moment the IRS was not hitting me right between the eyes. The case was in transition from one law firm to the other, and Sheldon Cohen and Miriam Fisher were getting current. Deborah Martin at the IRS agreed to stand down until they were ready. The white and pink dogwood blossoms sat delicately on their leafy branches. I ran hard each morning, skirting the Potomac River, passing below the Watergate apartments and the Kennedy Center, up and around the Lincoln Memorial. Sometimes I stopped at the Vietnam Veterans Memorial to touch a few of the fifty-eight thousand names of the dead inscribed on the black granite wall that rises from the earth as if pushed up by some elemental force of nature. It may be the simplest monument in this city full of monuments, but its simplicity is stunningly beautiful and very moving.

I shuttled between home and the restaurant in Georgetown and the CNN building near the Capitol on the other side of town. Driving a car had never been part of my routine. My father discouraged me early on when he sat fretting and stewing beside me in the front seat, until I pulled over, got out, and said, "Here, you drive." Howard always drove—always—and I was always the passenger. In too many ways, I was the passenger. But now the car was my sanctuary. I listened to music. Listened to my thoughts. And when I needed to, I cried. Sometimes at a stoplight the driver in the next lane would notice me, blubbering at the wheel. If it was a good enough cry I arrived at my next destination—home, school, restaurant, show, lawyers—refreshed and ready to move on.

I asked Martha, "Do you cry?"

"Yes," she said.

"Where do you cry most often?"

"In the car," she said.

After Howard died, Martha and I spent a lot of time together. It was odd that Howard and I had been together for twenty years and only now were Martha and I getting to know each other. Howard loved her, as he did his parents, calling on their birthdays and on holidays, but we saw them rarely. Howard wanted it that way. Now I think he was afraid of what they might tell me about him. I had to push for more frequent visits. When Spencer was born we got together with Martha more often, but by then Howard's father was dead and his mother was lost to Alzheimer's. The visits would usually be at the family home in Alexandria, or later in Delaware, after Howard and Martha had moved Mrs. Joynt there so she could be closer to the home Martha shared with Vijay in New Castle. They had one son, Zal, who was at Vanderbilt. But only now did Martha and I have time alone together. The more I looked at her—across my kitchen table, or across booth 26 at Nathans—the more I saw Howard's face in hers, the same brown eyes, the same white hair. She was trim and fit, a dedicated rower.

One night Martha and I were in the kitchen having a glass of wine before dinner. I'd just tucked in and given a kiss good night to Spencer. Suddenly I spontaneously blurted out that Howard had hit me. More than once. I leaned against the kitchen counter and looked down at her, sitting at the table, expecting to see her jaw drop.

But, no. She didn't appear surprised. Instead, looking down at the floor, she said, "It happened before."

My jaw dropped. I stopped what I was doing and sat down. "No! You're kidding!" I couldn't tell if Martha did or didn't want to talk about it, but I had to know. I needed her to help me bring this stranger, this intimate stranger I'd lived with for twenty years and once thought I knew, into focus. Howard was like an iceberg. The dangerous part was beneath the surface. That was the dark part I had glimpsed only in alcohol-fed rages. But I was not going to be the *Titanic.*

There were bits and pieces he had told me along the way, about feeling alienated from his parents, about fearing his mother's wrath, but weren't these normal feelings of a child toward a parent? I know he felt he had never lived up to his father's expectations, that he was told he was a disappointment—and often made the disappointments possible, getting kicked out of boarding school and then college for a range of shenanigans, including drinking. There was a lot of in and out of therapy, at his parents' insistence, but he had said, "I just sat there and said nothing until the session was over. It was pointless. I hated that they made me go." His self-esteem was low but he masked it so well—with the clothes, the posture, the good manners, the wit. Until, of course, the deep rage bubbled up to the surface. I needed Martha to tell me what had happened before.

"It will only help me understand him better," I said. "It won't make me love him less." She told me there had been "incidents" with the wife before me. "I don't know a lot, but I know in one case she ended up in the hospital. There was a split and talk of divorce but it didn't happen. They patched it up." She made a bitter face that told me she didn't want to go any further—like discussing Howard's tax fraud.

"I almost called the police once," I said. "I picked up the phone, started to dial, but couldn't go through with it. He stood there practically daring me, and then I hung up. It was my weakest moment." I always thought I could turn it around, that the next day would be better, that when he sobered up he'd see my reason and get help, get fixed, get something. And eventually, he did.

"Well, if it's any comfort to you," I said, "when he got on Prozac his rages stopped. It calmed whatever needed to be calmed. It was a total turnaround."

Martha's revelation meant I wasn't to blame for Howard's outbursts. It was him, not me. I know that's what the books say, and it's what my psychiatrist told me, too, but learning that I wasn't alone, that he'd hit another woman who was close to him, a woman he must once have loved, the mother of two of his children—that took away some of the shimmer and gloss I had given the man. Slowly a more realistic portrait was beginning to emerge.

Every time we got together Martha asked, "So, what's the latest on Nathans?"

"As we sit here I've got spotters at the bar. I hate to do it but all the big boys tell me I have to track the theft. It's always going on but apparently, just as Howard had often said, there are acceptable levels and unacceptable levels." At that moment I didn't appreciate the irony.

I should have had spotters trained on Howard. "I've got a lot to learn," I said to Martha.

Customers I trusted told me that Bob Walker, the night manager, was knocking back the Grand Marnier on the job and often appeared drunk by the end of his shift. He had a wife and children, and he drove home every night. "I don't mean to sound like a nanny but I worry that he's on the road like that."

"What does Doug say?" Martha asked.

"'Not my problem.' That's what he says."

I told Martha that I needed to hire my own bookkeeper to get the books together—a straight set of books, because "Howard kept two sets and I don't know if the one I've got is the straight one or the crooked one." We laughed about that. But the laughter was thin. In fact, there was nothing funny about it.

Invariably Martha would ask, "What *was* he thinking?" I had no answer to that. She also said, "You'll make mistakes. You know you'll make mistakes. But you'll figure it out and pull through."

At my age, a few years shy of fifty, I was experienced enough to avoid the big blunders, and if I did mess up I recovered quickly and smartly—but that was in journalism, the profession I understood. In the restaurant business I wasn't sure I'd recognize a mistake until it hit me in the face, or the backside. There were no tutorials. I asked myself, What would Howard do?—a foolish question. All I had to do was look at what Howard had done to see how foolish the question really was. The ruins were all around me.

Slowly I got settled in at Nathans. While the office, and what went on in the office, confused me, there was a greater comfort level with the dining room and the kitchen. If I brought any restaurant expertise to the business it was that for twenty years Howard and I had dined out at the best restaurants in the world, and by exposure I had developed a sophisticated palate and an appreciation for a wide range of foods—from the street to the highest end. I could talk the talk. Also, we had eaten at Nathans occasionally and I liked the food. After a few months I felt comfortable getting more involved.

I met with the kitchen staff in the empty dining room between shifts, our chairs in a circle. Apart from the senior cook, Lore, no one spoke English. I talked. They nodded. A lot of smiling and nodding. Lore translated from English to Spanish. I spoke effusively about my appreciation of their work, my love of restaurants, and my vision of Nathans' role in the community, and asked if they had questions about my thoughts on food, the menu, or how I wanted the kitchen to operate. They nodded and smiled. There was only one question. Lore translated: "Do we keep our jobs?

Doug seemed reluctant to help me understand how Nathans worked so I went for a tutorial to Fred Thimm, president of the hugely successful Palm restaurant chain. It had started small in New York and grew to a megamillion-dollar corporation on a winning formula of huge servings of steak and potatoes with the occasional supersized lobster. Nobody messed with the formula. The headquarters were now in Washington. Fred and I sat across from each other in puffy leather chairs in the company's conference room, Nathans' financials spread out before us. He looked through the profit-and-loss spreadsheets and copies of the "daily sheet," which showed a more specific breakdown of day-to-day business. "This doesn't even tell you how many covers you did! How do you find that out?"

I didn't know what a "cover" was.

"It means the number of tables served," he said. "You need more information. What's on this spreadsheet just makes the job easier for the guy counting the money. Do you know what it costs to open each day? Has anybody told you that?"

I shook my head.

"I wonder if anybody knows," he said. I was beginning to feel woefully stupid.

"Well, you've got to find that out. You've got to know what you're paying for rent, for food, for payroll, wine and liquor, taxes, all of that. That has to be inside your head. You have to know the numbers and understand them." I didn't tell him that I'd flunked high school math.

"Right now, these numbers look to me like you have some days where you're just working for your staff and the landlords. You open up for the courtesy of paying employees and vendors, but not yourself.

You've got a lot of tightening up to do. Your rent is outrageous but there's probably nothing you can do about that. Your payroll is way high. I can't believe Doug is getting one percent of the gross. Where did that come from?"

Fred talked rapidly, forcefully, and confidently. He was a regular businessman who just happened to have the looks of Jon Bon Jovi, if Bon Jovi wore a pin-striped suit.

"Do you get along with Doug? I bet you don't. I bet in his head he's the only one who knows how to do it and he hates having you there."

"Fred, I've looked around the restaurant and I see places where I can make a difference. I want to get it painted. I'm going to buff up the back room. We need more fresh flowers."

Fred sighed and shook his head. "You don't get it, Carol. That's the fun stuff. Your place is in critical condition. You don't have time for the fun stuff." He grabbed a piece of paper. "This is what you have to do." He leaned over the conference table, writing quickly. When he finished, he took the piece of paper and turned it toward me. On it he'd written:

1. *A new lease.*
2. *A bookkeeper (Are you making or losing money?).*
3. *Settle with the IRS.*
4. *A strong general manager.*
5. *Rebuild Nathans—its brand, its image.*
6. *Sell it, or learn to enjoy it.*

"You think I can do all this?" I asked.

He pulled one of the chairs closer and sat next to me. He put his hand on my shoulder. It was a friendly, almost brotherly gesture.

"I know you can. You're smart enough and strong enough. But you have to stop being a victim and a martyr and start being a survivor and a winner. Carol, you're in denial and you've got to get over it. This is your problem. It's your problem and nobody else is going to fix it for you. Only you."

AFTER MEETING WITH Fred, I picked up Spencer at school, took him home to the babysitter, returned to Nathans' basement office, and made some calls to *Larry King Live.* Then I asked Doug Moran to join me in the quiet back dining room, which was empty in the lull between lunch and dinner. His mop of blond hair was still wet. He'd just returned from the health club. We sat at a round table by the windows. Bright afternoon sunlight was streaming through the glass. The spring weather was beautiful. The sidewalk outside was bustling with shoppers, tourists, students.

"We have to find a way to work together," I said. "It's not good for the staff to feel we're at odds."

"It's hard for me not having Howard here," Doug confessed. No matter what their disagreements, they had been a team.

"It's hard for me, too, but there's nothing I can do about that."

"I worry that you don't know what you're doing," he said. "And I worry you'll go up to New York and meet someone and get married and he'll take my job."

I was flabbergasted. "Doug, the only husband I want is the one I just buried! I'm trying to do the best I can here. My entire focus is on Spencer, Nathans, the IRS, and *Larry King Live.* That's all. I have no room in my life for anything else."

"Are you going to lose the business?" he asked.

"I don't know," I said. "I hope not. I have new lawyers and I'm hoping for the best."

"Well, I know you can't run this place without me," Doug said. "If I'd died instead of Howard, Nathans would be closed already."

"Yes, Doug, you've told me that before."

Chapter 12

"THIS IS HOW we think Howard was working out the math," Miriam Fisher said. She, Sheldon, and I were sitting in their conference room as she explained the details of Howard's tax crimes. Thick legal binders were stacked on the table. It had been almost six months since Howard died. My new lawyers were now read up on the case. I trusted them. I liked them.

Everything circled back to Howard and his father. Mr. Joynt was involved in the restaurant from the moment in 1969 when he decided to buy it for his son. He bought out the founding partners and negotiated a lease with the landlords' lawyer, Dimitri Mallios. It wasn't a very good tenant lease. It heavily favored the Halkias family, who owned the building. Howard had agreed to pay property taxes, insurance, and upkeep for the entire building. He had waived any number of rights. He couldn't assign the lease without the permission of the landlords, and the lease set a very high base rent for the time—according to real estate experts, the highest per square foot in the city. It was a fabulous location but the rent was unrealistic for a 2,500-square-foot bar and restaurant that served a limited number of people. "If you were using the whole building to serve booze and food, that would be one thing," Fred Thimm had told me. "You pay rent for the whole building and use only one floor. You have the potential to raise your gross from $1.7 to $5 million."

With that 1969 lease agreement, the Howard Joynt era of Nathans was launched, and Nathans became a white-hot focal point of Georgetown and Washington nightlife. Fans stood five deep at the bar. Critics loved the northern Italian cuisine, new to Washington in the early 1970s. The fettuccine Alfredo, prepared by Chef Giuseppina, was sublime. The *Washington Post* ran a front-page political prognostication story with the headline AT NATHANS, THEY SPLIT ON CANDIDATES. But even with business booming, my lawyers said, Howard had financial problems. Nathans often needed money and Mr. Joynt provided it.

Miriam and Sheldon uncovered an earlier tax evasion. It happened in 1977, just as we were beginning our romance, possibly simultaneously. The IRS hit Howard with a bill for $700,000 in back taxes. I was speechless—a reaction that was becoming a pattern in meetings with my lawyers. "His father advanced him the money, bailed him out."

Was that the wedge in the marriage that was ending when I met Howard? I wasn't going to ring up the ex-wife and ask her, but it entered my mind. Sheldon and Miriam estimated that over the twenty-eight years Howard owned Nathans, his father had knitted up the shortfall to the tune of $2 to $3 million. Miriam said that in the 1980s, Mr. Joynt advanced Howard even more money to keep the business afloat. "His last loan to him was for $500,000, and before he died"—of prostate cancer in 1989—"he forgave the debt and gave Howard the promissory note. Howard probably figured he was paying the money back to himself. He didn't consider that income—he was just repaying the debt—so he didn't pay tax on it. Also, he didn't give himself a salary. He just figured what was Nathans' money was his money, not unusual in a small business."

"And this will fly?" I asked.

"We don't know," Sheldon said, flattening his hands on the table, "but that's where we are."

A welter of emotions was running through me as I left that particular meeting. The news weighed me down with dismay and sadness. Were my last twenty years just one big lie? Were Howard and I *that* different? How did he carry around these burdens? *Were* they burdens? Maybe not for him, but they were for me.

When Mr. Joynt died, Howard's safety net vanished. He was on his own, no more bailouts. Without Mr. Joynt's subsidy, Nathans couldn't afford itself. The landlords had no interest in working through tenant problems. If there was an issue, they simply ignored it; what they cared about was the rent. The rent was too high and Howard's lifestyle—*our* lifestyle—was too expensive. Howard was a beneficiary of the trust established under Mr. Joynt's will, but the income wasn't enough. And then there was everything he passed through the business.

Howard faced a choice: Pay the rent or pay the taxes, and he chose to pay the rent. I couldn't comprehend how he could forgo giving the feds their withholding tax. Miss one month or two months, maybe, but consistently over five years? That's not an accident; it's larceny. You have to have some real guts to do that, but the courage, if that's what it was, was misplaced. Howard knew the landlords would definitely miss a monthly payment, whereas the federal government would not, at least not immediately.

Howard had liked playing the pirate, the bad boy. He wasn't the first man who grew up soft and well off, secure and with a safety net, who liked living dangerously. The Runyonesque romance of the saloon business encouraged a boys-will-be-boys attitude and made it possible to believe that laws were for grown-ups, not for cowboys on barstools. Howard spent his working hours among the daytime barroom clientele—bookies, gamblers, drunks, fellow saloon owners, and others who lived life on the margins. Many of them seemed to be hiding from something, trying to stay off the radar to avoid a society in which most people played by the rules. In Howard's case, this game didn't pay. Somehow my husband had lost his way, and it pained me that he hadn't wanted to tell me.

I wondered if the dependence on his father was at the root of his deeply buried rage. It can't be easy for a man—and a proud man at that—to rely so much on his father's largesse. It wasn't money Howard could take at will; it had to be bestowed, and usually with a lecture about not getting the job done, not measuring up. Where's the manliness in that, especially if with each bailout, as helpful as it was, he felt like less of a man? Eerily, it was not too far removed from my accepting gifts after one of Howard's violent episodes. Did his tirades at me occur within days of receiving money from his father? I'll never know.

I was beginning to understand the nights I would roll over in bed in the wee hours and notice Howard wide awake, staring at the ceiling. But when I met with the lawyers, I kept those thoughts to myself.

Miriam and Sheldon didn't pass judgment; they just rattled off numbers and possible adjustments. They were confident that some of the items could be negotiated down or away. Where the IRS would not budge, they said, was in the matter of withholding. The government was understandably intolerant of an employer who withheld taxes from employees and then put the money in his own pocket. It was the government's money. There would be no mercy.

"I'm selling things," I told them. "I'm sending stuff to auction, to consignment, selling it to friends. Whatever, wherever."

"That's good," Miriam said. Her expression changed. The lawyerly veneer gave way to a more compassionate face. "This is hard, isn't it?" she said. I nodded and probably betrayed my sadness. "I know. But you're doing the right thing. We don't know how this will turn out, but you have to be prepared." She moved her hand toward mine on the table. She didn't touch me, but the gesture was sensitive. "How are you holding up?"

"I'm okay," I said. "But I hate this. I'm so afraid of losing my home. I can't imagine what effect that would have on Spencer. To lose his father and then lose his home . . ." I was worried about the effect on me, too. I was not ready for that kind of ripping away. I could give up a lot, but I would rather live in our house with cots and sleeping bags and paper plates than have to let it go. It was the one solid thing in our lives.

"Don't worry about that right now," Miriam said.

"I want a summer there," I said. "We need the summer on the Bay."

"I can't say you won't have to sell it, but you can have a summer," she said. "I promise you that."

Miriam said she would meet soon with Deborah Martin, the IRS agent. "And at some point you have to tell me about yourself and your life with Howard. The whole story. This will be a large part of your defense. But I'm not ready for that yet."

How could I share the whole story with Miriam, with anyone? Which parts did she need to know? The love story was real. He had swept me off my feet. He was my prince, and I still loved him as much as ever. It would be easy for me to tell Miriam about the fabulous times we had together, with all the fun, beauty, adventure, and affection. They were real, or at least I thought so. I was holding on to them like trying to remember a dream, even as the good parts begin to fade as the day wears on until eventually, sadly, all you can remember is that it was a good dream. Or should I just go right to the version of our lives that was emerging, the darker version in which Howard was coming more clearly into focus as a tragic charmer who lived large and fell the same way? I knew this: He had loved us, and he didn't want to hurt us, but by doing what he thought was helping, he *did* hurt us. His tragic flaw was his passion for the "lifestyle." You see it in all of literature's lovable rogues. In fiction it may be charming, but in real life it leaves a mess.

Arrangements were made to inventory our possessions. Two friendly enough strangers came into my home and fingered, fondled, and assessed everything from our socks and underwear to books, lamps, knives and forks, plates, chairs, tables, towels, Spencer's toys, appliances, clothing, and carpets. Every last thing we owned, everything that was dear to us, was given a dollar value. The appraisers would ask me what something cost and I would hazard a guess. They would ask, "Are we lowballing or highballing?"

"What?"

"Do your lawyers want the estate to come out worth a lot or a little?"

THE PSYCHIATRIST SAW me once a week. That was barely enough. No matter what, I fit him into my schedule. I couldn't afford him. Neither could I afford Spencer's therapist. But we couldn't afford not to have them. At least our health insurance paid for part of it.

"Talk to me about anger," he said in one session. "What are you doing with your anger?"

"I don't feel any anger toward Howard, if that's what you mean—at least none that I recognize." I thought I spoke truthfully then. "I try to understand what happened but I bang into walls," I told the doctor. "I just don't have room for negative energy." At that time succumbing to anger would have been like hooking an anchor to my life. It would have weighed me down, stopped me in my tracks. Everything was about survival; everything was about getting through the day, getting through the nightmare. Anger would have to stand in line to own a piece of my flesh, my soul.

To survive I had to stay positive, and I was determined to survive.

"Did he think I wouldn't love him if we didn't have a Jaguar in the driveway or a suite at the Carlyle?" I asked the doctor. "That stuff was fun but I didn't love him for his cars."

Spencer recovered at his own pace. He had good days and bad days. Sometimes he was ahead of me, sometimes he lagged behind. I made time for us to be alone together. We took walks. We had picnics by the Potomac. One night we slept in sleeping bags under a starry sky on the lawn of our home on the Bay.

"Do bugs live forever?" Spencer asked me. "I want to find out what lives forever and make it so everyone can live forever. I want you to live forever, Mommy. I don't want you to die."

"We all die," I said. "That can't be changed. Remember the 'Circle of Life'?" That was Elton John's great song from *The Lion King.* I had taken Spencer to see the movie when he was three years old, soon after Disney released it. In it the father lion dies, leaving behind his young son. We both liked the song and when Howard died a little more than two years later, the film resonated with Spencer and me, especially Tim Rice's lyrics to the "Circle of Life." Spencer and I decided together to ask our friend Judith Owen to sing it at Howard's memorial service, where we hummed along, affirming that the circle moves us through our despair "till we find our place on the path unwinding."

"I'm going to change that, Mommy," Spencer said. "I'm going to invent something so you won't die." I kissed his sweet head. I couldn't hold him tight enough. I wanted to blanket him in love.

Another evening, in his bed, we listened through a toy stethoscope to the beating of his heart and my heart. He asked me, "What was it like to feel Daddy's heart stop beating?"

"It was very peaceful," I said. "Like he was being lifted up by angels." Spencer grabbed Baby closer, stuck his thumb in his mouth, and settled into deep five-year-old thought.

It was a quiet evening at the apartment. Spencer was tucked in and asleep. I poured a glass of wine and sat on the floor in the den to sort through old photographs, putting them in groups and loading them into a storage box. Our life together was there in the photos: A Polaroid from our first picnic beside a stream in the Blue Ridge Mountains. My brother's pictures from our wedding, when Howard playfully kissed me with a mouthful of cake. Our honeymoon in Bermuda, both of us on mopeds, tan and smiling. Standing near the surf on the rocky coast of Maine; on a sandy beach in the Caribbean; in Utah during a cross-country drive; on the California coast, my hair wildly frizzed by the salt air; with Spencer between us, only minutes after his birth. So many Christmases, birthdays, anniversaries. Laughter at dinner parties with friends, caught in a flash frame. Silly moments. Somber moments. A portrait here, a portrait there; images of us young, and older, but never old. That's the photo we'd never have.

In the midst of all the drama and complications of being a solo parent, of having the IRS and Nathans on my back, of the continuing revelations about Howard's past, sometimes I needed simply to step away and grieve. The pictures made that happen. Tears spilled from my eyes, falling onto the photos. Oddly, as painful as it was, this kind of pain felt better than the pain of coping with Nathans or worrying about where I'd end up with the IRS. Widowhood had its touchstones. Crying over old photos is part of the grieving process. But there was no guide for what I was going through with Nathans and the IRS.

I put all the photos in a big box, sealed it with heavy tape, and packed it away.

Chapter 13

EARLIER I HAD learned that we owned a boat I didn't know we owned—the Hinckley sailboat Howard sold in Maine—but there was also a boat I knew we owned, one that was usually tied up at our home dock, a thirty-eight-foot powerboat named *Arcadia,* and I could sell her. In fact, I *had* to sell her, and fortunately she sold fast and for a good price. The money went into the estate account destined for the lawyers and the IRS, not into mine. Shortly after Memorial Day and just before the boat went off to the new owners, a dear friend, Randy Parks, helped Spencer and me stow our personal gear into canvas bags. We passed them from the afterdeck to the car like a bucket brigade.

"Today we're saying good-bye to *Arcadia,*" I told Spencer.

"But why, Mommy, why?"

"Because Daddy was her captain, and a good captain, and I would probably just run her into the rocks." He thought that was funny, thankfully, and didn't question me further.

After this we would be down to just one boat, Howard's eighteen-and-a-half-foot Herreshoff, the *Carol Ann,* which to me seemed small enough to keep and too sentimental to let go. I had fantasies that Spencer and I would take her out. Or, perhaps, he would grow up to want her for himself. Regardless, she was a keeper.

When we finished unloading everything, we sat in the cockpit. It was comfortable and familiar. Howard, Spencer, and I had enjoyed some happy family hours on *Arcadia.* I found a half-full bottle of Mount Gay rum in the galley and on my last trip up, I said, "Don't want to leave this, do we? Let's have a sip. A toast, really."

"Why not?" Randy said. "Howard would approve." It was eleven a.m. I poured some rum into two Dixie cups and handed one to Randy.

"To Howard," Randy said.

"To *Arcadia,*" I said. We touched cups together and knocked back the rum.

"I want some, too," Spencer demanded.

"Honey, it's rum. You can't have rum," I said.

"I want to do a toast to *Arcadia* and Daddy," he said.

"Okay, a little toast—but you aren't going to like it, I promise you." I poured half a teaspoon of rum into a cup and handed it to him.

"To Daddy," he said, then reenacted the way we had tossed the rum down our throats. Before it got past his tongue he spit it out, spraying wide and hard. That brought laughter to what was otherwise a sad farewell. I locked the hatch, fastened the canvas cover, and stepped off the boat. It was the first of many good-byes to the life we'd known. I resolved not to look back. If I didn't look back I would be okay. Go forward. Always forward. Forward. Forward. Forward. And I did.

WE WERE INTO summer but it didn't feel like any summer I'd ever known. Every day was a battle or an avalanche. At Nathans, Doug Moran and I paced warily around each other, watching. The staff sensed the tension, and I didn't like that. They were also beginning to hear about the IRS case, and I didn't like that, either. It's not that I expected to keep it secret, but I couldn't talk about it publicly, and the rumor mill, as it usually does, was certain to make a swordfish into a whale.

On the home front, I had to downsize and fast. I asked a real estate agent to sell the Georgetown apartments—two, factoring in the studio down the hall—and help me find a house, "something not too big, not too expensive, but the right size for a mother and a little boy." When I was honest and told her about my IRS issues she reared back like I was suddenly radioactive. I knew it would be this way now. Even if I was earning my own money fair and square, I was branded.

A friend recommended a family financial planner, a nice woman who met with me at the apartment. She arrived in a conservative suit, with a little bow tie at the collar of her blouse, sensible shoes, and carrying a smart briefcase. I greeted her in a T-shirt and jeans. We sat in the den. She opened her briefcase and handed me some forms. I brought her up to date on everything that was happening to us. I told her about the IRS, the debt; Nathans, its debt; the lease; the risks that filled the road ahead. When I was done, she closed the briefcase.

"You don't need me," she said with a thin smile. "You need a lawyer." She stood up, turned to leave, then stopped. "No. You need *lots* of lawyers."

I RETURNED TO New York in June to help produce the *Larry King Live* broadcast that previewed Princess Diana's dress auction, followed a week later by the live show covering the auction itself. Christie's had a party for the princess. Diana was approachable, friendly. I had written her a lot of letters requesting an interview and gotten only polite rejections in reply. She flattered me, though, by remembering the letters. Leaning toward me in the "mosh pit" at Christie's, Diana said, "So much effort for so little result." She laughed. "But really, I'm not doing any interviews."

In all, I made three trips to New York that June of 1997. I didn't like to leave Spencer, but he took it well, and even better when I returned home with a surprise in my suitcase. My trips were on weekdays. We talked on the phone every morning and evening. He was in daylong summer camp and happy to hang out with his pals and babysitter. But I missed him. It was us alone in the world and seeing him each day made the drudgery of survival less draining.

The auction broadcast was a ratings winner. We were "live" from a raised platform in the middle of Park Avenue, attracting attention with lights, cameras, and comedian Joan Rivers. She cohosted from the New York location while Larry ran the show from our "home" studio in Washington. Drag queens gathered around the platform to wave and shout for her attention. Joan loved it. In the middle of it all fire trucks roared past, which added to the raw excitement of live TV. The national audience got a raucous taste of New York. My primary job was to get successful bidders out of Christie's, across the street, and up onto the platform with Joan.

The event won me points back at the office. I needed them. Our executive producer, Wendy Walker, was sympathetic to my plight but still had a job to do, and she expected me to work at full capacity for her to be able to do it. Full capacity from me—with Spencer and Nathans and the IRS all clamoring for my time—had become a challenge. Wendy made clear that being a productive and hardworking member of the *LKL* staff had to be moved up on my priority list. Our working relationship was strong because I did what she asked me to do—land the biggest gets, the hard-to-book people who draw winning ratings. When I first took the job, before Howard died, Wendy and I discussed it over lunch. "I need someone to go after the interviews Barbara, Oprah, and the *Today* show are trying to get," she said. "I need someone who can write the letters, make the phone calls, take the meetings, negotiate, and get it done." I told her that it sounded good, that it was what I wanted to do. Because of Spencer, I asked to set my own schedule, which amounted to a half day in the office.

"If I get the people you want me to get it won't matter whether I'm ever in the office," I said. "If I don't get them, it won't matter if I'm in the office all the time." She agreed. Becky, the show's senior producer, was not enthusiastic about the arrangement, however, and she was not shy about making that clear to me. Wendy said, "Don't worry about Becky. I'll deal with Becky." That was fine when I delivered, but Becky's doubts and objections had more influence after Howard died and my performance weakened.

The main office of *Larry King Live* was a warren of cubicles on a top floor of the CNN building, a stone's throw from Union Station and the Capitol. In the middle of the office was a "booking board." It was big—about seven feet by eight feet—and displayed two calendar months. As soon as a producer had a confirmed booking, the name of the guest, the studio location for the interview, and the producer's initials went up on the board. Nobody wanted white space. As a producer, you wanted your initials all over it. Once upon a time mine were everywhere. Now, not so much.

"I can't imagine what you're going through," a sympathetic Wendy said during a meeting in her office. "I think you have too much to do. I'm going to lighten your load." While I appreciated the gesture, she took away the least heavy part of my burden: the books. Authors don't say "no" to network interviews, least of all to Larry King. The challenge with the book beat was to let a publishing house down gently because you might very well have to call the next week to ask a favor. I didn't want to give up books because that beat kept my initials all over the booking board. After my load was lightened, my get list was daunting. The pope was still there and the queen of England and "other royals," plus Paul McCartney, Mick Jagger, Madonna, Woody Allen, Oprah, and Michael Jackson.

I never treated Wendy's requests with anything less than absolute seriousness—nothing ventured, nothing gained—and so I pursued a meeting with New York's Cardinal O'Connor regarding the pope. We met in a handsome reception room at St. Patrick's Cathedral, resplendent with silks and brocade and important art. He was friendly and chatty, but his message was clear: "The pope is not going to do an interview." No surprise there.

"We've heard there's something in the works with Barbara Walters."

He said nothing, but his expression was priceless.

With Michael Jackson, I made repeated calls to one of his Los Angeles handlers, Sandy Gallin. He never took my calls but had an assistant leave a recorded message: "Mr. Gallin wants you to know that Michael Jackson will never do your show so don't call back." That didn't stop us. Oprah's people always took my calls, always took my pitches seriously. But Oprah would only do the interview if Larry came to her in Chicago, and Larry did not like to travel. I dogged Lisa Marie Presley but she was as elusive as a hummingbird. Wendy's personal obsession was to bag an interview with Doris Day. No matter how much Wendy may have wanted her, though, and how hard I tried, Doris Day was not to be gotten and that was that.

I brandished my target list at Wendy and begged for mercy. "Please give me some people who are gettable. I need some easy stuff."

"Carol, you weren't hired to go after the easy stuff."

Chapter 14

WIDOWS WEAR BLACK and people take that to mean they've shut down—suppressed their emotions—but really, they don't. There's still a living, breathing woman inside and the emotions are similar to what she felt when she had a living, breathing husband. Coping with loss, grief, and survival puts a damper on thoughts of romance, including sex, but they don't go away entirely. More than anything I needed a hug, arms around me, a shoulder, but there were also instinctive stirrings for something more. In the months after Howard died, I thought about kissing, and men in general, in an abstract way. I thought about past kisses rather than future kisses. When I thought about sex, I wondered whether it would ever happen again. I was a mother in my mid-forties who was accustomed to marital sex. Everything was familiar and comfortable. The idea of having sex with someone new caused me agony. It felt like betrayal. Also, I was clueless. It sounds ridiculous, but I felt as if I didn't know how to have sex now. What about AIDS? What about condoms? Aaaarrgghhh! It scared me. It had been too long since I'd been in the world of singles, and now all the singles were half my age. The last time I was single we hadn't heard of AIDS. I was part of the pill generation, not the condom generation.

I REMEMBER MY first real kiss. It was from my boyfriend Tom Harvey when we were in our early teens. It was a Sunday summer afternoon, sunny and breezy. We sat at the edge of a dock on a creek. I wore a yellow sleeveless shirtwaist dress and sandals and he was in khakis, a blue short-sleeved oxford cloth shirt, and loafers with no socks. Everything about him was attractive, even his ankles. His dark blond hair was straight and he nervously ran his hand through it, brushing it away from his forehead. He was a year older. He was shy, but not as shy as

I was. We sat side by side, our arms occasionally brushing, and talked about nothing for a while before he leaned over and kissed me. I had waited for that kiss for weeks and when it happened I wanted to shout with joy. I kissed him back. I thought I would dissolve.

My first kiss from Howard was equally wonderful. It didn't happen right away. In fact, for the first two weeks we dated, and even though we spent practically every night together talking, driving around, and getting to know each other, there was no physical contact. There was affection and flirtation, but he didn't make a move on me and I didn't make a move on him. Then it happened, one afternoon, in the kitchen of my apartment in Washington. I was yammering about something and he pulled me toward him and shut me up with a kiss. It was deep and long, and it blew out my nerve endings. That night we made love for the first time, too.

Soon after, driving in the car, listening to music, quietly taking in the views along the highway, he slowed the car, pulled over to the side of the road, and parked. Before I could ask him why he had stopped he took me in his arms and kissed me hard. He kissed me with more passion than anything I'd known before. My blood turned to steam. And then just as purposefully he pulled back, settled into his seat, and eased the car back into traffic. "I just had to do that," he said. "I couldn't help myself." Of all the thousands of times we kissed, that's the one I remember best.

When I did think about widow sex, my mind was not on any particular person. I noticed men. I noticed men all the time. At stoplights, for example, I sat in my car and watched men cross the street, wondering about their bodies and what they might be like as lovers. In a government town like Washington, these fantasies were, well, like Washington. "First," I'd say to myself, leaning on the steering wheel at a red light, watching a man, "you've got to get him out of the pinstripes." Second . . . actually, there never was much of a second.

Sooner or later most women who've lost a spouse have to face the myth of the merry widow, as if the death of a husband turns a woman overnight into a sex-crazed party girl hot on the prowl for the next Mr. Right. It's odd. Widowers are treated like lost dogs who need to be taken in, spoon-fed a fresh casserole, and fixed up with good women. Widows, on the other hand, are on their own. I can't speak for every widow, but I wasn't even remotely on the prowl. If anything, it was the opposite. I didn't want a new other half. I'd been so content in my marriage, and motherhood—especially the last five years—that I only wanted my own marriage back. Early on, some close friends, Trish and Mark Malloch Brown, invited me to the movies and included an unmarried male friend who was visiting from out of town. It was not an official "date," but he was a man and he sat next to me in the theater. Because we were a foursome, two couples, I was uncomfortable. I wasn't used to being with another man this way, even if only a friend of a friend. It felt like I was cheating. I fidgeted through the entire film and couldn't wait to get home. I missed having a man, I missed intimacy, and I hated having an empty bed, but I wasn't ready to invite him, whoever "he" might be, into it. I wasn't about to jump into his, either.

Sometimes men showed up at my doorstep, unannounced. Too often they were husbands of friends, and I would obligingly invite them in for a glass of wine and some conversation. Usually they didn't know why they were there—or, if they knew, they couldn't act on it. I was relieved when they went home. Other men kept a polite distance, as if I wore a widow's black veil. They didn't know what to say to me after we'd covered Howard's death, the IRS nightmare, trying to balance my CNN career, Spencer's well-being, and Nathans, always Nathans. In their eyes I was a widow bereft and cut off below the waist. Bereft was one thing, but I wasn't cut off below the waist.

The only man who treated me like a woman, fresh on the planet, feminine, soft, desirable, and dearly in need of a kiss happened to live and work in New York. Without even seeing it coming, but desperate for something that made me feel good, I ignored my best instincts and fell into an easy, comfortable, and romantic flirtation with Paolo, who had been a friend to Howard and me and who was married. His wife lived in Europe most of the time and they had an agreeable "understanding"—very French. Paolo was a chef on Manhattan's fast track. His downtown restaurant, Umbria, was pretty, stylish, acclaimed, and packed. He was the son of an Italian mother and a French father who had divided his time between both countries when he was growing up. He was younger than me by about five years, full of enthusiasm and love of food, wine, cooking, restaurants, and New York. His accent was an irresistible Euro gumbo that matched his sexy floppy hair and brooding good looks.

Our first meetings were innocent enough. When he generously offered to help me understand this complicated business that had landed in my lap, I was over the moon. He would guide me through the mysteries of chefs, menus, wine lists, and kitchens. We would meet around eleven p.m., after my live show and his dinner service. He'd park his motorcycle on Madison Avenue and walk into the lobby bar of the Carlyle hotel looking practically edible in black—always in black—leather jacket, jeans. Black suited him as handsomely as his starched white chef's jacket. We'd sip tea or wine until both of us were too tired to keep talking. He had the grace and masculinity of Baryshnikov, if Baryshnikov had been a little younger and a little taller and with a full head of dark brown hair.

I'd bring menus, spreadsheets, and profit-and-loss statements to our rendezvous. One night as I blathered away about one restaurant issue or another, he slid his hand over and placed it on mine and left it there, his warm skin caressing mine. I didn't know how much I had missed the feeling until I felt it. I wanted him to never let go. I stopped talking, almost breathless.

"Sometimes we want things we can't have," he said softly, "but that doesn't mean we can't want them. The first time we met I thought you were the most beautiful woman I'd ever seen." I remembered the first time, too, when Howard and I had looked him up at a mutual friend's suggestion. He had been the new chef, and the culinary next big thing, at an Upper East Side bistro. As he emerged from the kitchen in his crisp chef's jacket and headed toward our table with a smile, my silent reaction was "Wow." I never thought of chefs as alluring until that day. But I was married and he was married and I put the thought away.

He wrapped his fingers in mine and leaned in close. "You are still that beautiful today." Now tell me, what widowed tax fraud defendant with a cash-strapped saloon wouldn't want to drink at that fountain?

He walked me to the elevator. As we hugged good night, and he kissed each cheek, I had the urge to crawl inside his leather jacket and live there. But I was scared and he was married. Been there, done that.

Howard was gone but I still felt very much his wife. Only the rules had changed. The new rules said I was free to do as I pleased. But what was that? I asked myself.

Paolo called me often at home in Washington around midnight. He'd be in his kitchen office; I'd be in bed, with the phone cradled by my ear on the pillow. We didn't talk about anything in particular, really; we talked *around* things, flirting. He'd gloat about good news. "The king of Spain was in tonight." Or the celebrity customer would be Woody Allen or Johnny Depp, his personal favorite. Tim and Nina Zagat were at a table and swooned over the food. The *Daily News* was about to do a review and he'd heard it was good.

At my end of the line I'd whisper, "Well, I got the spotters' report and only two of the bartenders are stealing and only one is seriously over-pouring. We got a $100,000 lawsuit from a woman who said she slipped on a butter pat and it ruined her sex life."

PAOLO WAS AN elixir. One flash of his smile threw off enough positive energy to bolster several days of my war-torn life in Washington. I craved a romantic dinner for two. I wanted us to behave like normal people, the way I remembered these things. I wanted to dine with him, drink wine with him, eat and talk with him. Yes, I had a crush on him. I was infatuated.

We made a proper dinner date and he picked the restaurant, owned by a friend. Paolo picked me up in a taxi and we rode together to the restaurant just off of Central Park West. The maître d' greeted Paolo warmly and led us to a corner table. It felt private. There was candlelight. A lovely tapestry hung on the wall behind us. We sat next to each other, nervous, both of us aware we had crossed a line. I'd brought no spreadsheets or P&Ls; this was no longer about two old friends talking shop. This was a romance, and Paolo was a man—strong, powerful, macho. He smiled and everything else in my head was vaporized.

"Champagne?" he asked.

"That would be lovely," I said.

We had easy conversation over dinner and our hands stayed on the table with the flatware, the food, and the wineglasses. We did no touching, no fingers grazing hands or arms. Paolo ordered a bottle of

Puligny-Montrachet. We talked about our pasts, our careers, marriage, life, and how we met. Over the course of our dinner the other customers left, the chef said good night, and the maître d' pulled off his tie and followed the chef. By dessert it was only us and the candlelight; the sommelier and waiter kept a respectful distance.

Paolo looked at me but said nothing. He reached out with his hand and took mine and pulled it over to him and kissed my fingers. He kissed them slowly, one at a time.

I leaned close to him and said in a low voice, "You are my secret."

He said, "You are my secret garden." I pulled his hand close and placed the back of it against my right cheek and held it there as if it were a precious possession. My eyes met his and we sat like that until the waiter walked over. We collected ourselves and Paolo asked for the check.

"You are our guests," the waiter said kindly. "There is no check."

Alone again, Paolo took my hand in his and kissed the back of it and turned it over like a leaf and kissed my palm. The tip of his tongue played with the soft skin inside my wrist. I closed my eyes. My breath caught. The fingers of my other hand played with his hair and moved over the back of his head to the nape of his neck. I tried with my touch to give him the same pleasure he gave me.

The waiter shuffled in the distance, snapping us back to reality. I picked up my small clutch and sweater. Paolo had no jacket. He wore a striped long-sleeved shirt of soft cotton. His cuffs were rolled up to just below his elbows. He looked good. We looked good together.

We walked along West Sixty-First Street toward Central Park, his arm around my shoulder and my arm around his waist. The air was balmy. The streets, even Central Park West, were quiet. It was almost one o'clock in the morning. "Let's walk a bit," I said. Under a streetlight, he stopped and turned and took me in his arms. I moved closer toward him, at first tentatively and then eagerly until my face was buried deep in the warmth of his neck.

He pulled back enough to put his hand under my chin to lift my face toward his. He kissed me, at first softly and then more urgently. He stopped and started, his lips softly pressed against mine, and then hard and harder, for what felt like many minutes. Paolo pulled back, his arms still tight around me. "We've got to get a cab," he said. Entwined, we hobbled to the street. A cab pulled up. Paolo opened the door and continued to kiss me. We climbed in, kissing. He came up for air only long enough to speak to the driver—"across the park"—and then he dove back into me. The windows of the cab, all of them, were open to the soft June air, and it buffeted us as we flew through the park, jostled by the cab and the bumps in the road, adjusting our kiss to the motion.

Paolo stopped. "We are not going to become lovers," he said.

"Yes," I said. "I know that. You're married and I'm not ready. Nothing more will happen."

"We are only kissing," he said.

"Yes, only that," I said. We flew back into each other's arms and kissed again. His hand ran along my back and down my thigh and across my tummy to my breast. I cupped his face in my hands and kissed his eyes and nose and lips. When the cab stopped at a light at Seventy-Ninth and Fifth, I gasped, "Let's get out and walk. I have to get some air."

We walked half a block before he grabbed me and embraced me and kissed me again. We stopped in front of an apartment building. He kissed me so vigorously that one of my earrings flew off and rolled across the sidewalk before it went down a grate. "These earrings were a gift from Howard," I said. "I think he just sent us a message."

"I hope it was approval," he said. Doubtful.

We walked along Fifth Avenue, the only people on the street. I walked backward with my arms around his neck, looking him in the face, exchanging more kisses. He pulled me closer and stopped us in our tracks and kissed me again. He held me so close our bodies were practically welded. He kissed my neck and my ears and my mouth. I was limp and warm and flushed.

At the entrance of the Carlyle we decided we should part right there, but each time he walked away he turned back and kissed me again. "Let's get away from the hotel cameras," he said, and pulled me into the shadows just beyond the entrance. He kissed me again.

"I must go now," he said. "It's late."

"So, go," I said.

He kissed me again. "I guess this was dessert," I said, nibbling at his neck.

"The chef's special," he said. "I must go," he said again.

"Go," I replied. He wrapped his arms around me, pulled back, kissed my eyes and my nose and my lips. "You have no idea how wonderful this is for me," I said.

"For me, too," he said, holding me tightly next to him.

"Let's not wake up in the morning and regret this," I said.

"We won't," he said, kissing my neck.

Before we parted we inhaled each other and pulled the scent up into our heads for safekeeping. And then all I saw was the back of him. He was gone, walking toward Park Avenue to hail a cab.

THE NEXT MORNING, swooning in my hotel bed, a smile pasted on my face, I called a girlfriend to tell her what had happened. I was in that goofy, heady, crazy state of mind that comes with a crush.

She would have none of it. She gave me only tough love, especially when I told her I wanted to call him.

"You can't call him! He can't call you! You can't go to his restaurant! You can't have anything to do with him. You made out with him. He's married. You can't have a relationship with him. You just have to back away!"

I knew she was right. I was being selfish, but for a moment I felt whole again. I had been kissed. I was a widow who got her first kiss.

Chapter 15

My days were an organized, well-oiled machine—with chaos lurking just beneath the surface. I zoomed here and here, and there and there. I timed everything. In my new world there was no wiggle room, no time for a delay, a backup in traffic, a meeting that ran over, or surprises. The real world had another plan. It worked on its own time, and inevitably a crisis would strike like a bolt of lightning.

This day began normally enough for mid-July. Searing heat by seven-thirty, too hot to run. A walk to the bagel shop and Starbucks and back home. A shower, then walk Spencer up the hill to his day camp. He was particularly talkative that morning. He was still chattering when I kissed him good-bye and left him at camp. I was in no rush. I would take my time walking down the hill to Nathans. My plan, though begrudgingly, was to give the day to Nathans, to be there, to roll up my sleeves and learn some actual restaurant skills. The morning may have been hot, but it was also quiet and peaceful. It was too good to last. Sometime after nine my cell rang. Wendy Walker was on the line. "Versace's been shot! Murdered! In Miami."

My jaw dropped.

"Get on it, Carol," she said. "We need it for the show tonight."

The fashion elite were still my beat, and this would be my story. As awful as it sounds, I needed a big breaking story like this to prove my value to the show. Journalism thrives on the misfortunes of others. As I walked I began making calls to the design houses of Valentino, Chanel, and Donna Karan, to reps for models such as Naomi Campbell and Cindy Crawford, and to New York PR people such as Susan Magrino and Paul Wilmot. A bee stung me on the toe, making me hop in pain, but still I juggled the phone. I got to Nathans, made my "good mornings" all around, and jumped on the phone at my desk in the basement, my toe still burning.

Wendy called again. "Carol, I think I'm just going to have them work on the show from here. I can't have you there and my not being able to control what you're doing. This is just too big. I have too much pressure on me. Tom [Johnson, the head of CNN] was just on the phone with me and I have to deliver. I just can't take the chance." She paused for a breath. "I hope you'll understand. You'd feel the same way about Nathans. You have too much to do there. You can't possibly give this the time it needs."

I said, "Wendy, I understand and I'll do what you want but I wish you would just give me a try. I can do it. I'm working on nothing else. I'm here. That's what matters at this end. Besides, this isn't any different from any of the other shows I've worked on from out of the office."

"Carol, this is a big breaking story," she said.

"I know. I know. But just give me a chance. Let's see if I can do it. If it gets over my head I'll be the first one to pull out. Why don't we wait till lunchtime to see where I am? I've already put out a lot of calls. I've been doing nothing else." She gave me until noon. I hung up, desperate, but also resenting that I was stuck at Nathans, where I least wanted to be, rather than at CNN with my colleagues, doing the job I loved. The business I owned felt like a cancer eating away at my career and there was nothing I could do to fight it. All I could do was try to juggle both.

The calls I'd put out there were rolling back in. Sometimes I was fielding so many calls that all three lines into Nathans were on hold and I was on my cell. Deliverymen came into the office, waiting for me to sign off on crates of fresh fish, cases of beer, and slabs of beef while I haggled over Naomi Campbell and Cindy Crawford.

"I know Naomi can't stop crying, but that will be okay for us," I pleaded into the phone while one of the delivery guys waited for his check. He gave me a strange look. An architect was standing at my desk, waiting to survey the upstairs. Doug was waiting for me to look over the newly reworked menu. I was juggling calls and taking notes. "Okay. Maybe Naomi can stop crying long enough to do a ten-minute interview with Larry? That's all we need. No? You don't think so? Okay. If she changes her mind, we want her."

Sylvester Stallone, Demi Moore, and Madonna said no. More pleading with Wendy. She extended my deadline. A wine salesman showed up with some of his top wines for me to try. I'd forgotten I'd made a lunch appointment with him.

Wendy was getting more nervous because the big designers—Calvin Klein, Valentino, Donna Karan, Isaac Mizrahi, as well as a half dozen big stars—looked like they were no-gos. I was sitting with the wine salesman at a table in the bar. He'd brought a vintage Oregon pinot noir and two rare rosé champagnes. Some of the summer college-student staff gathered around while he showed them how to uncork a bottle of champagne properly. When he got to the part about the importance of keeping a thumb on the cork so the cork won't fly out, saying "that happens about one in a thousand times," the cork shot out with a loud *bang.* It caromed from the ceiling to the floor to the bar and every man sitting there ducked. I laughed out loud. The salesman did, too.

Wendy called. I pleaded for time. "I'm waiting for a big call. I think I'll have it soon."

"Okay, Carol," Wendy said, "but that's it." I knew this time it really was "it."

A waitress approached the table. A call from Paris was holding for me. It was the Chanel rep, with whom I had a good relationship. Karl Lagerfeld would do the show via satellite. *Jackpot!* I called Wendy, who was ecstatic. "That's huge, Carol!" she said. "Wow! You did it."

I beamed. I needed this booking to prove my worth, to stay in the game. I returned to the table and said to the salesman, "Well, I get to keep my job for another day." He had no idea what I was talking about.

IN THE MIDDLE of all this, Miriam Fisher called. She needed me to pull more numbers together and went through a list of issues that were coming up in the week ahead, such as the final tally of my total debt and a meeting she had scheduled with Deborah Martin at the IRS. "Deborah's very relaxed, so far," she said. I chose to interpret that as a good sign.

A friend had suggested I stash away some money for Spencer and me—just in case. He suggested offshore accounts. I ran this idea by

Miriam. She put the kibosh on that. "In light of your debt and the circumstances," she said, in her most serious, lawyerly voice, "the government would charge you with fraud."

So much for that dumb idea. "Okay, Miriam," I said, "I'll get the numbers for you."

Chapter 16

LATER IN JULY Martha invited us to join her, Vijay, and Zal, at a summer rental on Chappaquiddick Island. I immediately said "yes." Spencer and I packed our bathing suits and sandals and headed for Martha's Vineyard. The "Casa Kumar" turned out to be an old fisherman's camp. We drove to the end of a long dirt road, took a treacherous drive along a lumpy beach, and followed one more dirt drive to the house, which sat at the water's edge. It was stripped down and ramshackle in a poetic seaside way, and we loved it. Meals were shared at a big table in the window-filled kitchen. We all cleaned up together. Spencer and I shared a room, but bedrooms were really just bunk areas divided by partitions. At night we could all talk to one another across them. The windows were open, the breezes blowing through.

In the mornings Spencer would don some goggles and grab his plastic bucket; I would slather him with sunblock, and off we'd go in search of what he called "nature." The water was knee deep for him. We stopped every few feet as he reached down for a rock or a shell. Sometimes when something he was after would suddenly move, he'd jump into my arms. "Mom, are there sea monsters up here?"

"No, honey, don't worry. Maybe some crabs and fish, but no monsters."

At Chappaquiddick, Spencer's world expanded beyond just our usual twosome. Sometimes he'd go off on a hike with his much older cousin, which, as he told me, made him feel "all grown up." As a family we cooked and ate lobsters. We played games, sat at the table, and talked. We listened to music and danced on the beach. Spencer put his little feet on the tops of mine and I waltzed him in the sand. It was altogether lovely. The mosquitoes, of which there were many, couldn't spoil that.

At night before his bedtime Spencer and I would sit outside and look for the brightest stars. I put my arm around him and we'd snuggle.

"Mommy, is Daddy up there or is he here?"

"What do you mean, sweetie?"

"Well, you said he's watching over me all the time but he's a spirit. I just wondered if he was up there on a star or down here with us."

"Where would you like him to be?"

"Here with us."

"That's where he is."

"Good."

Spencer's childish interpretation of death was endearing, a balance to my own acceptance of the hard reality: Howard was completely gone. He was a life form that had vanished. I had no idea when Spencer would come to terms with that view. Over time he did, but for the longest time he looked up and believed his daddy was there, in heaven, keeping an eye on things. Who would want to rob a child of that hopeful notion?

MY FATHER WAS seventy-nine years old and in failing health. He suffered from diabetes and Parkinson's disease. When my brother David called to say Dad had been admitted to the hospital with a heart problem, Spencer and I raced to his bedside in rural Virginia. My other brother, Robert, who lived near my father, was there when we arrived. David had made it sound like the bell was tolling but when we arrived the doctors said that while Dad was in rough shape, it was not his time. I treasured my visit and gave him loving assurances and kisses, but afterward I told Robert, "You and David have to handle this. I'm tapped out. I can come see him, I can spend time with him, but I can't handle the heavy stuff. There's no more of me left to pass around." And there wasn't. He died within the year and was buried with full honors at Arlington National Cemetery, where I read the eulogy. Spencer and I, with my brothers, walked behind the horse-drawn caisson to his grave.

While seeing his grandfather was fun for Spencer, seeing him in a hospital brought up too many memories of his father. As we walked out into the fine summer day I asked, "Would you like to hike a mountain stream?" The hospital's location was close to the Blue Ridge Mountains. It was a weekend. We had time. Spencer beamed.

We drove up, up, and up a twisting mountain road in the Shenandoah National Park and parked near a familiar trail. I'd been there years before and recalled it as tame enough for urban folk. We looked for "nature" and right away we found it in the form of a snake. It was gray with white stripes and we decided it had to be poisonous. "Mommy, you're not the one who knows how to kill snakes. That's Daddy, and he's not here. We shouldn't be around a snake without Daddy." He pulled me away.

We held hands and walked deeper into the woods, away from the snake. I held him over a stream so he could drink from the clear mountain water. This he declared "cool." Later, at a roadside country store, he wore down my resistance and I bought him a plastic Davy Crockett rifle. He cradled it in his lap. "I'm a real mountain man," he beamed. On the highway, headed home, Spencer stared out the window for quite a while then turned to me and asked, "Mommy, if you marry again will you tell me if it's an alien?" I promised him that I would.

Chapter 17

THE PACE OF my life was quickening. While June and July were packed with enough New York high life, professional success, and personal excitement plus an escape to the Vineyard to make me believe my problems had gone away, August reminded me they had stayed put, waiting for me. I may have been changing but my problems remained the same. Sometimes they overwhelmed me, but apparently it didn't show.

"You don't look the same," a French friend told me soon after we returned from the Vineyard. "You always used to look like a woman carrying a burden, head down, very serious. Now you look like a woman who's walking on the Champs-Elysées with your head up and smiling." Odd that before Howard died, when I didn't have a burden I looked like I did, and now, with nothing but burdens, I looked stress free.

My psychiatrist noticed it, too. "Something in you that was dormant is waking up," he said.

"Not a moment too soon," I replied. I knew I was changing. I stood up straighter and my step was more purposeful. I could see it, feel it. But I couldn't explain it. My troubles in the real world were as daunting as ever. I guess Nietzsche was right: That which does not kill us makes us stronger.

The staff at Nathans needed a lot of attention. The night manager, Bob Walker, asked for a raise. I used his request as leverage. "I don't mind giving you something but in return I'd like you to knock off the sauce when you're on duty." He didn't look happy. "Look, Bob, you're the responsible grown-up here at night. I worry about your driving home. You're a father. I really want you to do this for me but if that doesn't work, do it for your family."

He nodded. As I walked away, he said, "Doug thinks all the managers should get raises."

I stopped, turned, considered what he'd said, turned again, and then continued to the office. His words got me rattled. Where was the money supposed to come from? They were the most highly paid managers in the city, their pay scale out of line with what the business made. Doug Moran knew I had the government breathing down my neck. I still couldn't figure out what he did for his hundred-thousand-dollar salary—and now he wanted more?

AT *LARRY KING LIVE,* Wendy called me into her office. "Here, Carol, I'll give you an easy one." She asked me to book George Stephanopoulos, who'd left the Clinton administration the year before. He was reportedly writing a book about his years on the campaign trail and in the White House. I was grateful for the bone she'd tossed me but I wished she'd told me that everyone else at CNN, including the network's White House correspondent, had pursued him without success. His publisher would be nuts to let him do any interviews before the book was even written. "These are the summer doldrums," Wendy said. "We need bookings." Stephanopoulos did not return my calls.

I would swing in and out of moods about the show. I loved the work, but what I used to think rocked the world now could feel shallow and pointless. I liked to take on world issues, but I couldn't get stressed anymore over whether Michael Jackson or Mick Jagger would do an interview. But I needed to be productive because I really needed the job. Stephanopoulos would have been a nice little coup. I tried, I failed.

At Morgan, Lewis, and Bockius, Sheldon and Miriam worked hard to find ways to bring down the tax debt. Miriam asked me to sift through five years of Howard's credit card charges, particularly restaurant charges, and to mark those that were business related. What qualified as a business dinner, I wondered? I recognized so many of the charges. Did champagne and steamed lobsters at a romantic window table at the Black Pearl in Newport, Rhode Island, count as a business dinner? It was October 1993, a sailing trip in New England, our first time away from Spencer, and I was anxious about leaving him. Howard pocketed the dinner menu as he always did when we ate out. In the restaurant world, did that make it a business dinner? Another restaurant owner told me, "You write off all your meals. Why else be in the business?"

"Why does Deborah Martin's report cover only five years?" I asked Miriam at one of our meetings.

"Because that's when they decided to stop looking. Deborah had enough. She had a good case. She could have gone further back and would probably have found more, but she said she had enough and stopped."

I WAS CUTTING my emotional ties to our possessions. I looked at the furniture in terms of what could go and what should stay. It came down to this: We've got to have beds, chairs, tables, a sofa. Almost anything else can be sold. I needed cash, desperately. Spencer and I operated on a third of the income we had had when Howard was alive. We weren't poor, but our household expenses cost more than what I had. It cost a lot to keep the Bay house and the apartment in good working order so they could be sold. I had to be smart—and legal—and try to find money somewhere to keep everything going.

Howard's estate was fat with money that I couldn't use. Dividend checks from his stock portfolio regularly arrived in the mail. They were in Howard's name and, with Uncle Sam watching, I had to put them in the estate bank account. The money from the sale of anything that was in Howard's name went into the estate account as well. The income from the Joynt family trust stopped the day he died. The way the trust was set up, when Howard died the remainder went to Martha and her son and to Howard's two sons from his last marriage. Since the trust documents and Mr. Joynt's will were written before Spencer was born, he was not mentioned. There was a lot of money around us, but none of it was mine or my son's.

I EXPLAINED MY IRS problems over dinner with Roger Cossack, host of a legal affairs program on CNN. I told him that even though my lawyers were "building a wall around me," letters from the IRS arrived in the mail every week. "They threaten to put liens on my bank accounts, to seize whatever property I own, to take my car and anything else they can get their hands on. They are really scary letters," I said.

"What do you do with them?" Roger asked.

"I open them, read them, and fax them to Miriam Fisher. Maybe I should skip the reading part and go direct to the fax. Might be better for my mental health.

"Once I actually called the IRS 800 number to tell them I had legal representation," I said. "That didn't impress the woman at the other end of the line. She started asking me when I was going to send a check for the full amount. You know, a few million dollars."

"You're on their radar," Roger said. "Most of us live our lives and never show up on it. We just hope to stay that way. You used to be off their radar. When this is over, you'll be off it again, but that may take a while. Don't be surprised if they audit you for a few years."

"But what about the people who can't afford a lawyer?" I asked. "I think about them every time I get one of these letters. They make me feel like a deadbeat, a criminal. Never a hint that I might be innocent."

Not that the IRS needed any guidance from me, but I was struck by how cold it is out in the cold. "If I didn't have lawyers explaining everything to me, calming my paranoia, I'd probably be locked in my house with the furniture piled against the door. I hope when the hearings on the Hill are done the IRS tones down its language. They need to hire Miss Manners."

"You forget that a lot of these people they pursue did commit fraud, did break the law." Roger was again the lawyer, but I knew he was right. "Those letters are crafted for the guilty, not the innocent."

Roger was a widower and his son was grown and out on his own. I told him about Spencer and how much it weighed on me each time I went to New York for the show. "It's tough because the trips are good for me but I worry I'm some kind of awful mother, leaving Spencer with the babysitter."

"Go," he said. "Give yourself the time away. Enjoy yourself. Spencer will be fine. If it makes you feel better, call him every hour on the hour and drive him nuts. But he'll be fine."

I GOT TO know another widow who had had her own experience with the IRS. It didn't turn out very well. Leona Helmsley served time in prison for tax fraud. Her case was in every public way the opposite of sympathetic. In her trial she was quoted as saying, among many other incendiary gems, that she didn't pay taxes because "only the little people pay taxes." In my pursuit of an interview for Larry King, I invited her to dinner. We went to the ultra-upscale French restaurant Daniel, which at the time was on East Seventy-Sixth Street. It was at the top of the heap among New York restaurants. I'd heard that it was a favorite of Mrs. Helmsley, who liked everything haute, including the cuisine and the wine. Mrs. Helmsley didn't eat in downscale restaurants. I supposed they were for the "little people."

A well-polished long black limousine pulled up on Seventy-Sixth Street outside Daniel precisely on time and out stepped the "Queen of Mean." She looked great, much brighter than she had been at an earlier lunch with Larry, his fiancée, Shawn Southwick, and me at the Park Lane, one of her hotels. Her short dark hair appeared soft and not the least like a helmet. She wore an attractive black linen dress that hit just above the knee. Around her neck was a double strand of pearls so amazing that later, during the meal, I asked if I could touch them. "Sure," she said, as if people asked her that all the time. The pearls were the size and weight of marbles. More haute than that you could not get.

As we walked to the table a number of people reached out to greet her. She was gracious. I did not sense any of the bitterness that had showed at our lunch.

"That man who just kissed me on both cheeks," she said as we took our seats, "he tried to outsmart me in a deal."

"What happened?" I asked.

"I outsmarted *him,*" she said, placing the napkin on her lap.

Daniel Boulud, the superstar chef, came to the table to say hello and to ask, "Can I cook for you?" We were not about to say no.

Mrs. Helmsley flirted with him. "You ought to come work for me," she said. "I've got a good restaurant over at the Park Lane. We could be a good team."

I wondered what this famous chef thought about her offer. He seemed to be appropriately flattered. When he walked away, she leaned into me and said, "He's good, you know. *Very* good."

We talked about her life, my life, her IRS story, my IRS story, her husband's death, my husband's death, her business, my business, and prison. "You know, they liked me there," she said, referring to her fellow inmates. "But I wanted out. *Every day* I wanted out."

I wondered what it would have been like for Howard if he'd been indicted, convicted, and sentenced to prison. I think the humiliation would have done him in. But Mrs. Helmsley seemed to be made of tougher stuff. I told her a few details of my case, including that the IRS said I owed them almost three million.

"Sell what you've got to sell," she said, waving her hand in a grand dismissive gesture. "Give 'em the money. Get on with your life."

I looked at her. "That's easy for you to say, Mrs. Helmsley. You're a billionaire." To my relief, she laughed. But it was true. "What properties do you own in New York, Mrs. Helmsley?" I asked. "How big is your real estate empire?"

She ticked off a list of impressive addresses. She was in the midst of selling a lot of them. "But I'm not selling the Empire State Building. I'm going to keep that."

"You go, girl," I said. "You keep the Empire State Building."

The wine made her cheerful. She cracked jokes, flirted with the handsome French waiters, and invited them to come work for her, too. She showed me a soft side that would win people over if she could only reveal it on television. I told her all the ways Larry made the hardest cases look good in live interviews. I suggested there would be a positive response from the public and media, especially if we put some focus on her large gifts to charities.

The soft side dropped away and she turned cold and serious. "It doesn't matter. They'd kill me," she said. "They'd kill me from the start. I could go on the show and Larry and I could have a good time together, but the next day the press would kill me. There's no way around it."

After dinner, at her car, I said, "Leona, come visit Washington. Come have dinner with me at Nathans. Come see the studio. See Larry. We'll all get together and have some fun."

"When I get my jet out of the shop, dear," she said, disappearing into the back of her long black car.

The next day her representative Howard Rubenstein was on the phone. "She had a good time, Carol, but she's not changing her mind about an interview. There's no good reason for her to put herself out there."

I would get the occasional note from her, but we never met again. There were no network interviews. She died in 2007, leaving an estimated $4 billion estate, $12 million of it in trust for her dog.

Chapter 18

When I found time to mourn, I mourned, fitting it in between all the moments when I had to be alert, in charge, responsible, and dedicated. Mourning is an emotional roller coaster. The lowest low always came after the highest high. Hairpin turns came suddenly, and then everything was upside down, the whole world on top of me, my feet in the air, speeding. Then, nothing. Full stop. A day or two or three later, the ride would begin again.

I was no longer surprised by how good I could feel one minute and how miserable the next. I understood that the mood swings were unpredictable. I learned to roll with them and move on. Spencer swung between being a happy-go-lucky, perfectly normal five-year-old boy and Damien, the Antichrist. I rolled with that, too. Only rarely now did Spencer ask me to kill him so he could be with his father "in heaven." But he told me repeatedly that he didn't feel like he fit in with his friends. That disturbed me, but his therapist assured me it was normal. He was a little boy trying to put Humpty Dumpty together again and set him back on the wall, intact and whole.

"I'm the only boy who doesn't have a father," he said, which was true in the technical sense of a living father in our particular circle of friends.

I told him, "It won't always be like that. As life goes on you'll meet other boys and girls who don't have a father, and you will be a step ahead and able to help them."

We didn't talk about the loss of Howard as much as we talked about the life of Howard. I wanted Howard to be part of our daily dialogue, as a reminder to Spencer that he did have a father and that his father was an important part of his existence. Many times I told him about the day I told Howard I was pregnant. "I came into the den in the afternoon with the little plastic stick that shows if a mommy is going to have a baby, and it showed that I was going to have you. He was reading a book and I waved the little wand in front of him."

"What did Daddy do?"

"Oh, he jumped for joy. We both did."

"How did you know it was me?"

"I just did. You were exactly who we both wanted."

Spencer could be incredibly loving and sweet. But he had his dark moods, too, and sometimes those moods were very dark. One day he said, looking very sad, "I don't have a daddy."

A therapist might have suggested I say, "Let's talk about it," or something in the therapeutic ballpark. But there was no therapist around at that moment. "Yes, you do," I said. "You'll always have a daddy. It's just that your daddy is dead, in heaven, and watching out for you from there."

In a fit of frustration he yelled, "I hate you. I wish you weren't my mommy." A little later he told me, "I loved Daddy. Not you. I still love Daddy. I love Daddy more than you. I wish you were the one who died." I let it roll off me, but there was a painful familiarity. Oddly, even though he was a five-year-old child, he sounded just like his father when his father was Mr. Hyde. Already he looked a lot like his father. That was fine, I thought; look like him, just don't be like him.

I did my best to handle Spencer's outbursts, but there was no guidebook. Typically I went with one part ignoring to one part reprimanding to one part "Let's talk about these feelings you're having." Later I could always think of other responses that might have been better, but maybe not. We were both grieving. He was five years old and had lost his father. It was hard. I was forty-seven and had lost my husband and simultaneously acquired his status as defendant in a tax fraud case and his debt to the government. That was hard, too. If the IRS didn't decide I was the innocent spouse, we might lose everything, including a place to sleep at night. I tried not to think about that. It was too terrifying.

I learned to be tolerant with myself as well as with Spencer. Children never realize how much they can hurt their parents until they're parents themselves. Often parents don't realize the depth and intensity of their children's feelings. But I was the grown-up. I had to keep remembering that. Sometimes I wanted to blow back at him, but, instead, I went into the bathroom and cried. I tried to ignore the pop psychology that paints a challenging picture for solo mothers, but still I worried whether I had the mettle to raise a son alone. Could I forecast the damage Howard's death would cost, head it off, and wrap him in enough love to protect him from the empty and lonely feelings? I would look at my darling little boy and wonder, Who will you grow up to be? I was not sure how much of his father I wanted in or out of the mix, or whether it was already genetically predetermined.

Our weekends at the Bay could be tough for Spencer. On the one hand he had me all to himself, but there was a big "on the other hand." From the moment we arrived I was busy with essential household tasks, which ranged from throwing out dead mice to dealing with the bad news in the mail to checking the phone messages and dealing with the bad news there. I had a phone stuck to my ear while I put away groceries, opened windows, swept, straightened, and organized. There were calls from Nathans, *Larry King Live,* and the lawyers.

When I got outside to play with him at last, I was whipped, spent, wasted, and brain-dead. "Come on, Mommy, let's play 'divers,'" Spencer would beg. "Let's dive for treasure." I was collapsed beside the pool, but I managed to toss a few toys into the water for him to go after. That wasn't good enough. "Mommy, Mommy, you have to be in the water, too. You have to be a diver, too." Eventually I'd kick myself into gear and fall into the pool where we played till he was running on fumes. I was already on empty.

In the house, Spencer and the dog followed me around as close as pilot fish, with Spencer saying, "Will you play with me?" "Will you read to me?" "Can I go swimming?" "Can we walk in the woods?" The dog, a small white bichon frise named Teddy, whined because he wanted me to go outside and throw his ball. When I went to the bathroom they both stood outside the door, Spencer knocking and the dog scratching. Sitting on the toilet, tired as I was, I had to laugh.

I TRIED TO be at Nathans during dinner at least three nights a week. Alone, I didn't know what to do with myself and tended to simply lurk in a back corner, staring at the customers. Staff would say "Excuse me," as they tried to maneuver around me. I was in the way. With Martha or a girlfriend—and sometimes Spencer—I could be in the place and feel like I belonged. Spencer enjoyed Nathans. He'd gobble down a plate of pasta while the waitstaff doted on him. When we could we'd include his friends and their parents, which he loved, because a whole group of us would sit around a big table with lots of food, chatter, and laughter. I liked it, too.

My favorite place to hang out was not in the bar but in the back room, and always in the red leather comfort of booth 26, which was well-centered, enabling me to keep an eye on the door where patrons waited to be seated by the maître d'. If people waited too long, I hopped up and tried to help. If someone I knew came in the door, I walked over to say hello. If someone got to the dining room, looked around, and then turned and walked back out the door, I wanted to know why. What had turned them off? What could we have done differently to make them stay? I wanted to chase after them and ask questions, which would likely have spooked them away forever, remembering me as the stalker restaurateur.

I adhered to my code of survival: Get out of bed every morning, exercise, go forward, laugh, and try to get a dose of friends whenever possible. Friends made the difference between a horrible day and a wonderful one. Something as simple as an unexpected phone call to find out how I was doing, or an invitation to a dinner party, would lift my spirits considerably. Or, another moms' dance party. Late-night phone calls from Paolo helped, too. He put such a big smile on my face. I loved the secret we shared, our clandestine teenage flirtation. My shrink said, "You're like a virgin again," to which I replied, "and in no hurry to lose her virginity."

Nobody knows what to do with a widow, and it's especially a challenge for married couples. My girlfriends were married and they might be able to come dancing on weeknights but weekends were husband and family time. In the first several months after Howard died, I was included as the third person or fifth or seventh at dinner, but in time there were fewer invitations, fewer phone calls. The calls always stopped altogether after six o'clock on Friday, not to resume until Monday morning at ten. Initially I thought this might be because I lived in Washington, a socially conservative community with old-school standards, more Eisenhower era than many would believe. But when I talked to other widows—different ages from far and wide—I'd hear the same complaint. Some felt they'd become invisible after their husbands died.

Friends would bring up the question of dating, as in when I was planning to start, but I wasn't the least bit interested. For one thing, I still felt quite married—only my husband was dead. With my harrowing schedule, it would have been nearly impossible to start a relationship from scratch. I couldn't very well tell people about my flirtation with Paolo. For me, it was just enough real and just enough fantasy. It was like we were both married, but flirting. I didn't have room for more. It would be something else entirely to come home to the same man every night with a rundown of my day. That would be the biggest downer—for him; it might have been a relief for me.

One Friday evening, I forgot myself and called a married friend to see if she wanted to talk or walk or go out for a drink. "Oh, Carol, I'm sorry, I can't. I'm doing something with Harry." She didn't mean to be unkind, but it felt like a door slammed in my face. She hadn't done anything wrong. In a couple-oriented society, her life was normal. It was mine that was not. I thought, "I used to be like that. I used to have that. I was a member of that club." Honestly, I got angry. I told the psychiatrist about the episode. He asked me how I handled it.

"I politely said 'Good-bye' and then slammed down the phone and muttered, 'Bitch.' "

"Good," he said. "That's a healthy sign."

IT WAS CRITICAL that Nathans get a new lease from the five landlords, all of them members of the Halkias family and in their mid- to late seventies. They'd come to the funeral home for Howard's visitation. A few weeks after that, Melina Halkias, who had the biggest share in the property, and her son joined me for coffee and cakes at Nathans. She wore black from head to toe, had a tissue tucked in her sleeve, and spoke halting English. Her son did most of the talking. It was clear they had deep concerns. Fear of my inexperience was now compounded by the tax fraud.

It was essential to keep them in the loop but also keep them pacified. "Call them every now and then, okay?" I asked Doug. "If you could do that I'd be grateful. Just check in with them. I want them to know that everything is okay here." Doug had a good relationship with the Halkias family, and I needed to keep them happy. For the moment, I needed them more than they needed me.

Attorney Jake Stein was negotiating the actual terms of the lease with the Halkias family's lawyer, Dimitri Mallios. Howard first retained Jake in the 1980s when he learned that some busboys and a manager were dealing cocaine in the restaurant. The manager was arrested, convicted, and sent to prison. Jake looked out for the interests of both Howard and Nathans then, and afterward Howard kept him involved in dealings with the landlords. These talks had been going on for some while, getting stalled periodically by my IRS issues and their own unrelated legal problems.

Meanwhile, I was faithfully paying the full rent each month. At one of several meetings in his office with Jake and me, Dimitri matter-of-factly said, "The family couldn't care less about what kind of scrape Carol is in as long as she pays the rent. That's all they care about."

Howard loved to tell me how each time the lease was up he simply sent one of his cronies—a bookie who called himself "Nathan Detroit," the very same bookie from whom Howard's father bought the first share of Nathans—to meet with the oldest Halkias male, Theo. "I gave Nathan some feta cheese, a bottle or two of retsina, and a bag of money. By the end of the day I had a new lease."

Was it true? I don't know. I was learning that for Howard a good story often mattered more than the facts. Neither Howard nor his emissary was around to verify it in any case. But no matter the truth of Howard's story—or the lack of it—I knew I had to play with a different and less colorful set of rules. There would be no retsina, no bags of money, not even a pound of feta from me. But I desperately needed the lease, because if the IRS did not grant me innocent spouse status, we might be able to negotiate a deal in which I paid the IRS not with my house but with the profit from selling Nathans. In order to sell Nathans, I needed a lease.

Chapter 19

When you're the defendant in a federal tax fraud case, you don't take or spend a dime without first calling your lawyers. The IRS has you by the short hairs. You are not sure what's yours and what's theirs. You call for permission on just about everything. Anxiety and sleepless nights become a way of life. Caravans of what-ifs crowd your private thoughts. And that's when you're innocent.

Miriam and Sheldon got us that one last summer at the house on the Bay, and I was grateful for that. I needed it, and Spencer especially needed it. I had to slowly bring him around to the notion that we would have to sell it and move. Even though "sentimental Carol" didn't want to give up the house on the Bay, the emerging "rational Carol" knew it was inevitable. When Howard was alive, it was our happiest place to be as a family: boating, swimming, cooking, gardening, hanging out, having friends over, being alone together, enjoying our son and each other. At night we left the doors unlocked and the windows open, and I slept like a baby. I loved that we were at the end of a long dirt road, isolated, with no neighbors in view in any direction. Now at bedtime I locked the doors, closed the windows, and turned on the alarm. Even then, any little sound woke me. I never slept soundly. There was a lot of maintenance work to do. We entertained rarely. Most often it was just the two of us and the dog, trying our best to move on and be happy but living too sadly with memories of the past. It was time to sell. But there was a major uncertainty: The lawyers weren't sure whether the money from the sale would go to Howard's estate and therefore the government, or to Spencer and me.

Washington was sweltering in a heat wave, which comes as regularly in late August as the cherry blossoms do in April. Miriam and Sheldon asked me to come for a summit meeting at their offices. My full army was at the table—lawyers, accountants, bookkeepers, and a lawyer friend who had volunteered to observe. Miriam started it off. She looked up from the stack of papers in front of her and smiled. "I have good news! The house is yours, Carol, not the estate's. At the moment Howard died ownership reverted to you. Its called tenancy by the entirety. T-by-E. All the property and everything in it are yours."

I wanted to jump up, spring over the table, throw my arms around her, and plant a big kiss on her cheek. But this was a law office, and propriety had to be maintained. So I lowered my head in thanks instead. The news was a big fat blast of sunshine.

"If you win innocent spouse status, you should be able to keep the proceeds from the sale. Everything else, everything in Howard's name—stocks, bonds, bank accounts, savings, boats, cars, whatever else—belongs to the estate, and therefore the government."

But. There's always a "but." I could feel it coming.

"But if you don't win innocent spouse status, I don't think you'll get to keep any of it."

I CONTINUED LOOKING for a house of our own, a house I could afford where Spencer and I would be happy. The sanest option was to stay in Georgetown because that's where the restaurant was. I went there every day, and I needed to be close to it. If I had to get there in a hurry—for whatever reason—I wanted to be able to simply run down the street. In the evening I was a full-time mother, but if a friend or VIP showed up for dinner I wanted to get the call, wing over, say "hello and thanks," and then run back home.

In 1997, the Georgetown real estate market was in a slump. Bargains were available. I wanted something manageable, affordable, and, if possible, charming. We poked around, with my agent, Jeanne Livingston, often asking, "But can you afford this?" The truth was I didn't know what I could afford, because I didn't know what I would have when the IRS was done with me, but I felt I had to go forward, as though somehow, someday, something would break our way. The good news from Miriam gave me hope.

Then one day I saw Frederica Valanos, whose son, Teddy, was the same age as Spencer and attended the same school. Frederica was in a giddy mood. "Well, we closed on our new house," she said.

"What do you mean, your new house?" I asked.

"We bought a house a block away and it's great."

"What about your old house?"

"We're putting it on the market this weekend."

Without hesitation I said, "I want it. Don't sell it to anybody else."

I knew the house. It was a modest yellow brick townhouse with a big bay window that overlooked the street. I'd been there a few times, dropping off Spencer for playdates or to visit Frederica and her husband, George. It was the right size for the two of us—two bedrooms and a small patch of grass in the back. I already loved it.

"Can you do it, with the IRS and all?" Frederica asked.

"I don't know, but I'll find out."

During the next seventy-two hours, Jeanne Livingston gave me a crash course in how to buy a house. A mortgage broker did a credit check and the results shocked me. "You have perfect credit," he said. "This will be easy."

"How can I have perfect credit?"

"Your credit cards have always been paid on time. You have no loans or debts. You're clean as a whistle. You have the highest score they give."

In another ten years my credit rating would be the lowest score they give, but at the time you could have knocked me over with a feather.

Jeanne asked when I wanted to close.

"Before I do anything else I have to talk to my tax lawyers and find out if I can even dream about this," I said.

I faxed a letter to Sheldon and Miriam basically asking for their permission to buy a house, which was really asking them to ask the IRS for permission to buy a house. Of course it was complicated. What I needed to know was whether I could use money from the estate account, or from Howard's stocks and bonds, to make a down payment—money I would repay when I sold the Bay house (and hoping the government ruled my way on innocent spouse).

It was a gamble. We knew the worst-case scenario was that the IRS would get everything. If I bought the house, "everything" would include it, too. Later that day, driving out to a mall in Virginia for lunch with an old friend of Howard's and Spencer and the live-in babysitter, Patricia, my cell phone rang. It was Sheldon and Miriam. "We've reviewed your letter. Can we go over it?"

"Yes," I said. They were on speakerphone. We all listened.

"We don't think you can use the estate money," they said. "Can Nathans make you a loan?"

"Nathans doesn't have any money," I said. "The estate is the only money I have access to."

They said they would consult an estate law expert and get back to me. "But you may not be able to do this. It could put you in violation of the IRS." My heart sank.

I hung up. We continued driving to the mall. Patricia sat beside me up front. Spencer was in the backseat, talking, as he often did, about *Star Wars.* I tried to keep up with his lively chatter, but I couldn't concentrate. Tears welled in my eyes.

"Guys, I need a minute," I said.

"You cry if you want to," Patricia said.

"Don't cry! Don't cry!" Spencer shouted from the backseat.

Patricia turned to him. "If your mom wants to cry she has every right to cry, Spencer."

So I cried. It seemed everywhere I turned, everything I did to try to put our lives in order got stopped by the words "in violation of." There was always something I might be in violation of. It made me feel that at any moment I'd be hauled before a judge like an outlaw.

"Are you still crying?" Spencer asked.

"I'm trying to pull it together. I'll be okay in a minute, Spencer. Just remember how you cried when you watched *Mars Attacks* and how the Martians scared you," I said.

"Yeah," came from the backseat.

"Well, that's how I feel right now. Just as scared. Like Martians are after me."

"Are we going to be poor?" he asked.

"Poor? Maybe not flat-out poor, but certainly poorer. But we'll be okay. We can get through this. We can do it together."

At lunch, Howard's old friend wanted to share his admiring memories, but I wasn't feeling in a very benevolent mood toward Howard at that moment. I wanted him to come back to life and walk in my shoes for a day, to find out what it was like to be stuck in the mess he'd left us.

The restaurant had a jungle motif to wow the children. Spencer was enchanted. With all the noise, though, I could barely hear my cell phone ringing. It was Miriam. "Let me get to a quieter spot where I can hear you," I shouted over the din. The crowded mall was as noisy as a football stadium after a touchdown.

I searched frantically for some quiet space. Finally, I spied a janitor's closet. I darted in and shut the door.

"Hi," I said. "I can hear now." I straddled a wash bucket and leaned against a rack of brooms.

"I have good news! You will be able to use the estate money because ultimately it was supposed to be yours."

"We know that will never happen," I said.

"Right," she said, "but when you get the proceeds from the sale of your home that money will go into escrow to pay back the estate. I wouldn't put too much money into the house, though, because it might at some point have IRS exposure."

Exposure. That was another word I hated, and in my case it got used a lot. *Exposure* meant my assets were hanging out there and the G-men could grab them any time. Exposure was something a person in my position did not want to have, but, as my generation learned from the Rolling Stones, you can't always get what you want.

"The bottom line is you can get your house!" she said, emphatically. Even though I had learned to protect myself from sudden happy highs, I gave in on this one. My heart filled with relief, joy, and wonder. The wonder was that something positive could happen in the midst of so much negative. I emerged from the janitor's closet like Superman from his phone booth. I raced into the restaurant to tell Spencer, "We're gonna get Teddy's house!" He lit up like I *was* Superman.

During the drive back to Washington I called Jeanne Livingston and told her the good news. "It's a green light," I said. "Let's get that house." From the backseat Spencer trilled about what he would do with "Teddy's room." His joy was the best possible part of the day. I didn't know how he would react to the news of our moving. I honestly didn't know how much he understood of what I was saying. But he was excited and happy and that's what I needed. I wanted him, in his own little-boy way, to be caught up in the idea of not looking back but moving forward.

Negotiations stalled on the issue of price, which I thought we'd agreed to on the back porch only days earlier. Suddenly George Valanos became a hard bargainer. I learned no deal is a deal until it's a deal. We finally came to an agreement, at a price only a fraction higher than what he told me he was looking for. Later Jeanne Livingston said she had a message for me from George. "He said he was sorry he pushed so hard. He forgot it was not a commercial deal."

"Does that mean he'll drop the price back down?" I asked.

"I don't think so," she said.

Though we now had a deal, Jeanne wasn't finished. As encouraging as she had been about buying the house, she now felt she needed to remind me of the negatives. "Well, you know it doesn't have parking. It may not have quick resale value. It's only two bedrooms. The kitchen is not great. The rooms are small," she said. I was confused.

"Yesterday it was all about the great garden, the charm, the beautifully finished rooms. What happened? Now it's all bad?"

"It's my job to make sure you're aware of the negatives," she said.

"Don't be a buzz kill," I begged. "I love the place. We're going to have a home!"

Our good friend and Spencer's godfather, the actor and comedian Harry Shearer and his mother, Dora, were visiting Washington from Los Angeles. We went to a Latin restaurant downtown and celebrated my good fortune with tapas and margaritas. At least I did. Harry, as always, stuck to wine.

My beeper went off. It was George Valanos. Right away I called back, worried that something had happened to the deal. "Congratulations," George said. "We're sitting in the garden having some wine. Do you want to come see your new house?"

Yes. We all did. When we got out of the cab, we took a moment to stand in the street and stare at what would be our new home. I was still stunned I'd pulled it off. George and Frederica led us to the garden where two other guests were having a glass of wine. It was a lovely September night. Crickets chirped in the bushes and tall trees. There was a full moon. The garden was beautifully lit from above and below.

When I looked back, the house was glowing from within. I was glowing, too. I couldn't believe my good fortune.

Pride, personal pride, was something I had not felt in a long time, but I took deep pleasure in getting that house. While booking people like Nicole Kidman and George Clooney for an interview with Larry King was fun and a professional coup, I took no personal satisfaction in it. It was my work. Nor was there anything I'd done at Nathans that I was particularly proud of. The restaurant produced mostly an abundance of fear and confusion. Finding a house and making the deal—putting a roof over our heads—boosted my ego and made me feel capable. Maybe I could take care of us on my own.

When Harry, Dora, and I left the house that night, I stood in the street and took one more long look. "You did good, Carol," Harry said.

To myself, I said silently, "Dear God, Please, *please* let us find peace and happiness here."

George and Frederica asked if we could delay the closing date until after the first of the year. This was good for me because I needed to get the other property sold before we moved. Also, I had to sell a lot more furniture and other things and get myself organized. Downsizing is a lot of work.

"May I suggest a date?" I asked.

"Sure, what's good for you?" they asked.

"How about February 1?" I replied. That would be the first anniversary of Howard's death. This way I could make that day not about what we had lost but about what we gained—a house of our own.

Chapter 20

Fred Thimm of the Palm had recommended a new bookkeeper for Nathans and on his word I hired Connie, who, dramatically, was the spitting image of a younger Peggy Lee; her hair was a big bouffant of blond and white and her hands were delicate, with long, beautifully painted nails—red, always red, like her lipstick. Her build was broad and strong, her demeanor world-weary, and she didn't take crap from anyone. While she came across as all hard and no soft, we got along just fine. I especially liked having another woman in the office, where we worked side by side, going over the books. The new books. The books she put together and that now gave me an accurate picture of my business—all the numbers Fred said I needed to know. The debt astonished me, but Connie was unfazed. "Everybody in the restaurant business carries a lot of debt," she said. "That's just how it is." I asked Connie to teach me about the numbers. Nobody could sugarcoat them anymore. I wanted only the truth—no matter how painful, and, believe me, it was painful.

Maybe it made me an oddball as a restaurant owner, but I wasn't comfortable with debt. I knew I was dense where numbers were concerned, but because I was dense I knew it was best for me not to buy what I could not afford. That way I wouldn't get in trouble. It was an unsophisticated point of view, I was learning, but it was within my comfort zone. I was also comfortable with rules. Not all rules, but most rules. And I was beginning to understand why the bar business attracted the kind of people it did—people, like my husband, who didn't like any rules. He had very few of his own and those he had he had made up along the way. The standard was to string debt out as long as possible, play by whatever cockamamy logic seemed to fit, and, most of all, not get caught. But Howard did get caught. Then he died, leaving me with the consequences.

After consultations with Fred Thimm and Paolo, friends who owned businesses, and Connie, I tried to institute some belt-tightening measures and management organization. I honored Fred's earlier tutorial, which denied me the "fun stuff"—a paint job, decorating, and the like—to focus instead on fixing what wasn't working and to keep a lid on the money. We did a much-needed revision of the menu. When I first inherited the place, we had offered the same specials night after night, and half the time the waiter would say they weren't available. It felt like a diner on the skids rather than a glamorous pub at the best corner in the city. There was a load of waste. The food costs were outrageous. It would have been one thing if the food was superlative, but after trying everything on the menu during many dinners at booth 26, my opinion was that much of what we served was tired, lacked focus, or was too ambitious. The customers seemed to feel that way, too, because most nights the dining room was only half full. I hoped the new menu would make a difference.

The menu was still northern Italian but cut down by half. We axed items that were rarely available or that never sold. Everything that was popular and sold well was still there. We couldn't lose the famous lobster fettuccine, a platter of house-made fettuccine noodles drenched in a creamy, rich Alfredo sauce and topped with steaming hot lobster fresh out of the shell. It was one of our most popular dishes. There were couples who became engaged over lobster fettuccine and who returned to have it again as they celebrated their anniversaries or their son's or daughter's birth or graduation from college. I liked that. When the new menu was done I was enthusiastic.

Right away, however, Doug wanted me to know that he wasn't pleased. "We're getting a lot of grief about the new menu," he said.

"People don't like change," I said. "Especially at the corner pub."

"Some customers say they didn't think it needed to be changed." We were at our desks in the basement office. He didn't look at me when he talked.

I looked directly at him. "And others say they like it, Doug. We'll have to tough it out. The old menu had too much waste. We need to do this."

To any member of the staff who would listen, I said, "If we don't make changes we won't stay in business." We tightened up the schedules and continued to cut back on overtime. While the high-turnover waitstaff, most of them college students, now treated me as less of an annoyance, the longer-term employees—behind the bar, in the kitchen, managing the floor—still considered my changes to be meddling. Whatever anyone wanted to call it, I had no choice. Nathans was a rusty ship, dead in the water. I had to fix the broken engine and props, crank 'em up, and get the thing going again. I didn't want to be aboard, but I desperately had to get it to dry land without sinking and avoid the enemy warship, the IRS, just over the horizon.

I was painfully aware that I was not winning over all of the staff. Perhaps if I could approach the business with a more obvious sense of humor, or more charm, or if I hung out at the bar and drank with them, bought everyone shots . . . but that wasn't me and experience had taught me that false bonhomie generally fails. They wanted Howard. They wanted payments under the table, the pink checks. I wasn't the fun one, the charming one, the generous one with the easy money. I was the one left holding the bag, stuck with having to save the business and their jobs. The colorful outlaw had died and they got stuck with a dull schoolmarm. What they wanted most of all was for everything to be the way it was. The sad truth, though, is that Nathans never was what it was. I'd been forcibly awakened from that dream. The others also had to see their dream of the old Nathans for what it was: a dream.

Again, with the guidance of Fred, Paolo, and Connie, my new rules were straightforward, the rules most office workers take for granted. Managers who worked four-day shifts now had to work five-day shifts. Staff meals were no longer free but offered at a 50 percent discount. Vacation time had to be requested in writing and not taken at will. A manager had to be on the floor at all times when meals were being served. An office manager would be hired to oversee the delivery of food and beverages, bill paying, and other routine work, to free up managers to work in prime time. The general manager—that is, Doug—would be expected to be on the premises on Friday and Saturday nights. For the sake of the cash flow, paychecks would now come out every two weeks instead of every week. And so on. Nothing very startling to anyone who's ever held a job but something in the nature of an earthquake to those who for a long time had been enjoying the freewheeling ways of the old Nathans.

I required all managers to show up for the weekly managers' meeting. We would institute more staff training, especially courses on wine and food. I would design new uniforms for the staff. We would replace the worn and tattered fabric on the walls in the dining room. We would get new lampshades and curtains. I would buy the flowers from a wholesaler and do the arrangements myself. I suggested we try some wine specials and perhaps a discounted "early bird" dinner.

Last but not least, there was the challenge of Doug and his pay. I followed Fred Thimm's outline. "Pay the rent, pay the IRS, pay the lawyers, pay the staff, pay the bills, pay me." Fred and Connie gave me a tutorial on how managers are typically compensated. Then I met with Doug to tell him how I planned to change his pay formula. He had been getting 1 percent of the gross, but if Nathans was to stay afloat and all of us were to keep our jobs, that had to be changed immediately to 10 percent of the net after "my objectives are met," paid on a quarterly basis. That still sounded pretty good to me.

"What are your objectives?" he asked.

I repeated Fred Thimm's mantra: "Pay the rent, pay the IRS, pay the lawyers, pay the staff, pay the bills, pay me." He shrugged.

For the next couple of days I labored on a memo that I intended to put on Doug's desk. I wanted him to know that we were all in this together, and that if he continued as general manager he had to help sell the new policies and procedures enthusiastically to the staff. I wanted a happy staff and that comes from candid management, a job well done, and the pride we could all take in having a roomful of customers who liked the food, the service, and the surroundings. It seemed simple enough.

I folded the memo, slipped it into an envelope, and set it in the middle of his desk. It was still there unopened the next morning and the next afternoon, set aside on a stack of papers.

"Doug," I said, "I actually wrote that with the intention that you would read it."

He looked up. "Yeah, I'll get to it."

"If only you could turn him," Fred Thimm said on the phone. "I keep thinking at some point he's going to wake up and get on board. But what does it take? I thought by now he'd be thanking you for keeping him on the payroll."

"Fred, he views me as an impediment. He sees me as competition! I don't know what to do. He thinks I want his job. He thinks I enjoy this work."

"Have you had a heart-to-heart with him?" he asked.

"More than one. But he always ends up pissing me off. He loves to tell me, over and over, 'If Howard had lived and I had died this place would have closed in a week.'"

There's more than one way to let a new boss know you don't like her policies, and at Nathans they sprung a new one on me. Someone cut the rat screens in the basement. In the rat universe, that's the same as hanging up a neon sign with the words OPEN HOUSE. As the building was more than one hundred years old, rats had made various holes in the basement walls that we routinely covered with industrial strength rat screens. One day the early shift prep staff noticed lots of signs of rats, and then more signs of rats and more and more and more. Doug poked around and discovered all the screens had been cut. He seemed frankly surprised and said he would investigate.

It freaked me out. I sat in the basement for hours each day. I didn't like to think of rats scurrying around my feet. But worse, why would anyone have cut the screens? Was the staff sending me a message? It was not only bad for me but for everyone who had a job at Nathans. If the health department were to come in, which they did randomly and often, Nathans would be shut down on the spot.

Doug asked around but said he'd learned nothing. Later, when I was in the office alone, Arnoldo, the day chef, tentatively poked his head in and asked to see me. Could we go outside? We stood on the sidewalk by the kitchen door on busy Wisconsin Avenue. Arnoldo, like all the kitchen staff, was from El Salvador. Because he was the oldest and the most experienced, the other men in the kitchen—many of them in their early twenties—deferred to him. He was quiet, proud, and hardworking. Nathans was his day job. He worked at another restaurant at night. I never had a problem with Arnoldo. Still, he seemed supremely uncomfortable to be talking to me.

"Mrs. Joynt, I'm afraid this business was done by some of the boys," he said. I knew he was referring to the young dishwashers. "I am very sorry and embarrassed."

"Why would they do that, Arnoldo?"

"Because they are young," he said. "They don't know better. They are macho." They may not have known better but they very well knew what they were doing.

"What can I do?" I asked.

"There is nothing. I have talked to them. It won't happen again. But I am very sorry. This was very bad."

"Arnoldo, tell them the next time I will call the police."

When I repeated to Doug what Arnoldo had told me, he said quite casually, "Yes, I'd heard that."

"Why didn't you tell me?"

"I figured I could work it out and I didn't want to bother you."

I asked Doug what I asked Arnoldo. "Why do you think they did it?"

"You've been cutting back on their overtime. They're angry."

"Great. Get the business shut down by the health department. That will help overtime a lot."

I got up and left the restaurant. I had to get out of there. I walked home, let the babysitter go, and took Spencer and the dog out for an extended hike. Their company was the antidote to every disappointment, frustration, failure, and tinge of anger. I could never overdose on Spencer.

Chapter 21

NATHANS' LEASE WAS still up in the air. Jake Stein's negotiations with the landlords' lawyer, Dimitri Mallios, dragged along, but it looked certain the lease would expire before we settled with the IRS. This is where it got complicated. While I was anxious to have a signed lease, Sheldon and Miriam didn't mind if it ran out. Their view was that if Nathans had no lease then Nathans would have no value and there would be nothing there for the IRS to come after. A restaurant with no lease is worthless. This was an important negotiating point for them, a point I would never have grasped without my lawyers. It could be achieved simply by the Halkias family giving me a month-to-month extension, which would keep Nathans in business but technically was not a new lease. The lawyers and I could live with that. We'd go month-to-month for the time being, which dropped the restaurant to its lowest possible value. Then, once the IRS issue was resolved, we would sign a new lease that restored the full value. I still had the dream of selling Nathans. For that to happen, I would need a new lease eventually. My plan was to settle with the government, get the lease, sell Nathans, and use the money to pay the IRS. Or, if fate went my way, I could use it to build a future for Spencer and me. I checked with Jake late one afternoon about his talks with the landlords' lawyer. I was at Howard's desk in Nathans' gray and cluttered basement. Doug sat at his and Connie was at a third. "How's it going?" I asked.

"I just sent a letter over to Dimitri," Jake said.

"I hope this means we're close," I said. "I'll feel so much better going forward with the IRS when I know the landlords will work with us. At least I know I'll have a way to pay them if it comes to that."

"Getting there," he said, and then he paused. "You know, I think I ought to tell you something Dimitri told me. The word on the street is that Doug is negotiating behind your back to get the lease for himself."

I was surprised but not shocked. I knew I was vulnerable, that my lease was in some ways up for grabs once it expired. But the thought of a threat coming possibly from the inside was upsetting. And there was Doug, sitting not more than fifteen feet away, going over some papers with Connie. So much for asking him to mind the landlords.

"If anybody would know, it's him," I said, being necessarily discreet but referring to Dimitri. "What does this mean for me? Is this an impediment?"

"Nah," he said, "I think it will be okay. But if it's true, it tells you something about your manager."

"Jake, what should I do?" I asked.

"Do nothing right now," he said. "Wait until you get your lease."

"Will I get it?"

"Yes," Jake said. "I believe so."

Jake's news about Doug upended my composure. I hung up the phone, queasy in the stomach. I could hardly breathe. Doug was at his desk, yakking to Connie. I winced in order to stop myself from crying. If true, was this his version of loyalty? Was this another warped way of giving me support? Like when I first inherited the place, and he blithely told me the business was $250,000 behind in accounts, as if his management played no role in accruing the debt. His attitude was "This is your problem, not mine." How could Howard have coexisted with such a person? Leaving me with him was almost as bad as leaving me with the IRS. I sat at the desk, fighting back the tears.

Both Connie and Doug looked up, concerned, and Doug asked, "Is there anything we can do?"

"No."

The phone rang. It was Spencer. "Mommy, when are you coming home?"

"Soon," I said.

"But how soon?"

"Real soon, honey."

"Mommy, are you crying?" Spencer asked.

"Yes, a little."

"Why?"

"I'll tell you when I get home."

"Why don't you go to the phone upstairs?" he suggested.

"Okay," I ran upstairs and picked up the bar phone. "Honey, I got some bad news but I'll be okay and I'll be home soon."

"Mommy, is the bad news that we're not going to get Teddy's house?"

"No, angel, we're going to get the house."

"Is it that I'm not going to get to go to my new school anymore?"

"No, honey. You'll go to your school as long as you want."

"Then what is it, Mommy?"

"I'll tell you when I get home. Now, sweetie, finish your dinner and I'll see you shortly. I love you." I called Connie on the intercom. I could trust her with this, largely because she shared my skepticism about Doug.

"Are you okay?" she asked.

"Yes, I'm okay. Can you come up for a minute?"

We met in the empty dining room. I told her about Jake's call. She was momentarily speechless. "I'm going home," I said. "If I go back downstairs I'll lose it."

"I'll see what I can find out," she said. "But, honestly, I can't imagine the landlords giving the lease to him, and he couldn't have the business anyway. Nathans is yours. He'd have to buy it. What's the chance of that happening?" Connie, of course, was right. I did own Nathans for better or worse. I loved the fettuccine but I wished the cement blocks weren't on my feet. Still, as Anthony Lanier warned me, it was the hottest property in town, my lease was potentially up in the air, and the sharks could be anywhere. Why wouldn't Doug have fantasies of putting together a deal and pulling an end run on me?

At home, after Spencer was asleep, I called Jake to talk to him more candidly than was possible in the office. I asked him to try to find out what was going on between Doug and the landlords. Were these "talks" serious?

"Will do," he said.

I sat in the kitchen alone and picked at my dinner while I considered this latest scary development. Was Doug acting alone among the staff of fifty-five—or was it a mutiny? Whatever it was, I had to be ready to handle it fast and smart. And how would I do that?

I cleaned up the kitchen, walked the dog, and returned to sit at my desk for an hour, paying what bills I had the money to pay and filing the letters from collection agencies into their already overflowing box. Just when I was taking my somber spirits to bed with me, Paolo phoned. At the sound of his voice, Nathans, the IRS, the landlords, Doug, the unpaid bills—all that was lifted from my shoulders. His charm and affection were a magic wand that transformed me from a middle-aged widow who'd inherited a bar she never wanted, along with far more debts than money to pay them, into a princess pursued by the handsome Prince Paolo. I was back in my teenage crush. It felt like such a good, safe place to be.

But I wasn't a teenager. I knew that. For a magical moment I was just reveling in the rush of romantic fantasy. That's what Paolo gave me, and it meant a lot.

Chapter 22

Summer was over. We invited friends to stay with us at the Bay house over Labor Day weekend. It would probably be our last good weekend there because going forward a real estate agent would be showing it to prospective buyers. Our guests were Yolande Betbeze Fox, a Georgetown grand dame as well as the 1951 Miss America, and her partner, Cherif Guellal, once Algeria's dashing ambassador to Washington, along with Yolande's granddaughter, Paris, who'd been to nursery school with Spencer. We planned a lazy weekend enjoying the quiet of the countryside, good conversation, grilling by the pool, briny breezes off the Bay, and a drink or two before going back to Washington, where life would heat up as the weather cooled down.

Spencer was scheduled to begin kindergarten on Tuesday and needed some distraction. He got it. He and Paris got along famously until they started pulling each other's hair. We would calm them down, and a little later the fracas would resume until we calmed them down again. As I said, it was a distraction.

After dinner Saturday evening, Yolande and I were relaxing in front of the television when news broke that the car carrying Princess Diana and Dodi al-Fayed had crashed in a tunnel in Paris. Early reports from the scene were sketchy but said that Diana was injured but alive. Britt Kahn, who had quit the staff at *Larry King Live* to work for ABC News, called me shortly after nine p.m. to tell me that Diana was, in fact, dead. It hadn't been made public. Britt was at work in New York and plugged in. She called me not to leak news but because we had a Diana bond. She was a fan of the princess. At a Washington dinner where Wendy, Larry King, and I first met Diana, I had pulled Britt across the room to present her to the princess. Britt didn't forget that, and she was grateful. "I can't believe she's dead," she said. "But we've got people over there at the hospital who have it confirmed."

I paged Wendy. She returned my page right away and without revealing my source I told her Diana was dead. Was I sure? Yes. Just to confirm, she asked me to call Mohamed al-Fayed's spokesman, Michael Cole, who worked for al-Fayed in London. Cole and I had a solid professional relationship. He answered on the first ring and could confirm only that Dodi al-Fayed was dead. I talked to Wendy again. She knew I always had the best sources and trusted my information. We tried to call everyone else on the staff but it was Saturday night on Labor Day weekend. Most were out.

Toward the end of one of our conversations I mentioned that Britt Kahn had given me the initial tip. She took a moment, then with a chill in her voice that would have frozen water, she began to rail. "How could you do that? She's a traitor! I can't believe you did that! Why did you talk to her?"

"We're friends," I said. "She has a Diana thing. She called me. All we did was talk about what happened. She had confirmation of Diana's death. That was invaluable."

"Did you tell her what we're doing?" she asked.

"We aren't doing anything yet, Wendy. We don't have a show until Monday. All I did was hang up and page you. So, no, I didn't tell her what we're doing."

"Carol, I can't believe you would do such a thing. Nobody at our show should talk to anyone from another show. *Ever.*"

"Okay." She went on to talk about other things, but before we hung up she came back to how "bad" I'd been to talk to Britt. What was all that about? I wondered. I'd never before been lectured for being first to call in with hot news, and Wendy usually liked it if I had bits of gossip from other talk shows. She liked to know what was up.

The next call was worse. Wendy and senior producer Becky wanted me to get on the next flight to London and stay for the week. "This is your beat, your baby, you've got the contacts."

I couldn't disagree. London was where I should be. I had outstanding contacts in "Diana world" and was good on my feet when news was breaking. It would have been challenging and exciting. However, I couldn't go. "Spencer's starting at a new school on Tuesday. I've got to be here." All of us knew I should be headed to the airport, passport in hand, but it was hard to argue with the widow whose boy was starting kindergarten at a new school. "I can reach everybody by phone from here," I said. They knew that, but it wasn't what they wanted to hear. In a dismal tone that foreshadowed my future with the show, they said they'd send two other producers. I'd been in major-league journalism long enough to know that this was a moment when stepping up was everything, and I could no longer step up.

YOLANDE AND CHERIF were glued to the TV while I was glued to the wall phone in the kitchen. Eventually they excused themselves to go to bed. For me, the calls and TV watching went on through the night. My primary assignment was to try to get Tom Cruise for Monday's show. He'd already called CNN's live coverage to complain about the paparazzi. After talking to Michael Cole several more times, I finally got to bed at about four in the morning. I was up again three hours later, fielding calls and making breakfast for everyone. One of my colleagues, Pam Stevens, another booker, called for my contacts and numbers. Generally such things are privileged but she said, "These are for everyone, Carol."

We had a staff conference call around eleven a.m. Wendy began with an admonition: "If I hear of any one of you talking to our competition at the other networks you better start looking for another job." Hmmm. It was decided I would keep after Tom Cruise, plus pursue Madonna, Demi Moore, the PR man Michael Cole, *Harper's Bazaar* editor and Diana pal Liz Tilberis, *Vogue* editor Anna Wintour, designer Zandra Rhodes, and Elizabeth Emanuel, who had designed Diana's spectacular wedding dress.

When I finally reached Pat Kingsley of PMK, who represented Tom Cruise, she was tired and weary of calls from bookers like me. "No," she said. "No to Tom." I left messages for Liz Rosenberg for Madonna and Susan Magrino for Tilberis. I talked to Paul Wilmot about Anna Wintour. But I actually booked Michael Cole. Score!

"Okay, Carol, I'll do it," he said. "I'll rest up for you." It would be two a.m. in London when we went live.

"Thank you, Michael." Cole agreed to be exclusive to our show.

He was al-Fayed's spokesman but also his stealth leaker. We'd had a few dinners together in New York where I worked through him to work through Mohamed al-Fayed to get to Raine Spencer, and through Raine to Princess Diana. Raine was Diana's stepmother and was close to al-Fayed. The al-Fayed family, particularly Mohamed al-Fayed, was obsessed with the royals. Mohamed went so far as to put Raine on the board of Harrods, more a British institution than a simple department store he now owned. There were times when Wendy, Michael Cole, and I would go through elaborate choreography to get Larry on the phone with Mohamed in advance of Mohamed's possibly being in the same room with Diana, to pass on a message. Unwittingly, perhaps, Mohamed served as a surrogate "booker." When Diana was al-Fayed's guest in the south of France that fateful June weekend in 1997 when she so publicly hooked up with Dodi, Michael called me regularly with practically by-the-minute updates about the goings-on out on the al-Fayed yacht. "Dodi and Diana are getting along *beautifully,*" he cooed. "They're like lovebirds. They can't keep their hands off each other!" Nothing for *Larry King Live,* but as far as gossip goes it was the inside skinny and pretty darn good.

The day rolled on, and the phone never stopped. I made beds with the phone wedged between my shoulder and my ear. I served lunch on the phone. Went crabbing at the dock on the phone. I closed up the house on the phone. The others helped, of course, and whenever I had a break I filled them in on the latest about what had happened in that Paris tunnel.

We got back to D.C. and there was another conference call with Wendy and Becky. "Why haven't you called Tom Cruise at home?" Becky demanded.

"Well, first off, I don't have his number and no one will give it to me. Second, he's not at home; he's in London starting a film."

"What's the film? Where's he shooting? Where's he staying?"

"I don't know."

They were delighted that actor Steven Seagal was available. "He's stayed at the Ritz," Wendy said. "He's been driven in that same car and he knows the driver. Paparazzi chased him in that same tunnel!"

"This is huge!" Becky exclaimed. You have to understand that in the circus that is entertainment television, "huge" isn't quite the same thing as it is in the real world. I was becoming increasingly cynical about the news that we in the business deemed critically important: the lingering tendrils of the O. J. Simpson saga, the macabre drama around the brutal murder of child beauty queen JonBenét Ramsey, the crisis of Christian televangelist and *LKL* regular Tammy Faye Bakker, any celebrity scandal or actor with a terminal illness, and now the deaths of Princess Diana and Dodi al-Fayed. We were turning their personal tragedies into a celebrity fest. The worst things in the world equaled monster ratings, and the ratings were everything.

Wendy, Becky, the other producers, and I compiled a wish list of knowns and unknowns that ran about three feet long, small print, single-spaced. It had more names than the Washington social register but for Monday's show we'd confirmed only Seagal and Michael Cole. We also had a few eyewitnesses, and we hoped to get French police officials and Scotland Yard. Then Becky said she wanted to speak with me privately. "Wendy only wants you to work on two people—Michael Cole and Anna Wintour. Nobody else! We're streamlining." Since I had Cole in the bag, it meant I was after only one person, Wintour, the longest of long shots.

I didn't see why Becky had to make this assignment privately or why Wendy didn't tell me herself, but this was television. "Okay," I said.

My colleague and friend Dean Sicoli called me at home that evening to tell me that Wendy didn't want the staff to talk to me. "She had Pam Stevens tell everyone 'Don't talk to Carol.'" Sometimes working in television was crazier than working at Nathans.

When I got to the *LKL* office on Monday, the morning of our first show about the Paris crash, Wendy wasn't there. She and Larry had flown to Los Angeles on previously scheduled business. I sent her an e-mail message. "I heard last night that you instructed Pam Stevens to tell the staff not to talk to me or work with me. Is this true?"

Finally Wendy responded. "What you heard was hearsay. This isn't my problem. You know the source. Settle it with her." Later, on a staff conference call, Wendy said, "We all love Carol. She's part of the team. We work with her and she works with us." What can I say to that? Not much. A job in the television pressure cooker always keeps a person on her toes.

But I still had a job, thank God, and all the phones were ringing nonstop. Every button on the receptionist's console lit up with a new call or flashed with an old one on hold. Pam and another member of our booking team were having a vocal tug-of-war over a potential guest whose publicist was on hold. The receptionist, Dorsey Edwards, wanted to give one of them the call so she could handle the other ringing lines. The argument got louder. Finally Dorsey stood up and exploded.

"All of you are so, so, so un-fucking-professional!" Her voice rose on every *so.* "So fucking rude! Fuck! Fuck! Fuck! Every one of you!" We'd had blowups in the office before, but this was the Mount St. Helens of eruptions. "You should all be ashamed. I've never seen anything like it! You butt in on phone calls, you interrupt conversations, you make impossible demands, and you bark orders like General Patton. I've never worked anyplace so unprofessional, and I worked in the restaurant business, for God's sake!" Dorsey sat down, put her head in her hands, and burst into tears. I was probably the only one in the room who got the picture.

Dorsey's outburst was the perfect aria for our seventy-two-hour office death-of-Diana media opera—and the opera had scarcely begun. It was only the end of the first act and everyone on the staff was coming apart. To top it off, and amazing as it now seems, Larry King and Shawn Southwick got married—suddenly—that same week in a Los Angeles hospital where Larry—just as suddenly—had been scheduled to undergo emergency coronary bypass surgery. He'd had heart disease for years. The ceremony took place at dawn; Wendy was a witness. They wanted to be married before Larry went under the knife. I'm not sure who wanted it more. At the last minute, the doctors decided Larry didn't need the surgery—that an angioplasty would do—but the wedding went ahead anyway. After the ceremony, the happy couple flew to New York for Larry's angioplasty. In the midst of the Diana frenzy, Wendy gave the full staff a report on Larry and Shawn's wedding in a late-night conference call.

And Tuesday morning I kept my promise to Spencer and went with him to his first day of kindergarten at his new school.

I'D GONE TO public schools and believed in their value, but at that time in Washington the city's public school system was something to be avoided if at all possible. Even city leaders conceded that fact. There were good schools within the system, but they were heavily subsidized by parents. The best required an application process similar to private schools. Most middle-class Washington families who wanted to send their children to public school moved to the Virginia or Maryland suburbs when their children reached school age. That wasn't an option for us. During all the back-and-forth with the IRS and my lawyers, I'd kept my moderate savings account out of the picture. I used every dime of it to pay for Spencer's school. Just in case our world went south, I paid the full tuition in advance for kindergarten through the third grade. I wanted Spencer's education to be a certainty. Even if the IRS took everything else away, he'd still have that.

The school I chose, part of the Washington National Cathedral, was solid and established, and most of his friends from preschool were starting there, too. I felt confident it would bolster him, make him feel safe. It attracted parents who were typical of Washington's comfortable and powerful "haves"—politicians, lobbyists, lawyers, journalists. Most of them were there that first day, too. I wasn't sure if I still fit in with those glossy, mannered mothers and fathers, or even if I wanted to, but it didn't matter. Spencer was happy to be there with his friends.

Parents stood around outside, chatting in small groups. Everybody looked good and spoke politely and was on their best parental behavior. I milled around in my jeans and blazer, saying hello to a few people I knew. I could tell from his exuberant mood that Spencer was reveling in having this time with me, making him like every other kid whose parents were there, and making us altogether more normal than whatever it was we'd become. Seeing his happy face, his confidence, I knew I had done the right thing in not taking off for London and leaving him to start school alone.

"Hey, Mom, look at this," Spencer said, pulling at my arm, pointing to a big green tube slide. "This is so cool." He jumped in and disappeared. From down at the bottom I heard a faint voice cry, "Come on, Mom, you do it, too."

I looked around self-consciously, making sure no other parents were watching, and climbed in. Before I could register what was happening,

Whoosh!, I was speeding down the chute at top speed. It swerved to the left, then swerved to the right before shooting me out at the end. Wham! Bam! Butt on the ground, feet in the air, splat in the sandy dirt. Not a particularly glamorous arrival but Spencer was delighted. He jumped up and down, laughing and clapping. The parents standing at the bottom of the slide looked down at me with a slightly puzzled expression. I got up, dusted off my jeans and jacket, smiled, and stuck out my hand.

"Hi, I'm Carol Joynt," I said. "Spencer's mom." We shook hands all around.

"Nice to meet you."

Spencer beamed. I was behaving, in his eyes, like a parent. Yes, for an instant, we were like everyone else, Carol and Spencer Normal.

Chapter 23

THE NEWS BUSINESS covers "real" people every day, and every day people in the news business think they understand the real world so they can tell us about it. In fact, some of them believe they're authorities on it; very few of them are. They do travel to a lot of places most people don't get to go and see a lot of things most people never see except on television—and they do it on somebody else's dime. (Actually dollars, and lots of them.) But the truth is, most of those in the present-day mainstream news business live sheltered, privileged lives, far removed from the reality most people face. Maturity and authentic life experience are not prerequisites for the job. How you look tends to matter more than what you are and what you know. Of course there are exceptions. They prove the rule.

Everybody likes to be pampered. The news business, particularly television, pampered me as much as Howard did, maybe more. Every day's mail brought a pile of new books from publishers. I took that for granted. We all did. Broadway publicists sold me the best house seats for the hot new shows. Nothing not to like about that. Every day was a little bit of Christmas. I was invited to important dinners with important people and got a good seat at a good table.

The grittier parts of the job were also touched with fairy dust. When Charlie Rose and I flew to San Francisco to interview Charles Manson, he was the one behind the bars, not us. We could walk in and out of the prison. We could view San Francisco Bay at will. A day spent with a paralyzed and wheelchair-bound Christopher Reeve, in the process of a taping for *Larry King Live,* was humbling but also a privilege few could experience. It was tedious waiting for Elizabeth Taylor to come down from her hotel room, get in the limo, and ride to the studio for an interview with Larry, but on the other hand, how many people get to spend an entire afternoon with Elizabeth Taylor?

My son got to meet some heroes, such as actor Bill Murray, who got goofy with him in makeup, and Titanic explorer Robert Ballard, who posed with him for a picture. Spencer; his new live-in babysitter, Erica Hart; and I were guests of Disney for the perk-heavy VIP maiden voyage of their new cruise ship.

Certainly my life at CNN was interesting and sometimes glamorous, but it was about as close to the real world as the Washington media's annual self-promoting lovefest—the White House Correspondents' Association dinner—where the "journalists" get dressed up in their finest duds to tell one another how great they are and to count the celebrity notches in their belts. When I was introduced as a producer for CNN, people would ask me about serious world issues or events in Washington, assuming I *knew.* After all, I was a producer for CNN. I had to know what was going on. You can get used to people assuming you know what's going on. They'll even grant you gravitas. Look at George Will, the poster child for gravitas. Almost anyone who's on television in Washington is granted the assumption of authority.

It was fun to live in that bubble of faux importance where it's so easy to believe it's all about you. It's not. People who forget that can find themselves quite alone when, voluntarily or forcibly, they leave the bubble for the chilly world outside. I've lived it both ways. Once I gave up the news business, and became only a saloon owner, nobody asked me about the world again. Ironically, owning a small business, being a solo parent, battling the IRS, I knew more about the world than ever before, but if I wasn't working for a network or a newspaper, what could I possibly know? That's life out in the cold. It's tough. I understood and didn't fault anyone.

After spending the day dealing with a recalcitrant general manager at the business I had inherited, or preparing my son for school, or listening to lawyers explain the latest restrictions put on me by the IRS, I would spend the evening reconciling my real and shrinking bank balance. That's why it became difficult to show up at *Larry King Live* with a smile and to take seriously whether I did or didn't have a home phone number for Tom Cruise. I didn't blame Wendy. She had a job to do. She wanted me to be the person she'd hired, doing the job she'd hired me to do. From CNN to Nathans, people wanted life to be the way it was when Howard was alive. I did, too, but I knew that was gone forever. I'd learned my lawyer talk: You can't unring the bell.

Of all the precious things Howard's death cost me, the worst was my faith in him, but what hurt the most at that moment was the way it set me up to fail at *Larry King Live.* I didn't actually quit the show for another year, but after Diana died I was a falling star who checked in, did what she could, and checked out. I played my hand. They knew my limits. I'd like to say I flamed out but no, there was nothing spectacular about the way my career faded away. Just a slow fizzle.

In the meantime, I loved being in the bubble when I could. I used any excuse for a trip to New York. The babysitter, Erica, was excellent and also the apple of Spencer's eye. She'd just graduated from Georgetown University and was taking a chill year. Nobody had to push me to go, and I could leave without guilt. I called Spencer in the morning, again after school, and at bedtime. Of course I missed him but I knew he would enjoy my good mood when I brought it back home. Sometimes, when the trip butted against a weekend and it was practical, I took him with me. We'd see family friends, wander in Central Park, tour museums, eat and play, and generally have a great time in the greatest of cities.

When I went alone, the trip was usually no more than two nights. I often spent one of those nights seeing Paolo. If it was a one-night trip, the night usually belonged to him. Everybody has a selfish pleasure and he was mine. I should have felt guilty, but I didn't. Not in an overt way. I had no overarching designs on the man. I didn't want him *that* way—happily ever after. I wanted him this way—here and now. I didn't want to upset his world, nor did he. We went to cafés and held hands under the table, we flirted, we talked endlessly. I loved his voice, his accent. We called room service for midnight meals in my room. We watched television. We made out on the hotel room floor, but when it came to sex, we were well matched in our restraint. In a world where sex was everywhere, we were in no hurry. Me because I still felt married. It was too soon. Paulo because he sensed my hesitation and had his own old-school and endearing moral code. We were in the same place and we liked it. We loved playing at being in love.

Sometimes when I was in New York I didn't see or talk to him.

Other times I felt I needed him. One of those times came after the September 8, 1997, memorial service for fashion designer Gianni Versace at the Metropolitan Museum of Art. The service was moving and sad. The Temple of Dendur was adorned with astonishingly beautiful white flowers, Andrea Bocelli's voice soared to the glass rafters, the grief on the faces of Donatella Versace and her brother Santo was palpably real. My own heartbreak overtook and surprised me like a rogue wave and, as Whitney Houston sang, I cried like everyone else. The service had become more than a tribute to a great designer, more than a collection of boldface names. It enflamed my own wounds, and my own grief poured out, even though it had been months since Howard died. My *LKL* colleague, Dean Sicoli held my hand, realizing, he told me later, that a funeral was probably not the smartest place for me to be.

I had not told Paolo I would be in town, but when the service ended and after I said good-bye to Dean, I hopped in a cab and headed downtown to his restaurant. It was closed during the between-meal break, but the front door was open. I tore through the dining room, past waiters polishing glassware, arranging silver, and freshening flowers, and charged boldly into the kitchen. Paolo's face told me I was the last person he'd expected to see. But he smiled, stopped what he was doing, and came around the large stove area. He seemed embarrassed to be in grubby kitchen clothes rather than his starched whites, but he looked good to me.

"I'm sorry," I said. "I just had to see you. I thought it would be a day trip but now I have to stay for a meeting tomorrow morning. I was at Versace's memorial service and I'm sad and I missed you."

"I don't know what I can do tonight. I have two big parties late." Paolo sighed and rubbed his hand across the stubble on his chin.

I leaned close, kissed him on the cheek, and placed my room key in the palm of his hand. "I know. I understand. But you know where to find me." And then I was gone, back in a cab and headed uptown.

Late that night, in bed, I heard a rustling at my door, a faint knock. I stirred from my sleep and dashed to the door. I unhooked the chain and turned the lock as I finished pulling on the hotel's terry cloth bathrobe over my silk night slip. I pulled the door open to see his smile. If nothing else I was seduced by his smile.

"I can't stay long," he said.

"Well, stay for a minute," I said.

"A minute," he said.

He looked irresistibly handsome. He was in his sexy professor mode in a dark suit, dark polo shirt, and wire-rimmed glasses. His hair was floppy on his head, wet at the ends, like he'd taken a shower.

"I'll order some tea from room service," I said.

"Chamomile, please. With lemon." It was two in the morning. The room was dark. I found some of the small votive candles the hotel provided for emergencies and lit them.

"Really, I'm not staying," he said. "I am so tired. I have a medical checkup first thing tomorrow, and we were so busy tonight and I just couldn't get out of there."

"Just sit down," I said, getting back in bed and pulling the covers over me. Often the hotel gave me this same room. I liked it because it was on the seventh floor and had two huge windows that looked out on the city. I would sleep with them open because I liked the street sounds of Manhattan—sirens wailing up Madison, trucks grinding their gears, taxi drivers laying a heavy hand on the horn. To me they were familiar, comforting sounds, and more soothing than silence.

Room service arrived quickly. Paolo took the tray from the waiter, placed it on the desk, and poured two cups of tea. He set them on the bedside table, sat down on the edge of the bed, and looked at me.

"Come over here," he said, patting the space beside him. He grabbed a couple of pillows and fluffed them up. "Come here and get comfortable." I slid across the bed and curled up beside him. He handed me a cup. We sipped our tea.

"It's nice of you to come see me," I said, "and tuck me in."

"How could I resist? If a beautiful woman gives you her room key you do not stand her up."

"Oh, that's your French half talking."

He shrugged. "You never know. Could be my Italian, too."

I sighed. He sighed, took my cup, and put it next to his on the bedside table. He turned back, leaned over, and kissed me. Slowly he eased the terry cloth robe off my shoulders. He kissed my neck, my shoulder, and then down my arm to my fingers. I closed my eyes and gave in to the rush. I reached for his chin and brought his face up to mine and kissed him deeply. I moved my hands through his hair and down his back and across his chest. I kissed his face and his neck and danced my tongue in his ear, nibbling on his earlobe. We kissed again. I clutched his head to my chest, rocking him, my fingers playing in his hair.

"I want to know something, Paolo. Are you afraid of falling in love with me?"

Candles flickered in the light breeze from the window. "I think perhaps I've done that already," he said, with an air of resignation in his voice.

"Don't be afraid," I said. "Don't be afraid of me. I don't want anything from you but the times we have together, times like this. They sustain me. You make me float when everything else is pulling me down. But I can't forget that you're married. Not ever. I just can't. I really, really don't want to disturb your marriage. I've been there. I've done that." I was thinking about Howard, about how when we first met he was married, though I had believed he was in the midst of a divorce. It didn't make any difference. An affair was one thing, but I did not want any man leaving his wife for me ever again. That road was tawdry and definitely not romantic.

Paolo leaned over and kissed my belly through the brown silk slip.

I sighed. "You like that part, don't you?"

"I like all your parts. Even the ones I haven't seen." He sighed and rolled over on his back. He rested his wrist on his forehead and stared at the ceiling.

"Don't worry about my marriage," he said. "It just is what it is. We all make peace with certain arrangements, and I've made peace with my marriage. I'm not guilty, not *that* guilty." He smiled impishly. "You shouldn't be."

I put my hand on his chest, and walked my fingers toward his chin. "You know, I like your parts, too. Particularly your neck right here." I touched him just under his ear. He pulled me down and we kissed softly and slowly.

"Should we make love?" I whispered.

"Yes, we should." But we didn't.

The next morning I was up early for a vigorous run in Central Park. It was sunny and cool, a beautiful autumn morning in New York.

I ran around the reservoir and felt revived. I was part of the world. I was among the living. And I was relieved that the night before with Paolo we hadn't done anything to complicate things further. It had been romantic and intense and I felt like Cinderella before the coach turned into a pumpkin. Fairy tales have their own reality. My relationship with Paolo was as real as that, and as satisfying.

As I ran, my mind was spinning. I adored Paolo. I was probably in love with him. He was like an addiction. I would arrive from Washington beaten by forces beyond my control—the government, Nathans, the show—with my self-esteem and confidence in the ditch. Then, after a dose of Paolo, I would feel good about myself again. I stood taller and welcomed the challenges ahead.

Maybe our liaisons did the same for him. I couldn't cast spells over the government or my work, but I could make Paolo smile.

BACK AT THE hotel I showered and dressed quickly. I was late for a meeting with a man from Christie's to discuss the best time to sell the antiques that Howard had inherited and were now thankfully mine and not the government's. It was a dreary occasion because I had thought these pieces would always be ours and would eventually pass to Spencer. Since he wasn't a named heir to the Joynt trust, at least he'd have something from the family. That wasn't an option anymore. We needed cash.

When I returned to the hotel room the phone was ringing. "What are you doing right now?" Paolo asked, purring into my ear.

"I just finished breakfast."

"Don't ask any questions. Put on some jeans and meet me in front of your hotel in fifteen minutes. Okay? Can you do that for me? Wear something warm."

"Okay. I will do that."

There under the awning at the hotel's entrance was Paolo on his motorcycle, the engine idling. He wore a light sweater, leather jacket, and jeans. He held out a helmet.

"I can't do this," I said.

"Yes, you can. Put on the helmet. We're going for a ride. You trust me, don't you?"

"Of course I do," I said. "But I'm an only parent. I can't take chances."

"You're wasting time," he said sweetly. "Get on."

I pulled the helmet over my head and wrapped my arms tightly around his middle. Paolo gunned it and we were off—up Park Avenue, a right turn on Ninety-Sixth Street, an easy merge onto the FDR Drive. I took a deep breath and gave in to the ride.

We zoomed along the Merritt Parkway and into the beautiful New York and Connecticut countryside. I loved holding on to him for dear life. My fear was overtaken by the sheer exhilaration of freedom. Paolo was strong and confident and made all the right choices. We rode for hours through woods and by lakes, passing rock walls and open fields—and then we were back in Manhattan.

"You needed this," Paolo said. "You needed this more than anything."

"Yes." We had shared many tender moments over the months, but this one truly was the best.

Chapter 24

THE TWO WELL-DRESSED men who walked in the front door of Balthazar were obviously accustomed to making the scene in New York City. I spotted them from the maître d's post where I was standing with my friend Susan Magrino. They were the type who didn't need reservations to get the best tables in the restaurant of the moment. In the fall of 1997, Balthazar was that restaurant. The men looked comfortable, secure, and stylish in an offhand American way. Their eyes scanned the room. When they saw Susan, their faces lit up.

"Hey, Magrino!" the bald stocky one called out.

"Susan, good to see you," said the other. He was handsome like a matinee idol: thick, dark hair and a dark moustache. He had the quiet assurance of a good-looking man who knows he makes heads turn.

If it hadn't been for Susan, I wouldn't have been at Balthazar at all. To get a table there, you had to be someone or know someone. Susan qualified in both categories. She was one of New York's most successful PR executives. Her long list of clients included many "names," such as Martha Stewart, as well as important corporations and publications. She was smart and attractive and had a good sense of humor. Her blond hair, bright eyes, and broad, generous smile set her apart from the high-strung, edgy stereotype of the New York PR woman. She also had an unforgettable deep voice. I'd met her in 1992 when she was doing publicity for Charlie Rose and I was producing the Washington segment of his nightly PBS talk show. When it came to Charlie, Susan and I shared mutual affection and exasperation. We loved Charlie but we also knew him too well to be adoring sycophants. Now, with my job at *Larry King Live,* we talked practically every week. But on this night at Balthazar, we weren't working; we were just friends out for dinner.

The room was large, loud, and crowded. It had high ceilings, banquettes lining the walls, and tables packed into every square inch—the look and feel of a Parisian bistro. Even the hum of voices sounded imported. The antique lighting cast a golden glow that was reflected many times over in the huge mirrors on the walls.

I felt good. I thought I looked good, too, in a short, stretchy skirt and matching T-shirt—funky and sexy, completely unlike anything I'd worn for the past twenty years. Susan introduced me to the two new arrivals, gesturing to the affable bald fellow, saying, "Carol, this is Bobby." Then, indicating the darkly handsome one, "And this is Keith." If she said last names I didn't catch them. "Carol is up here from Washington. She's a producer for Larry King." We shook hands.

"We've done business before," Bobby said. "You've booked some people through me. Tell Larry I said 'Hi.'" He must be Bobby Zarem, I thought, one of New York's public relations legends.

Keith moved closer to me. "So, Larry King, eh?"

"Yeah," I said, "Larry King." He was beguiling, and he knew it.

"I watch that show all the time," he said. "I love Larry."

I laughed. "Yes, he's very lovable."

"Have you been there long?" he asked.

"Not long. About three years."

"Why are you in New York? Got a hot date?"

"Well, that's a thought"—I laughed again—"but no, no hot dates. I went to the memorial service for Gianni Versace. We want Donatella on the show."

"Oh, you do, do you? You want Donatella Versace?" He was full of himself, mocking me, flirting. It made me blush.

Susan and Bobby stood to the side, deep in conversation.

"What's this outfit you've got on?" Keith asked, moving closer.

"You like it?" I asked. I was flirting, too.

"Yeah. I can see right through it," he said.

"No you can't," I said, laughing again. "But go ahead and dream."

The hostess interrupted. "Ladies, your table is ready."

Susan and I excused ourselves. Keith was so close I had to squeeze past him.

"You and Keith sure hit it off," Susan said when we were seated. "Another second and he would have been all over you. Do you know who he is?"

"He's in PR, isn't he? Like Bobby," I said. "PR people are always like that once they hear Larry's name."

"Carol, you don't know, do you?"

"No," I said, "I guess I don't."

"He's a baseball player. Keith Hernandez. He's a retired Met. Two World Series. He's a star, a hero in this town, and a notorious lady killer."

A look of shock lit up my face. "Wow," I said. How could I not know who he was? I hoisted myself up in my seat and craned my neck to look back at the front door. He stood there with Bobby, looking at me. He gave a small wave. I smiled back, embarrassed that he'd seen me gawking. The cocky expression on his face suggested that he knew we were talking about him. I slid back down on the banquette to face Susan.

"Could you go for that?" she asked.

"He might be too exciting for me. But he is handsome. There's no denying that." The men had been joined by some young women and were being led to a table up front. "I've never really been into jocks but who knows. It's a new world for me now."

We ordered a carafe of red wine, steaks, and fries. When the waitress brought the fries there were so many of them they spilled out of the bowl and onto the white paper covering the table. It was a delicious sight. A bounty of French fries. They were long and skinny and dark brown and crispy. I nibbled away at them, loving every bite. People stopped by to say hello to Susan. We ate, shook hands with visitors, talked, and ate some more. Half the people I met handed me business cards and pitched ideas for Larry King. "There's nothing in Washington like this," I said to Susan. "The energy in this room could power a small town."

The route out of the restaurant took us by the table where Keith and Bobby sat with a dozen people, many of them attractive young women. As we inched by, Keith whispered, "Everybody here is staring at you. I think it's that skirt."

"The one you can see through." I laughed. I wasn't usually that brash. I put out my hand to shake his. "It was good to meet you."

"We should keep in touch," he said. "I'd like to hear more about Larry King."

Susan and I shared a cab uptown. "I have no idea how to deal with men," I said. "I mean, he was flirting with me and I had no idea what to do. I was reduced to gibberish."

"How long were you with Howard?" Susan asked.

"Almost twenty years."

"You really are sheltered," she said. "Give yourself time." The windows of the cab were open. We were flying up Park Avenue with all the lights in our favor. I liked the speed, and the fresh air whooshing through the backseat.

HOME AGAIN IN Washington I told the story of Keith Hernandez to anyone who would listen. At Nathans the boys at the bar were at long last impressed with something I'd done. Martha, a baseball fiend, quickly faxed me all his stats and then in a phone conversation explained what they meant. At CNN, when I told Larry King, he said, "I love Keith. He's one of my favorite people in the world."

I reminded Larry that in the next week, when we were in New York to do an interview with Martha Stewart, I would be taking him and Shawn to dinner as a wedding present. "We're going to Daniel, remember, where we went with Al Pacino?"

"Oh yeah, sure," he said. A haute French restaurant was not exactly Larry's top choice but Shawn was dying to go there. I liked Shawn and was pleased to make her happy. It was much more difficult to please Larry, but I had an idea.

"What if I invite Keith to come as my guest?"

Larry beamed. I wondered what had possessed me to think of inviting a man I barely knew and who was clearly accustomed to having women fawn all over him. As Becky the senior producer faithfully told any colleague who would listen, I was out of my mind.

"Okay, Larry, I'll do it."

I called Bobby Zarem and asked, "Is Keith married?"

"No," he said. "Why?"

"I want to ask him to dinner next week with me and Larry and Larry's new wife."

Bobby said, "I'll call him." About an hour later the phone rang. It was Keith. I was at my desk in Nathans' basement, where Connie the bookkeeper and I were paying bills. His voice was soft, intimate.

"It's something different to have a girl ask me out," he said, "but I'd love to come to dinner with you and Larry King." We agreed the four of us would meet at the restaurant after the live show.

Just like that. Not even two minutes later, we hung up. "Oh, my God!" I said, looking up at Connie. "I have a date!"

"What do you mean, you have a date? You don't just have a date, you have a date with Keith Hernandez!"

This particular New York trip was jammed with work. I had a meeting with someone who was trying to help us book Lisa Marie Presley; I had a meeting with Hamilton South, the gatekeeper for Ralph Lauren; and I had a meeting with Ed Filipowski, who was the U.S. publicist for Donatella Versace. We had live shows with Martha Stewart and Kitty Kelley and a daytime taping of Chanel's Karl Lagerfeld with Anna Wintour of *Vogue,* who agreed to come in because it was with Lagerfeld. All of them were my gets, my responsibility, my shows. But my focus was on the date.

The two cocktail dresses I had brought from Washington, the pride of my dwindling collection of designer frocks—I'd sold the others—hung in the hotel closet. I chose the little black one. I anxiously zipped up the dress and put on the pearls Howard had given me for our tenth wedding anniversary. I was careful not to muss my hair and makeup. All I needed was the man and the corsage and I was ready for the prom.

My reflection in the mirror made me grin. I hadn't fussed over myself this much in years, and I felt a little foolish caring so much about how I looked. It felt odd, too, to be headed out the door alone, not to have a man beside me or waiting for me downstairs. The last time I had been on a "first date," I was twenty-six years old. It was the first time Howard took me out to dinner.

It had been eight months since Howard died, but he was still a presence in my life. Every month I marked the anniversary of his passing. He was in my dreams and fantasies. I'd made progress, but I didn't think of myself as a "single" woman. Paolo and I had kissed like teenagers—in secret and in shadow. He had, in some mysterious way, freed me. But I wasn't sure I was ready for this. A date? There was only one way to find out.

Shawn was good company. We stopped briefly at a party, but I was anxious to get back to the hotel. "It's near the restaurant," I said to Shawn. "We can relax and watch the show there." Well, Shawn could relax but I was pacing. "What do you think? Should I change my dress?"

"Carol, you're fine. Don't change a thing. Just try to relax." She was concentrating on the television, on Larry. It was 9:45. Fifteen minutes to go and the show would be off the air and we would head to Daniel. "Let's not arrive right on time," she said. "We should be five or ten minutes late, so you're sure he's waiting there for you. He can watch you walk in."

"Okay," I said, cheerfully. "That sounds like a plan."

We waited. I checked my watch and waited some more. At ten-ten I said, "Can we go now? Please? Shouldn't we go?" She nodded. I gave one last check in the mirror. Little black dress, check; pearls, check; subtle but good makeup, check; beautiful shiny hair, check; sexy, strappy stilettos, check. I hadn't looked this good in ages. Who could resist me?

The maître d', Bruno Jamais, met us when Shawn and I walked in the door. I looked around. No Keith. "Are we the first ones here?" I asked, only slightly disappointed that Keith would not watch me arrive. "Is our table ready?"

"Yes," Bruno said. He showed us to a table near the middle of the room. It was the restaurant's most visible table and it was set for three. That was odd. Somebody had backed out, and I knew it wasn't Larry.

"We were supposed to be four," I said.

"Ah," sighed Bruno in the most consoling tones, "Mr. Hernandez called and said he cannot make it. He left a number. He would like you to call him."

My thought: Forget that!

Larry charged through the door right on schedule. He was still pumped with the adrenaline from an hour of live television. Diners turned or looked up. Larry started to walk the short distance to our table as the chef, Daniel Boulud, reached his side, eager to greet the star. But that was of no matter to Larry. "Where's Keith?" he boomed.

"He couldn't make it," Shawn said, quietly.

"What? He stood you up?" His voice boomed. He was still standing, looking directly at me, as if I'd lost an important guest for the show at two minutes to air. "You mean, Keith Hernandez stood you up, Carol?" Everyone in the room could hear him. I wanted to kick him in the shins. "Why would Keith stand you up?" Larry repeated. "Did you have any idea?"

Well, no. Shawn hustled him to sit down and tried to change the subject.

Larry could not be appeased. Food was no consolation. I knew Larry well enough not to take his reaction personally. It was just Larry being Larry. Sometimes he took his disappointments like that of a little boy whose toys have just been snatched.

The chef had to have recognized that the table was dysfunctional, but he leaned over to ask what I would like. My appetite was gone. He went to Larry, eager to suggest a variety of delicacies from his famed kitchen: foie gras, caviar, short ribs, crusted halibut. Since his angioplasty, however, Larry was eating a bland diet.

"For me?" he growled. "Grilled chicken with the skin off and some steamed carrots." Larry could have been having a quick piece of chicken at Joe Allen—what he preferred after a show—but instead he was at this fancy French restaurant where the food would clog his arteries, and he was there for only one reason: Keith Hernandez. And no Keith!

"Why did Keith stand you up?" Larry asked, unable to let it go.

Shawn rolled her eyes and patted his arm. "Give it a rest, Larry."

"I have no idea, Larry. Believe me, it's not the way I wanted it to turn out." We were both in the same dark mood. We'd both been stood up. But I put my chin up and moved us on to other topics. I asked about the night's show, about his day. Shawn tried to make some jokes, but we were both hauling rocks through a sea of mud.

Bruno walked over. "You have a phone call," he said.

I took the call near the coat check. It was Keith. "I'm so sorry," he said. "I was just too tired." He gave me a list of all the tough things he'd done that day, including being honored by the Mets with the retirement of his jersey, number 17, and now he was whipped and ready for bed. "Can I call you tomorrow and maybe we'll have a drink or dinner?"

"Sure, Keith, you do that. Good-bye." I hung up and returned to the table.

Larry, Shawn, and I were out of there in forty-five minutes, soup to nuts. The chef came out from the kitchen, astonished that we were leaving so early. "Larry moves fast," I said as we raced past him and out the door.

I walked Shawn and Larry to their car. It was a gorgeous evening. Breezy. Cool. Dry. Full moon. Soft, soft air. The city was alive and vibrant. It was the kind of night I loved. But there I was, in the middle of it, rejected and alone. I struggled to hold back the tears as I walked through the lobby of the Carlyle, rode the elevator up to my floor, walked down the hall, and jammed the key into the lock. Once inside, I slumped against the door. "Goddammit. I want my husband back. I want my marriage back. I want my life back. I don't want to be a widow."

I took off the slinky black dress, the sexy heels, and the pearls, washed the makeup off my face, put on a white cotton T-shirt and boxers, and crawled between the crisp white sheets. I was not going to be a victim. "I'm not going to let any man get me down," I said to myself. "If they want me they'll have to come after me." I wasn't miserable. My ego had been bruised but it was already bouncing back.

The phone rang. "Tell me all about your date," Martha said, unable to restrain her excitement.

"He stood me up!"

For a moment she was silent. "You're kidding," she said. Another pause. "No, you're not."

"Can you imagine? A widow goes out on her first date and gets stood up?" Suddenly we both burst into laughter. We laughed until we said good night. I turned out the lights and drifted off to dreamland.

Here was my problem: I couldn't go back to Washington without at least a base hit. The boys at the bar were counting on me. It was a matter of saving face—Nathans' face, not mine. I had to return to Washington with some kind of success story about me and Keith Hernandez.

The next day Keith paged me four times. After six hours and two more pages, I returned his call. He invited me for drinks and dinner. "We'll see how the drinks go before I commit to dinner," I said.

Shawn had advised me to arrive late. "And play it cool. Play it real cool."

I arrived late but I don't know how cool I played it. At Keith's suggestion we met at the opulent bar of Le Cirque. "Carol!" He got my attention. I walked over, sat down slowly. He was as handsome as I remembered. Dark. Serious. He appeared nervous, shy, and appealingly contrite. We both ordered martinis; mine vodka, his gin.

We made small talk and big talk. During the time we sipped our drinks we covered the highlights of his career as a ballplayer, that he was divorced, that I was a widow, that he had three daughters, that I was a single mother, that he lived in Midtown, that I lived in Georgetown, that he had split up with his girlfriend, that I had a restaurant and a TV job, that he was in retirement, that I had an IRS problem, that he'd once had an IRS problem, and that it was a big no-no to stand me up.

At that point I agreed to have dinner with him. He chose the Park Avenue Bistro on lower Park Avenue. We sat side by side. He insisted I wear his World Series ring, which engulfed my finger. Celine Dion sang in French over the sound system, and he sang along; we ate roasted chicken and French fries, and drank a lot of red wine. He was very affectionate. He put his arm around me. He tried to kiss me.

"Whoa," I said as he deftly moved in for a smooch. I don't know how he played on the ball field but he definitely had major-league moves on the banquette. "We don't even know each other."

"Then let's get to," he said, pawing my arm.

"I'm not ready for this," I said, gently easing away.

"How many guys are after you?" he asked.

"None," I said.

"Can I spend the night with you?"

"No." This was everything I feared a date with a single man would be.

"What if I just sleep with you? No sex?"

"Do I look that naïve?"

"Can I see you again? Will you call me to let me know when you're coming to town again?" he asked, nuzzling my neck, nibbling on my ear.

"Yes, yes, sure."

In the cab outside my hotel I gave him a quick kiss good night. Not twenty minutes later the phone rang in my room. It was Keith. "Are you in bed yet?"

"Just about," I said.

"What are you wearing?" he asked.

"I can't believe you only just met me and you are asking me this. You are something else!"

"I had a good time tonight," he said. "I like you. I can't wait to see you again."

Keith thoroughly confused me, but it was not his fault. He was a red-blooded unmarried male and entirely available. That scared me, in a screwy widow way. Keith was the opposite of what attracted me to Paolo. My head was spinning. At least I had a story to take home to the boys at the bar. I regaled them with the glossiest version, but I knew that one night the man stood me up and the next he crawled all over me. Either it was just a baseball thing or I'd entered a brave new world. I hoped I was brave enough to handle it.

Chapter 25

SALOON OWNERS HANG out at the bar. If you want to find one, that's the first place to look. You'll find him—yes, most of them are men—there most nights, moving from table to table greeting guests, hobnobbing with them, pouring drinks, playing the jovial host. It's the first law of the barkeep. I wasn't typical. I wasn't typical at all. It was hard for me to play by those rules. I wanted to spend most of my evenings with my little boy.

Almost nine months after Nathans fell into my lap I still didn't feel comfortable playing the role Howard had played so well. I was delighted to see people packed five deep at the bar. I thanked Howard every day for having created one of the best-looking rooms in the city with yacht hulls and marine prints and charts and other nautical memorabilia. The polished teak floors, the dark navy walls, the antique fans, and the low lighting gave the room unique charm and character. If a Hollywood production designer was asked to create a Georgetown bar, it would look like Nathans. When James Brooks shot *Broadcast News,* he filmed there for a whole day. (Alas, the scenes didn't make the final cut.) The room at its best buzzed with the low hum of conversation broken by frequent peals of laughter and music floating from the jukebox. The bar gave off the warm and intimate aura of an earlier time.

But I was a backroom girl. Always had been. That's where Howard and I had dinner on the rare occasions when we had eaten there. It's where Spencer and I ate pasta. And it's where Martha joined me one October evening for one of our regular dinners together in booth 26.

We faced each other on the cozy red leather banquette. She ordered her usual—a glass of merlot with a side of Diet Coke. I felt the need for a real drink. The waiter obliged with a supercold Stoli martini. Much to my delight, the other tables were filled. The place was hopping. Miles Davis soothed through the multiple speakers that lined the ceiling. The staff seemed happy. I prayed that it would last.

Lying between us on the red-and-white checked tablecloth was the reason I wanted the support of a Stoli martini: the outline Miriam Fisher and her team had prepared for my defense. It included the "story of Howard and Carol." I needed Martha to read through the outline, to make sure what I had told the lawyers about Howard's life before we met was correct. I could only tell Miriam what Howard had told me, but Martha had lived through it.

I wasn't proud of what the report said about me, but not because Miriam got the facts wrong. She got them right. That was the problem. The report showed the truth, and the truth made me cringe. It hurt. It made clear that in my marriage I had given over control of my life to another person. I was too trusting. *Sheltered* would be the polite word. *Idiotic* seemed more like it, even *stupid:* "Throughout her career and her adult life Carol steadfastly avoided getting involved in financial matters, because she knew they were complex and she did not understand them. She would hire professionals or defer to her father or husband." I was proud of my professional career, where I was more than competent, I was good. I'd gotten awards and acclaim. How, then, did I let things slip into this, this . . . ignominious state of affairs?

When the report didn't make me feel like a fool, it made me feel like a concubine. That wasn't a good way to feel, either. "Carol met Howard in May 1977 when she was twenty-six and he was thirty-eight years old," Miriam wrote. "They fell in love almost immediately. Carol was enticed and overwhelmed by Howard's ability to make decisions and get the job done, and his obvious comfort in a good life she had never before experienced." I'd been hired by Walter Cronkite when I was twenty-two, for God's sake! I'd lived in New York, the West Indies, and France.

"For a girl who had worked since high school and who furnished her apartment with camping equipment, this was an exciting and exotic new world." Well, yes, it was exciting and new, and Howard made me feel like a princess. I could love him for that alone. He made me feel marvelous. Beautiful. Desired. And he made me laugh. It was all magic carpet and, with his adoration, I was not alone. He made everyone he focused on feel they had wonderful, hitherto hidden qualities that he could see at once. He made us feel better about ourselves. That is a great gift. I wondered how he had felt about himself as his life caught up with him and slipped out of his control. I would never know the answer to that.

"At twenty-six," Miriam continued, "Carol had never owned anything, never had investments, never had a loan, never owned a car; her only financial responsibilities had been rent, food, clothes, and the phone bill." Yes, and I liked it that way. "She fell in love with Howard believing he would be able to take care of her and would never let anything happen to her. That was her Faustian pact."

Faustian pact. There it was, the truth that haunted me, the truth I was unable to speak. My version of a Faustian pact. It was that. It always was that. I'd sold myself for what I thought would be a better life. In terms of possessions and the roof over my head, it was better. I was a good wife, homemaker, and mother. I stuck with our marriage when it was rough and savored the pleasures when it was good. I didn't realize I was living in a fairy castle built on sand. When the tide came in, my lovely castle was washed away. I had to believe I genuinely loved Howard, but our life together, which had appeared so solid and "real," was only as solid as that sand castle, as a dream. Dreams have their own reality, but no matter how vivid or real, upon waking the dream passes like a shadow. None of what I had savored was ever mine. I should have probed. I never did. I didn't ask questions. I didn't insist on answers. I didn't want to know. It was marital don't ask, don't tell. I liked my comfortable world where I was safe and protected and, well, innocent. But there are all kinds of innocence, and while I clearly qualified for innocent spouse by the IRS code, it was largely because I was stupid and silly. I'd preferred ignorance and innocence to knowledge. I wasn't proud of that.

In booth 26 I sipped my drink. We put off ordering. I wasn't particularly hungry. My anxiety level was high. Martha had walls around her when it came to the IRS case. It was too ugly, too disturbing, a fiery car crash with her brother—and to some extent her family—in the wreckage. She didn't know what to say or how to make it right, and she chose to remain at a safe distance. I granted her the buffer, but now I needed to hear what she had to say. She was the only person who could vet Howard's story about himself. Martha read the report while

I watched her face for reactions. They started almost immediately. She stopped reading and looked up at me.

"Howard didn't graduate from Choate," she said.

"He didn't?" I asked. "He told me he did."

"No," she said, "he was at Choate for a while and then returned to Washington and graduated from St. Stephen's."

"He talked about it a lot, graduating from Choate."

"Well, it's not true." She read more and stopped again.

"He didn't go to Harvard," she said, a droll smile crossing her face. "Did he tell you he went to Harvard?"

"Yes. He said he went there for six months before getting kicked out because of 'a case of booze,' and he transferred to the University of Pennsylvania."

"That part is true. He did go to Penn. But I think he got kicked out of Choate for drinking. He didn't go to Harvard, unless I missed a big chunk of his life, and I don't think I did."

"Why would he say that? It's not like Penn was chopped liver."

Martha returned to the report but stopped again when she got to the part about the Joynt family trust and Howard's inheritance. Her eyes popped. Miriam reported what Howard had told me: that he received twenty thousand dollars a month from the trust.

"That's just wrong," she said. "That's just plain wrong! It's not even close to twenty thousand." She laughed. "A ridiculous exaggeration. What was he thinking? Why would he do that, Carol?"

I took another sip of my drink. "Because the money was coming from here," I said, "from Nathans, and that was his cover."

"This is amazing," Martha said. "I had no idea he told so many fibs."

"Lies, Martha."

We drank in silence for a few moments, trying to absorb all this. My tangled emotions dueled somewhere between gladness and sorrow. Glad because my principal motivation was to survive and Martha's revelations would help my defense. Sorrow because each new truth moved me a greater distance away from the man I loved. The more Howard came into focus the less he was the man I knew.

"Martha," I said, "you've got to help me. You've got to talk to the lawyers with me. You've got to tell them everything you've been telling me. They have to hear it from you. Your pieces of the puzzle are critical. They could save me. Please, Martha, help me. I'm alive with a son to support. Howard's dead. None of this can hurt him now."

A meeting was hastily scheduled in one of Miriam's conference rooms. One of the lawyers who'd assembled the report was there, too. The lawyers sat on one side of the table, Martha and I on the other. Martha's expression made clear she would rather be anywhere than where she was. The process started slowly, tentatively.

Miriam took the report and read off a point. "Howard graduated from Choate before attending Harvard University and then the University of Pennsylvania."

"No," Martha said, her voice low. "He didn't last at Choate. He graduated from St. Stephen's in Alexandria. He didn't go to Harvard. He did go to the University of Pennsylvania."

"Did he graduate from the University of Pennsylvania?" Miriam asked.

"No, he didn't last a year. He transferred to Georgetown."

"Did Howard receive a payment from the Joynt family trust of approximately twenty thousand dollars a month?"

"No. He received a quarterly payment, and at most it was about fifteen thousand."

"His ex-wife was of Spanish royalty, a princess of some sort?"

Martha laughed out loud for the first time. "She was part Spanish and part Russian. I'm sure she thought she was a princess or royalty, but she wasn't."

Point by point Miriam went through the report, with Martha making corrections and the lawyers taking notes. Martha was not as forthcoming as she had been over dinner, and I knew why. She loved her brother. She had always been the responsible sibling, always there for him. She didn't want to feel as if she was betraying him. Me? I'd stepped outside myself at that point, wanting only to get a nod from Miriam that this information would bolster my case.

"I know this is hard for you, Martha," she said. "But this will help Carol and Spencer a lot. These shadings of the truth show a pattern in Howard's behavior that backs up our argument that he didn't tell Carol how he ran his business. This will make a difference."

"I'm stunned by all this," Martha said. A lifetime of Joynt family honor was at stake. You could see it in her face, the anguish and embarrassment. When we were finished she was drained dry. I wasn't. As inappropriate as it may sound, I was enthused. Through his sister, Howard had come to the rescue, giving me help from the grave. He seemed to be in the room, saying, "Here, take these flawed pieces of me and use them to save yourselves."

We stood up, walked out of the conference room without speaking, and waited quietly at the elevator. I broke the heavy silence. "Thank you, Martha. I know you didn't want to do this, but it will help so much."

"I hope so." Martha stood in her proper suit and sensible shoes, holding her handbag, looking resigned and uncomfortable. "Carol," she said, "there's something I didn't say in there, and I didn't say it because I figured you didn't need to know."

The bell rang, signaling the arrival of the elevator. "What was that, Martha? Try me."

"I don't want to cause you more pain."

"That's okay." More pain? I'd become nearly immune. "I can take it. What is it? You can tell me."

The elevator doors slid open. It was empty. We stepped in. "You believe Howard had two marriages before you. He had another wife you didn't know about. A first marriage. You aren't his third wife, Carol, you're his fourth." I put out my arm to stop the doors from closing.

This time I really was shocked, and it showed on my face.

"I didn't want to make it look worse," Martha said. "He was in high school. He forged her signature for the license. It didn't last long. Only a few months and then it was annulled."

"Martha, this doesn't make it look worse." I was recovering from my shock and beginning to smile. "This is better. Don't you see? It will help our defense even more. That's not bad news at all. We've got to go back and tell Miriam. Come on, we've got to tell Miriam now. I pulled Martha out of the elevator and back into the law offices, calling, "Miriam, Miriam . . . Where are you? . . . Wait till you hear this!"

Miriam finalized the report by the end of October and submitted it to Deborah Martin. My fate was now in the hands of the Internal Revenue Service.

Chapter 26

I'M NOT A blabbermouth. Journalism, while based on digging out the facts from the rumors, teaches discretion. You learn to keep what you know between yourself and your editor and you learn to build trust with sources by protecting their confidentiality. Why, then, was I sharing what had befallen me with friends, colleagues, and even casual acquaintances? This was not my normal MO. A lot of people in my shoes—maybe most—would have reacted like Martha—lips shut, locked, and the key thrown away. Me? I talked. The cascading revelations about my tax-cheating, mysterious stranger of a husband had knocked me for a loop. I needed to air them with someone beyond the lawyers and the psychiatrist. It was part of my coming to terms with him, with our marriage, and with myself. I wanted my friends and my colleagues at *Larry King Live* to understand this wasn't simply a matter of my husband's death. I hoped they would cut me some slack. Howard's death had changed my life, and was continuing to change it in ways I could never have foreseen. The aftershocks seemed to go on and on and on.

From Howard's and my friends, though, I needed more. Was I the only one who had missed it? Had they looked at our lives and seen the masquerade and just assumed I was in on the ruse? Had they known what Howard was up to? Some told me later they had had their occasional doubts about "where it all came from," but most had taken Howard at face value. He was larger than life, with so much natural grace, wit, and intelligence that it was hard not to be impressed by him, to like him, and to like being around him. Without him, life would have been a lot less fun. Maybe that's the artistry of the world-class liar. Plus there was the plausible backstory, including the family money, which was real, and the packed bar at the best corner of the city's best-known intersection. Only people who knew the saloon business, people such as Fred Thimm at the Palm, understood that the visibly packed bar didn't necessarily translate to a profitable business, especially when there was an owner who was deft at shenanigans. But outside of the bar business, there were few friends who got the picture.

I had a long, late kitchen dinner with someone who did understand: Terence Smith, who lived near us on the Chesapeake Bay with his wife, Susy Elfving. As couples go, we had spent more time with them than any other. For Howard, a man who really wanted and needed only one friend—me—his friendship with Terry was refreshing and welcomed. Terry's no pushover, and Howard liked that. He can be full of himself sometimes, and Howard liked that, too. He came up through the *New York Times,* in the tracks of his father, the legendary sports writer "Red" Smith. We met when he was a White House correspondent at CBS News. Now he was with the *NewsHour* at PBS. Like Howard and me, he was also a sailor. Terry was a good reader of people. He'd met plenty of men who live life by a roll of the dice.

Susy, at the time a top official at the Commerce Department, was away on a trip. Spencer was tucked in. It poured heavy rain outside as Terry and I ate dinner, drank wine, and talked. I let it all out about the tax fraud, the illicit write-offs, and the money Howard had taken from Nathans. "It's hard to accept how this happened," I said. Then I brought up another matter, one I'd discussed with nobody but Martha. "There are rumors going around that Howard committed suicide."

Terry was taken aback. "You don't believe that, do you?"

"No, I don't, but Martha wonders. She wonders about it a lot. She thinks he might have considered it his only way out. She can't understand why he didn't go to the doctor. . . . He didn't have to die. Maybe if I'd been here instead of New York . . ."

"Carol, he was a grown-up. You did all you could do. He was very ill, possibly—obviously—not in his right mind. He might have been too sick to recognize how sick he was."

"He might have gone to jail, Terry. He couldn't face that."

Terry was silent.

"If Howard had gone to trial and then to jail on top of the IRS taking every single thing we owned . . . well, I can't imagine. I simply can't imagine. Can you?"

"No," Terry said.

"Even if he didn't go to jail, the IRS would have taken everything they could get their hands on. He would have been mortified. No, that's too weak a word. . . ." I was beginning to think Martha had a point—not that Howard had actively killed himself but that he just let himself die because he saw no alternative. On the other hand, Terry knew Howard was smart enough that he could have figured it out. "He wouldn't have rolled over," Terry said. "There's no way he would have abandoned Spencer. None."

I believed Terry was right, but how well can we ever know another person, I thought. How well do we know ourselves?

SPENCER'S FIRST WEEKS of school went well. He loved kindergarten. He loved his backpack with the multiple key chains hanging down. He wore it proudly as he marched out the door to wait on the street for the school bus, with me and Teddy the dog in tow. He came home with elaborate stories about teachers and friends and antics on the playground. He regularly brought home artwork, including a family portrait of stick figures with names below them: "Mommy," "Daddy" (with a halo and wings), "Teddy," and "Cecilia."

Cecilia? "Who's Cecilia?" I asked. "Does she live in your room with you? Is she invisible to me?"

He didn't reply.

Later, at a parent-teacher conference, his teacher said to me, "You didn't tell us about your daughter. That was a surprise."

We were seated across from each other on pint-size chairs at a pint-size table. "My daughter? I don't have a daughter."

"Cecilia?" Instantly I understood Spencer's "family" drawing.

"Spencer told the class about his sister, Cecilia, and that she's away at boarding school."

"There is no sister. Cecilia's the product of his very active imagination." I laughed, but I was concerned.

When I mentioned Cecilia to his grief therapist, Ellen Sanford, she said not to worry. "He's just trying to make your family like the families of other kids in his class. Don't be surprised by that. Again, he just wants to fit in. He wants desperately to be like the other children."

She asked if Spencer was aware of the death of Princess Diana, if he'd seen any of the funeral coverage on television.

"Yes, we talked about it. I asked him what he would say to William and Harry. He said, 'I would tell them I miss my daddy a lot and that it's okay to cry.'"

As much as I tried to be there for him during his at-home hours, my record wasn't perfect. I almost always got home in time to meet the afternoon school bus, but one day in the first months of school (the babysitter was off-duty) I was late. I was walking down the street toward the waiting bus just as it pulled away. The driver wouldn't leave children at the bus stop unless someone was waiting for them.

"Stop!" I screamed. "Stop!" I yelled to pedestrians closer to the bus, "Don't let that bus go!" I was running as fast as I could in a straight skirt and heels. I cut through some office buildings to try to catch the bus one street over, but it picked up speed and I could not keep up. All I could think about was my little boy on that bus wondering what had happened to his mother. At almost six years old he certainly wasn't thinking that I had been delayed and was likely chasing the bus in four-inch heels.

I ran home, grabbed the car keys, and bolted for the car. I called the school to tell them I was on my way. My heart pounded. My poor boy. What must he be thinking? How sad must he be? I beat the bus to school by one minute. When it pulled up the driver opened the doors and Spencer stepped down, head hung low, eyes moist, dragging his backpack and holding a piece of artwork in his hand. He wore the saddest expression. "It's going to be okay now," the driver assured him in his lilting Jamaican accent. "Here's your mum."

Spencer didn't say a word. He fell into my arms, pressed his face into my side, and stayed like that. I rubbed the back of his head and kissed him. "Mommy's here. I'm so sorry, angel. I love you so much and never meant for that to happen. I ran after the bus as fast as I could but you guys were too quick for me."

I stepped back and knelt down so I could see his face. He didn't smile.

"Is it going to be okay?" I asked, holding his arms in my hands. Spencer nodded. "Why don't you take me into school and show me around? I bet there are all kinds of new things to see."

"Okay," he said, taking my hand. "I'll show you the science department where the animals live. We have lots of animals."

"Can I tell you something for the future?" I said. "If this ever happens again, if the bus stops and I'm not there to meet you—and I hope that will never happen again—but if it does, please remember to do this: Look out the back window to see if I'm running after you!"

"Okay, Mom, but you better stay in shape so you can catch it next time."

Chapter 27

EVEN THOUGH I didn't know when I would fire Doug Moran, I knew I would do it. The place needed a strong manager and unity at the top. Doug was not a good manager, and the top was more fractured than unified. But how to fill the job? And how to teach the new guy how we do business at Nathans? Maybe better to say how we'd *like* to do business at Nathans. That's when it occurred to me to bring in a future manager first as an efficiency consultant to look the place over thoroughly, stick his nose into everything, and learn how everything works and who does what. He would give me a report on what's done right, what's done wrong, and how it could be fixed. I patted myself on the back for that one. I patted Connie the bookkeeper on the back when she said, "I know just the man. Vito Zappala."

He'd owned a restaurant that had failed, which concerned me, but Connie said, "It doesn't matter. It wasn't his fault." Hmmm. Nothing about the restaurant business made sense to me, so why should I treat this bit of news as unusual? "It didn't work out but he's good and you'll like him. He's a grown-up." Where is he now? I wondered. "Works in the golf business, but he's tired of that. Wants to get back to restaurants."

Vito and I met not at Nathans but at another restaurant. Connie was right—I liked him. Not only did he have the lyrical name of Vito Zappala, but he looked like a Vito Zappala. He sounded New York and looked as Italian as a bowl of spaghetti carbonara. He was in his fifties, not tall, not short, not thin, not fat, dark haired, bearded, walked with a slight limp, wore a nice suit. He was in the midst of a divorce and had a daughter the same age as Spencer. He was extremely forthcoming about the ways he felt he could help me run Nathans. He understood that when the day arrived to fire Doug he would have to step in quickly and keep the business from crashing—and with no guarantee going forward that the IRS would even let the place stay open.

Vito showed up toward the end of October. He rolled up his sleeves and immediately involved himself in every part of the workings of the restaurant. The staff perked up and worked like professionals. Even Doug answered questions, opened files, showed up on time, and was agreeable and helpful. For a moment I felt guilty. Was I wrong about Doug? But then I realized Doug was behaving toward Vito the way he should have behaved toward me. I mentioned it to Vito. "Oh, it's simple," he said. "For one thing, I'm a man. For another, I'm not you."

I got out of the way and busied myself with the pursuit of a chef. We'd been using line cooks. They did an adequate job, but I thought a real chef would send a message to the community that Nathans, which had been foundering even before Howard died, was back in the game. The bar seemed to take care of itself. It wasn't broken, so there was nothing to fix. But the restaurant was another story, and food was an area where I could make a difference. I could put my stamp on the place with the food. During one of our midnight calls, I told Paolo that I was going to hire a chef. Paolo thought I was nuts. He believed I could run the kitchen just fine with a strong team of line cooks, *strong* being the important word. I heard the same thing a few evenings later over dinner with my dear friends Patrick O'Connell and Rinehardt Lynch, who had created The Inn at Little Washington in rural northern Virginia. My idea of hiring a chef drew guffaws. "They're all nuts," Rinehardt said.

Patrick, a renowned chef himself, agreed. "We are." The three of us broke into laughter.

What Paolo, Patrick, and Rinehardt couldn't grasp is why I wanted a chef: If I had to be in this business, I wanted a creative collaborator, someone to help make the ordeal more interesting, possibly even fun for me, even though I could hear Fred Thimm saying I was a long way from the "fun" stage.

THE PROCESS OF interviewing chefs was an eye-opener. A well-dressed middle-aged man came in with a thick book of clippings—all from high-end French restaurants. "You understand this is mostly a saloon?" I said.

"Oh, maybe it won't work, then." He closed his book and departed.

A young navy cook showed up, brimming with ambition and enthusiasm. "What are your specialties?" I asked.

"I can cook spaghetti," he said.

"And, what else?"

"Well, I can cook all kinds of spaghetti."

There was another young man I liked a lot. He had notable credentials in New American cuisine and listed some hot restaurants on his résumé. But there were so many of them. He was like a frog—hop, hop, hop. I called a restaurant owner friend who was—remarkably—on his list of references. I say *remarkably* because the owner had three words: "He's a drunk."

At the eleventh hour Paul Wahlberg called. He came with an outstanding reference, Nora Pouillon of Restaurant Nora, an acclaimed Washington restaurant and one of my personal favorites. Paul said the place where he worked had just closed and he was ready, willing, and able to be Nathans' head chef. Moreover, he had the qualifications.

Paul and I hit it off right away. He loved food and had grown up in a big family, where I got the impression he may have been the short-order cook. He was from the Dorchester section of Boston, complete with the accent. His manner was unassuming, almost shy. I can say he looked like the older brother of the movie star Mark Wahlberg because he *was* the older brother of Mark Wahlberg, a fact he revealed to me later, after he was hired. He had substantial experience as a chef and as a kitchen manager. He'd worked hotels and restaurants in the Boston area before moving to Washington. His wife had been relocated here by Crate & Barrel, where she was a manager. He was in his midthirties, he didn't drink, and he really loved to cook. His exuberant enthusiasm was infectious. We both thought an audition was a good idea. I was eager to see his game.

He showed up on time, dressed in a clean white chef's jacket, got along well with the line cooks, and prepared several delicious American dishes. "What do you think?" he asked, standing beside me at the table in the bar where I was sampling his food.

"I love everything," I said, sincerely. He made a spring roll of potatoes and crispy duck that was inventive. He made a salad of julienned prosciutto, goat cheese, roasted red peppers, and pine nuts on romaine that was delicious. He made salmon in a broth of fennel and truffles that I wanted to eat every day.

He sat down. "I wanted to make you some fried clam bellies but the clams weren't right. But I think I do fried clams better than anyone."

"I can't wait," I said, already imagining the salty sweetness of the clams. The next day I offered him the job and he accepted. Vito Zappala thought hiring Paul was a good move.

If Doug Moran wondered about all this activity and what it meant for him, it didn't show. He welcomed Paul. He did not interfere with Paul's plan for a complete redo of the menu, moving it toward American food. I liked Paul's ideas. Paul, Vito, and I felt like a team, with Doug on the sidelines not paying much attention.

The scenario the lawyers provided at this point was that if the IRS let me keep the business I would probably be making payments to them for years to come. It was essential that Nathans become as profitable as possible, so that I could sell it for top dollar. Every choice and decision I made was based on that goal. How would the customers respond to a new menu? Well, I had made changes to the old menu and though there were grumblings at first, they stopped eventually. I expected the same reaction when we switched from northern Italian to American. If we did a good job and put great food on the table, who really was going to bitch? This was an all-American saloon. It should have American food. Paul's was such a winning personality. He gave me courage. He was also a real captain of his kitchen. We gave him a budget and left him alone.

Things were looking up at the restaurant, but across town at *Larry King Live* my career was going from bad to worse. Three important bookings slipped away, and I'd worked hard on all of them. I'd been pursuing Ralph Lauren for months, wooing him with flowers and letters. I met with him in his surprisingly small New York office. We hit it off, and I thought he seemed favorable to an interview. Hamilton South of his staff told me Ralph had never done a big network interview. All the major talk shows seemed to be after him at once, but in the end his communications chief called with the news. "He's decided to go with Diane Sawyer and *Primetime Live.* He feels more comfortable with the taped format. He's afraid he won't do well on live television and that he'd make a fool of himself."

Then the possibility of Frank and Kathie Lee Gifford began to fade. They were a hot get at that moment because Frank had been caught in a tabloid sex scandal involving another woman and some hotel trysts. Kathie Lee was Regis Philbin's cohost on the highly rated *Live with Regis and Kathie Lee*. An appearance on *LKL* would be a sure ratings winner. In the summer, their public relations man, Howard Rubenstein, assured me that if they gave an interview, "Larry would be the one." Now in the fall he told me, "They're leaning toward Barbara Walters. Frank feels she's been good to him."

I said, "If he talks to Barbara she'll want him to cry." Howard said nothing. I kept pedaling. "Okay, let's say Frank goes on Barbara. Let's say that's a done deal. Here's my idea: Have Frank go on Barbara and cry and apologize and then have Frank and Kathie Lee appear together on Larry to make up. And do it just before her Christmas special. It will be more in the spirit of things and America can believe Kathie Lee is happy again." Howard said he'd find out. No promises. The couple planned to do only one interview. The sum of our conversation was that Larry King would not be the chosen one for Frank and Kathie Lee. That's what mattered to Wendy.

The biggest loss was Sarah Ferguson, the Duchess of York, the infamous Fergie, who, shortly after the Paris crash, said she would do one interview on the subject of Princess Diana's death. Her New York publicist, Jeffrey Schneider, told me Fergie had decided Larry King would get that interview. Wendy was elated. Suddenly, in October, when I met with Jeffrey, the deal had changed. He said, "It's now between you and Oprah." I sat across from him in his Sixth Avenue office while he called London and negotiated with her office on Larry's behalf. I heard him tell Fergie's people, "*Larry King Live* should be first." But then she, too, decided to go with Diane Sawyer. It happens. Sometimes you're on a roll and sometimes you're not. Right now I couldn't afford the *not*.

All I had in the pipeline was Marv Albert, the sportscaster who was in the middle of his own sex scandal, which made big headlines due to his alleged fondness for biting his lover and wearing women's underwear. That came out in a trial prompted by a former lover who had accused him of biting her. As always with talk TV, sex was a ratings winner and made Marv a white-hot get. Howard Rubenstein was his representative, too. Rubenstein pointed out that every major interviewer wanted Marv. When I was in the middle of my spiel about the relative merits of Larry versus Barbara, Diane, Katie, or Oprah, he interrupted. "Well, let me tell you who else has asked for the first interview. You won't believe it: RuPaul!"

"RuPaul!" I exclaimed. "That's who I would go with. Hands down." He chose Barbara instead. We would be second, but that was okay because we announced before she did, using a clever promotional tactic, touting the show as Marv's first "live" interview. We always found an angle.

While I was enjoying booking Marv Albert, Wendy understandably was focused on the ones that got away. Losing Fergie and the Giffords did not go over well with the boss, and she was disappointed about Ralph Lauren. Wendy didn't expect Lauren to pull big ratings, but he would have been a prestigious interview.

"I need to talk to you," Wendy said, inviting me into her office. I sat in the chair across from her desk. Becky was sitting on the sofa behind me. I could feel her chill on my back. "The McKinsey people have done a study of CNN and they have looked hard at our show," Wendy said in a tone that expressed more frustration than anger. McKinsey & Company is a global management-consulting firm that CNN hired to assess ways the company could trim budget fat. "Atlanta isn't going to tolerate anymore the way I have you in a staff position but only working part-time. I'm going to have to make you a freelancer." In the past she would have fought for me, but those days were over. Now, my career, which had been teetering on the edge for some months, was falling over the cliff.

"I feel bad about this," I said. "Can I think about it over the weekend?"

"Don't," she said. "Nothing's going to change. This arrangement will be better for you. You can concentrate on what you do best."

My long career in network news had taught me many things; one of them is that when a boss says, "This will be better for you," it means nothing of the sort.

"But, Wendy, I've been able to give much more time to the show lately. I'm working the same number of hours as when Howard was alive."

"You've only booked Rosie, Marv, and Calvin Klein," she said, shorting me by several other solid bookings. "And what about the pope? You haven't booked the pope. He's the number one target of Barbara Walters."

"Wendy," I said, "are you serious? Do you actually believe that if the pope were to do his first television interview it would be with Barbara Walters?"

"I have to end this," she said. "I have a call to make." The meeting was over.

This turn of events was more humiliating than heartbreaking. As I sat there talking to Wendy, I also stood outside my body watching myself beg for my job while Becky sat behind me saying nothing.

Later Wendy said to me, "My God, Carol, you have a full-time job at the restaurant and a child to raise. I don't know how you think you can do all this." She paused. "Tell me something. Is it that you want the job, or that you need the job?"

"Wendy, it's both. I want and need the job."

"We'll talk again," Wendy said. "We'll try to work something out."

The next morning, a Sunday, I went for my usual run. Along one of the prettiest stretches of the running path, where it skirts the Potomac River in front of the Kennedy Center, I took a bad fall, landing on my hands and knees, ripping open my running pants, and tearing the flesh. I pulled myself into a sitting position and rested my back against the railing, with the river behind me. My hands and knees were bloody. I sobbed like a little kid who had fallen off her bike on the playground, but I wasn't crying over my physical wounds; I was crying over all of it—Nathans, my no-longer-brilliant career at CNN, my debts, the IRS, the uncertainty, the fear, and now my bleeding leg. I sat in a heap on the running path feeling sorry for myself. Then I got up, wiped myself off, and limped home.

Sometimes—and this was one of them—I felt that Spencer was the only thing that kept me going.

Chapter 28

DEBORAH MARTIN FROM the IRS contacted current and former members of Nathans' staff who had received the notorious "pink checks." She wanted to tell the employees the obvious: The pink checks were income that had to be reported on their tax returns. The money had come from a slush fund Howard had created with the withholding tax money that he hadn't sent to the government. Miriam assumed that Howard had told Doug and that Doug had advised the staff that nobody needed to report it. But this off-the-books money was recorded in a checkbook, not doled out the old-fashioned way, in cash and under the table. A check is a check is a check; it's a paper trail. When Deborah did her audit, the checkbook was right there in Doug's desk.

The employees were as scared as I had been when the IRS first landed on me in February, which now seemed like a long time ago. Several of them were immigrants and the attention of the IRS made them crazy. Doug Moran asked what we could do to ease their fears. "What do we tell them? Do they have to get lawyers?"

I wanted to help the staff, but I was struggling to satisfy the IRS myself and I had no money to pay for any more lawyers. "If they declared the income, then no, they have nothing to worry about," I said. "If they didn't declare the income then they should contact at least an accountant."

"Well, no one declared the income," Doug said. I still remember the pink oxford-cloth shirt and flowered tie he was wearing that day, and that he hadn't shaved. Maybe he was growing the stubble that was coming into fashion.

"I figured that," I said. "But, Doug, I'm the least smart about this stuff and even I know if an employer gives you a check and you cash it, that's income and you have to report it. There's a paper trail. It can be traced."

"This was Howard's doing," he said.

I wasn't about to let Howard off the hook, but I had no doubt that he and Doug had worked in tandem. "Well, you didn't declare it as income," I said. "So a lot of the staff probably thought they didn't have to, either."

"A lot of them think Nathans, meaning you, will cover their tax debt."

Later I asked Miriam if I was personally liable for their debt.

"No," she said. "You have your own debt and the corporate debt, and that's that. You got what they got a thousand times over." Nonetheless, Miriam agreed to come to Nathans to talk to the staff, to answer their questions, to try to calm them.

Miriam arrived on a Thursday morning wearing a black suit and carrying her briefcase. She was in serious lawyer mode. About a dozen staff filed into the office, finding places to sit on the tattered sofa or on chairs they'd brought with them. Some leaned against the counter that held the copy machine and the paper cutter. The kitchen workers were in their white jackets, black-and-white checked pants, and aprons. It was an hour before opening and the rest of the staff was dressed casually. With the gray walls and the low ceiling, the room felt cramped. The atmosphere was quiet, expectant. When Miriam spoke, one of the Latino staff quietly translated. To me, their need for a translator underscored their vulnerability. It made me sad.

Miriam's talk was tough. She stood in front of my desk and I sat behind her, watching their faces. They looked shocked and helpless when she told them they could each owe thousands of dollars. Watching their reactions I could feel only sympathy. They'd been duped, just like me.

A full half hour after the meeting began, Doug ambled in, eased his way through the group, and tossed his keys down on his desk. He went about his business as Miriam continued talking.

"Because this income was not reported, the IRS now expects you to pay the taxes owed," Miriam said. "You may want to hire a lawyer to represent you in this matter."

Hire a lawyer? With what? Miriam was making clear she couldn't represent me and them.

Doug continued shuffling papers on his desk, acting as though we weren't there. Both Miriam and I gave him the eye, and he stopped shuffling and began to pay attention. When the meeting came to its dismal conclusion, after the last questions had been asked, the busboys, cooks, waiters, and managers had climbed up the metal stairs to get back to work, and Miriam had packed up her briefcase and prepared to leave, Doug cleared his throat. "There's something you don't know that may be important," he said.

"Yes?" Miriam said, turning to face him.

"Some of the kitchen staff get two checks under two different names," he said. "I thought you might want to know."

"Has this gone on a long time?" I asked.

"For a while," he said. While I was no longer shocked to learn the questionable ways in which Nathans paid the staff—on the books, off the books, or even, in this instance, paid twice—I wondered how many other dark secrets were still unrevealed.

"Have you put a stop to it?" Miriam asked.

"No," he said, "but I will."

Miriam sighed. "This may be a problem down the road," she said, sounding exasperated. "We'll deal with it when we get there."

Before dinner that night I was playing with Spencer in the den. I was Darth Vader and he was Luke Skywalker. The phone rang. It was a man who'd worked at Nathans a couple of years back, before Howard died. He'd been the bookkeeper, and he was among those who had received the pink checks and had heard from Deborah Martin.

"You bitch, you fucking bitch, you selfish bitch, I can't believe what you are doing to us!" he screamed before I could finish the word "hello." Spencer looked up, wanting me to get back to our light-saber duel. "You dump this on employees who don't have any money and you don't offer to pay it for us, and just who the hell do you think you are?" His voice was scorching. "Do you know how much money I owe? The IRS wants almost five thousand dollars from me! I don't have this kind of money. Where am I going to get it? You are a goddamned selfish bitch!"

Shouting back wouldn't help. I let him scream himself out before I spoke. Spencer wanted my attention. I was worried he could hear the man's voice through the phone receiver. He was ready to climb up my arm. I held my index finger to my mouth.

When I opened my mouth to speak I was calm, or sounded calm, anyway. "Look, I'm sorry," I said. "I wish I could pay everyone's debt, but I can't. I also wish all of you had reported the income. You did the books, for goodness' sake! If you were getting money on a check, didn't you know there would be a record?"

"Thanks for the sympathy, Carol."

"Hey, it's not that I'm unsympathetic. I know all too well what you're going through. The IRS has me against the wall, too. I'll trade places with you, how's that? Did you know I owe the government almost three million dollars? Why don't you take my debt and I'll take yours?"

There was a pause. "Oh, fuck," he said. "I had no idea. This landed on you, too?"

"Yes, it landed on me, too. It landed on me like an avalanche, like one avalanche after another. It hasn't stopped yet."

"Does the staff know what you owe?"

"I don't know. I don't go around talking about it to them. I know they know I'm in a bind. They've probably heard rumors. But they have their own problems. I'm not going to drag them into mine."

"I hope you're mad as hell," he said.

"Well, no. There's too much else on my plate right now. Mostly I'm scared."

"Carol, I'm sorry I said what I said. Really, I had no idea you were in the same boat. Please forgive me."

"I understand. It's terrible for everybody, and if people want to call and yell at me, that's okay. They can't yell at Howard and there's no point in yelling at Doug."

I served our dinner at the kitchen table. Spencer talked nonstop about whatever was on his mind. On any other night this would enchant me and we would chat back and forth. But on this night I played with my food, staring into the middle distance, lost in thought. "Mommy, don't ignore me," he demanded.

"I'm not, angel, I'm not. I just have a lot on my mind. I never ignore you. Honest. Even if I look like it."

But I was ignoring him. In my head all I heard was the violence and rage in the voice of the former bookkeeper. That wasn't an experience I was accustomed to, and I tried to find a place to put it. I felt terrible for the employees. I feared their anger toward me would undermine my effort to move Nathans forward. I was afraid stealing would become rampant. I wished I had money to pay their debts, to make everything right, but I could do nothing except try to save the business and protect their jobs.

In the day's mail, along with the past-due bills and dire threats from collection agencies, was an envelope that got my attention. At first I put off opening it, because I saw it was from a lawyer. Oh, God, I thought, not another lawyer! I'd reached my daily threshold for bad news. I tossed the letter on the desk and did a dozen other things before I came back to open it. Howard's previous wife, the third wife, and their two sons were filing a claim against the estate, wanting their piece of the presumed pie. This was a shock, because when Howard died his share of the family trust had passed on to those sons, making them rich. Spencer was born too late and had no claim to his grandparents' estate.

I called Miriam at home. She was unfazed. "They can stand in line behind the federal government," she said. "They always get their money first, and when they get done with Howard's estate there won't be any money left."

As much as Nathans careened around, steeped in employee rage and frustration, there was satisfaction in rebuilding the business, making it new again. We had to get the buzz back. But, you know, for a phoenix to rise, it first has to be ashes. Vito Zappala wrapped up his analysis and presented me with a five-page report. Bearded and looking like a pinstriped bear, he was smiling broadly as he handed me the neatly typed and stapled pages. He was back in his chosen game and he liked it.

In sum, the report said that there were opportunities for change and improvement in every department of Nathans. Vito outlined the steps that needed to be taken. He assessed the building ("falling apart"), the financials ("obviously Nathans needs to make more money"), and the staff ("their good attitudes should be used to improve the restaurant"). He wrote, "What is needed is a view for change as well as the leadership to make the change happen." I gave a copy to Doug Moran.

JAKE STEIN AND I had a meeting with Dimitri Mallios, the lawyer for Nathans' five landlords. We were no closer to a new lease. We just continued to go round and round. Jake asked, "Will the landlords mind if Carol fires the manager?"

I was afraid he'd say they'd want him to have the lease. Instead, Dimitri smiled like a Cheshire cat. "All the landlords care about is that they get their rent checks in full and on time. Period."

After the meeting, Jake and I walked together, his arm looped through mine. He had a way of asking me questions or making statements that were unexpected. Soon after Howard died he asked, "What did you think of Howard?" I was so surprised all I could come up with was, "I loved him." Now, as we walked, he said, "Widows have it the worst, don't they?" I couldn't answer for all widows, but at that point in my experience it was a decided yes.

I moved ahead and offered the general manager's job to Vito, contingent on my removing Doug. "I want you to be ready to slide right into Doug's chair, because after I fire him I don't plan to let him back in the building."

At *Larry King Live* I redoubled my efforts to demonstrate to Wendy how much I wanted to keep my staff job. In my head it was so simple: I would settle with the government, sell Nathans, return to television work full-time, and live happily ever after. "Please don't give up on me," I begged. I booked Dominick Dunne for his O. J. Simpson book. I had Marv Albert on deck. I made progress with Donatella Versace, scheduling a "get to know you" meeting for her and Larry in Washington. Wendy was delighted.

My colleague Dean Sicoli said, "You're back in favor. Wendy's mellowing. Maybe it's because Becky is away for three weeks. You can make this time work for you." Dean was right. With Becky away, I gained ground. It was better but not without bumps in the road and odd requests from the office. I give Wendy credit for many strengths, but above all was she was fearless about pursuing shows, an essential for a talk-show boss. Her motto: If you don't ask, you'll never know.

Wendy got excited when the *New York Post* had an incendiary item saying that lawyer Alan Dershowitz had accused Sarah Ferguson of being an anti-Semite. "Call Fergie to see if she wants to come on tonight and defend herself."

Sure. Why not? What the hell? If the report was true—or even if it was false—I couldn't imagine the duchess wanting to get anywhere near such an accusation. But from Wendy's point of view, no guts, no glory. I phoned Fergie's publicist and my good friend Jeffrey Schneider at Howard Rubenstein's agency. "I'm calling to talk to you about the *New York Post* item and to find out whether the duchess wants to come on to defend herself tonight against the accusation she is an anti-Semite. Before you say anything I want to be on the record as having asked."

"You are," he said, "and the answer is N-O! But, Carol, I want you to know that you and the *Sun* are the only media to call and ask for an interview about this." The *Sun* is a sensational and gossipy British tabloid.

"Well, what can I say? The best and the brightest, eh, Jeffrey?"

"You got it, Carol."

A few weeks later and quite out of the blue, Jeffrey called to say the duchess had finally agreed to go live for a full-hour interview with Larry. It could be wide ranging but, the duchess insisted, was not because of Alan Dershowitz. The downside was that we would follow Oprah. Jeffrey was beside himself with apologies and hoped that following Oprah wouldn't get me in too much hot water with Wendy. It didn't. Wendy was fine about it. Once again, we would promote it as her only "live" interview. Larry was delighted. Wendy rewarded me by asking me to book King Hussein of Jordan, Benjamin Netanyahu, and Yasser Arafat to come on together. Oh, and, "put in a bid for Saddam Hussein, too."

I rolled my eyes. "Sure. Why not?"

The evening of the interview, the duchess arrived at the CNN Washington studios with a small entourage and gifts for Larry, which she presented to him on the air. They were a random assortment of sweets and included gooey chocolate caramels that she fed to him on camera. Standing on the sidelines, I asked one of her entourage if the treats came from England. "No," he said, "she cleaned out the minibar back at the Four Seasons."

LARRY AND I needed to be in New York in November. It would be a long trip, almost a full week. Larry had shows to do, and together we had a few important meetings. I'd been yearning for the isolation, for the sight of Manhattan and the ease of a hotel room. The trip would be a tonic; the work would be interesting. Wendy, in a moment of compassion, said, "New York is medicinal to Carol," and she was right.

The high point of the trip was a meeting I had managed to get with Tariq Aziz, the deputy prime minister of Iraq under Saddam. We planned to get him live on the set in New York with Bill Richardson, at the time the U.S. ambassador to the United Nations. The interview excited me. It was hard news, my former expertise, and it would be big. Lots of Wendy points.

The Iraq Mission to the United Nations was housed in an elegant townhouse on the Upper East Side off Park Avenue. Outside, some police officers and a few reporters were staked out. The reporters were curious to know what Larry was up to. "Hey boys," he greeted them. "Just a little meeting. Nothing else."

We met in a large upstairs space that was probably once a ballroom. The Iraqis had furnished it sparsely with a silk sofa and chairs near a large fireplace. The meeting was a formality. We knew Aziz would do the interview. "But you won't get Richardson to appear with me," he said. "He won't have the guts."

The Iraqis pulled cameras from their pockets and politely asked Larry to stand with various officials while I took their pictures. The Iraqis wore expensive tailored suits. Larry wore a windbreaker.

I had a solid, friendly, and professional relationship with Larry, and we had plenty of time alone together. We talked a lot. Sometimes on assignments like this I thought of bringing up my struggles at the office. But I didn't. Larry was the star, not the manager. Nothing would be gained. He'd likely say, "I'll talk to Wendy," and mean it, but he couldn't change the complications or untie the knots. The only certain result would be a divide between us, and I didn't want that.

Later, back at the hotel, I worked out arrangements with Richardson's staff. Aziz was right; Richardson would not appear with him on the set, but he would go on solo. The public information officer at the U.S. Mission said, "We don't even want to pass him in the hallway, because if we do he will put out his hand to shake Richardson's, and Richardson will not shake his hand."

That night we performed an elaborate hallway choreography, which kept Aziz out of Richardson's sight. Richardson and his people were stationed in one room, Aziz and his people in another, and we posted staff in the hallway to make sure the two men did not come face-to-face in makeup or the men's room. I poked my head in each room just before air. In Richardson's room he and his entourage were stiff, tight-lipped, and tense. In the Aziz holding room the men seemed to be having fun—laughing, smoking cigarettes, talking trash, and making plans for the night. Richardson, who went on at the top of the show, was hustled out of the studio and through the CNN newsroom to the elevators; seconds later Aziz was hustled out of his room, through the newsroom, and into the studio. This maneuver had to be polite and deft and completed within a commercial break. It was dicey but we did it.

When the broadcast was over, the Iraqis said they were off to dinner.

"Where?" I asked.

"Harry Cipriani," said Aziz, adding that it was his favorite place in New York.

"Well, that's right in the middle of the action," I said. I wondered what would happen if Richardson walked into the same restaurant. Would the maître d' at Cipriani have to conduct the dance of the diplomats we had just performed or was that posturing reserved for the media only? Later, as my cab passed by Cipriani, I saw the Iraqis' limousines parked outside. Inside, I'm sure, they were enjoying good wine and pasta and probably didn't fuss much about the policies of the U.S. government. That would come later.

My mind was on something else. I was off to a dinner date with Keith Hernandez, who still called faithfully late at night to ask what I was wearing to bed. Even if I was in something skimpy, I'd say, "flannels and a sweatshirt." He was fast and furious to my slow and uncertain. We met at an uptown French restaurant, a corner table. He was movie-star handsome, flirtatious, and playful. He asked to wear some of my lipstick, had me apply it, tried to kiss me with it on, nibbled at my ear, and got his hands all over me like a tickle monkey. When the check arrived he paid it and declared, "Let's go to Elaine's." I was up for that. Elaine's is legendary, and I had happy memories of visits there dating back to my first weeks in New York in the '70s. In the cab Keith put his arm around me and moved in for a kiss. When I demurred he pulled back.

"Tell me something, are we going to have sex tonight?" he asked matter-of-factly. Oh, it was tempting, but I had nowhere near the self-confidence to play in his league. Keith had come along about a year too soon in this widow's romantic reawakening.

"No, no, I don't think so. But can't we still enjoy the evening?"

Elaine's was packed. We stopped to say hello to the Yankees' Derek Jeter and his posse of friends before joining the table one over, a group that included owner Elaine Kaufman, the actor Chris Noth, and his date. Elaine lit up when Keith took the chair next to hers. "Carol owns a bar in Washington," he announced as my introduction. Elaine acknowledged the information but couldn't have cared less. I didn't blame her. "She also produces *Larry King*." That got her interested.

I watched Elaine be Elaine. I swear she had eyes in the front, back, and both sides of her head, and they focused on everything from the front door to the back door to the bartender and waiters to the famous faces at a long row of tables. She watched them come and go and smile and frown, all the while jumping in and out of the chatter at our table. She was everything a restaurateur should be. I admired her but knew her skills were unique and instinctive, and that I was not Elaine.

KEITH WAS AFFECTIONATE and attentive, but it was late and I was tired. It had been a long day and I had an early breakfast meeting. When I whispered that I planned to head back to the hotel he nodded and pulled me close. "Would it be okay with you if I just put you in a cab and didn't take you back to the hotel myself?"

"Sure." I was relieved. "No problem," I whispered in his ear. "After all, if you're not going to get laid you might as well get drunk, right?"

He pulled back and looked at me. There was a long pause, and then he burst into laughter and gave me a good night kiss. Like a gentleman, he helped me into the cab, handed some money to the driver, and blew me one more kiss as I sped away.

Paolo and I talked on the phone, but we didn't see each other that trip. He was busy; I was busy. It was okay with me. In the morning when I checked out there was a bag waiting for me at the reception desk. In it were pastries and cookies and a card signed "XXX OOO P."

Chapter 29

I DIDN'T GO to college or to business school. Newsrooms, TV studios, and the stories I covered were my college education, and Nathans was my business school. The lessons I learned about business turned my natural instincts upside down. What I loved about the world around me became threats that could keep customers away from Nathans. Long summer days meant people didn't start drinking till sunset; a beautiful snow or rainstorm may have fed nature, but they didn't feed me. People stayed home; they weren't at Nathans. The beach, the mountains, a swimming pool, a tennis court, a congressional recess—all took money from my pocket. And I haven't even gotten to the Weber grill. The primary lesson I learned about business, though, was that it was normal life, minus the humanity.

In business school, I imagine, learning how to fire an employee is equivalent to that moment in medical school when a student first cuts into a cadaver. You just take a deep breath and do it, but the fact that it's a person who has a life, a career, and perhaps a family, too, has to be set aside. In my television career I had been a boss. At *USA Today: The Television Show,* I put together the Washington bureau and ran it. I felt I was a good boss—effective, organized, able to communicate, and compassionate. But I never had to fire anyone. I was a producer at CBS News during the bloodbath of the 1980s when Laurence Tisch bought the company and downsized radically. The firings were brutal. Friends were let go in the morning and had to have their desks cleaned out by the end of the day. Security guards were on call to escort them out the door.

There was no question I wanted Doug Moran out of Nathans. Yes, for me it was emotional, but it was also business. For whatever reasons, he seemed to resent me. He didn't want to work with me, he sometimes actively worked against me, and he mocked and insulted me. If he hadn't been so handsomely paid—$100,000 a year, with perks—he probably would have quit. But why would anybody quit a paycheck like that, especially with the leverage he conceivably had? My lawyers worried about what he might know about Howard's activities that the IRS might like to know, too. But once Sheldon Cohen and Miriam Fisher submitted my defense to the IRS, Doug lost some of that leverage. When Dimitri Mallios told Jake Stein and me that the landlords didn't care if I fired Doug, indicating they weren't going to give him the lease, his leverage disappeared altogether.

Nonetheless, firing him troubled me. He was a married man with a family, and his wife had recently lost her job. We were coming up on Thanksgiving. These factors weighed me down and fueled my guilt. But then Connie the bookkeeper sat me down. "If you had cancer would you keep it there? Wouldn't you cut it out? Would you care what kind of day the cancer was having? No. Most restaurant owners would have fired him months ago. You had your reasons, but still. You're the boss of fifty-five people, and it's time for one of them to go. Besides, you've got Vito waiting in the wings."

I phoned the various lawyers to tell them I was about to fire Doug Moran. No one tried to stop me. My research and everyone I talked to recommended the same procedure: Do it off premises, don't let him back in the office, have all his personal items boxed for delivery, and immediately change all the locks. Jake Stein offered one of his conference rooms for the deed. I took it.

Miriam Fisher said, "If he starts to argue with you, don't respond. Just let him talk. Let him say whatever he wants but no matter how mad it makes you, just let him talk. If you have to say anything simply acknowledge that he has a right to his opinion. But don't let it go on too long. Keep the meeting short."

THAT MONDAY MORNING I stood outside with Spencer to wait for his school bus. He played with his new Giga Pet, a small plastic toy that was all the rage in 1997. Shaped like an egg, it had a small screen that displayed a moving image like an ink drawing. At the beginning, the image was a tiny fuzz ball, then the fuzz ball matured into a baby bird. The child pushed buttons to tend to its needs. One button fed it, another button cleaned it up, another played with it, and yet another determined the pet's mood. When it wanted attention, the plastic egg made an annoying chirping noise that was hard to ignore. If not tended to properly, the pet "died" right there on the screen. I'd bought it for Spencer on Saturday. He'd fed it, played with it, and kept it alive through the weekend. Monday morning the image on the screen was a happy baby bird.

When the bus arrived Spencer hiked up his backpack and placed the egg in my hand. "What's this for?" I asked.

"Mom, we're not allowed to take them to school. You have to take care of it for me, okay? *Don't* let it die! Please!"

"Spencer," I gasped. "What do I do?"

"Mom!" he said, looking back at me as he climbed into the bus. "It's fine. I've fed it and cleaned it and played with it. Just don't let it die!" The bus driver smiled at me as if to say I wasn't the first parent left standing at the bus stop with a Giga Pet in hand. Spencer disappeared into the bus, the door shut, and off it went. I looked down at the Giga Pet, which was momentarily quiet. I looked at the screen. It was an electronic drawing of the little bird. I smiled. The bird smiled back. When I got dressed for the day I tossed the Giga Pet into my own backpack.

Doug and I were scheduled to meet at ten a.m. in Jake Stein's office. When I called to set the appointment, he didn't ask any questions, just said, "Okay, I'll see you there."

Miriam advised me not to go alone. "Take someone. You need a witness to what goes on."

I picked up Connie outside Nathans. "I'm so nervous about this," I said as I navigated rush-hour traffic. She wore a bright turquoise dress that set off the brilliance of her platinum hair. "What if he starts yelling at me? What if he refuses to be fired?"

"Do you want me to do anything to help you, anything at all?" she asked.

"No." The traffic was terrible. "No. But thank you. Just sit there. Be my witness. Give me strength."

When we walked off the elevator into Jake's lobby, the receptionist said, "Mr. Moran is in the conference room." To shore up my courage I recalled what Doug had done and said to me in the last months. I remembered him disparaging Howard, demanding a partnership, and reminding me over and over that I wasn't qualified to run the place. The day Jake called to tell me Doug was trying to get the landlords to give him the lease—that memory gave me resolve.

The conference room was small, standard law-office décor: a polished rectangular table and six black leather chairs—one at each end and two on the sides—and a few nice but unexceptional prints on the walls. Doug had taken the seat at the head of the table. He wore a sport coat and tie. I sat on one side of him and Connie sat on the other. I put my small black backpack on the floor behind me. We all shook hands and gave one another tight little smiles. The atmosphere was tense. Doug and Connie both looked at me, waiting for me to speak.

I took a deep breath. "Thank you for coming, Doug. You've worked for Howard for a long time and for me for almost ten months," I said, looking directly at him. His eyes were cold. "Howard had his Nathans team, and now it's time for me to form mine. For that reason I'm going to let you go, terminate your employment, effective immediately. You will continue to be paid for another month while you look for a new job. You'll have health benefits during that time, too. You'll have to return your parking pass. Everything that's personal from your desk has been put in a box and will be delivered to your home."

The room was hushed. Doug stared at me with contempt in his eyes. Finally, he said, "I thought this might happen. I saw it coming." I gave him my full attention but said nothing. "You can't run the place by yourself," he said. "You don't know what to do. You'll run it into the ground." My face was fixed in an expression of serious attentiveness, Connie's the same. When Doug stopped speaking, the room became as quiet as a vault.

From my bag on the floor came a birdlike sound. "Chirp-chirp," and again, "Chirp-chirp." And then again and again. I looked at Connie, she looked at me, and Doug looked at both of us. I looked at him and nodded. "Continue."

"Chirp-chirp."

"You have some skills," Doug said. "You think you know what you're doing, but you don't. You'll be closed in a year."

"Chirp-chirp." I suddenly realized the sound was coming from the backpack at my feet. The damned egg was hungry or constipated or bored or something. It wouldn't stop bleeping.

I continued to look at him, my face expressionless but resolute. He continued to talk. Slowly his demeanor began to change. Before my eyes he went from strong and angry to vulnerable and weak. I could see it in his eyes. Reality hit him. He'd been fired.

"You'll go under. You'll see."

I couldn't tell him this, but I was afraid he might be right. I was in over my head and I knew it.

"Well, Doug, you have a right to your opinion. That is all I have to say. I have to go. I wish you well."

"Chirp-chirp."

I grabbed my bag, nodded to Connie, and we left the room.

Connie and I remained silent in the lobby as we waited for the elevator. I bit my lips while rummaging in my backpack for the damned Giga Pet. When we finally got in the elevator and the doors were safely closed, I shrieked and slumped. "Oh my God, we did it!"

"What was that incessant noise?" Connie asked. "A pager?"

"This," I said, pulling the yellow plastic egg out of my pack. "It's Spencer's Giga Pet." Connie looked perplexed.

"Don't ask," I replied with a groan. I looked down at the egg. There was the little black bird, frowning. I held it up for Connie. "I think it wants to play," I said. "At least it's not dying." I pushed some buttons on the side of the egg. The bird calmed down, smiled, and returned to sleep. I slipped it back in my bag. "That was awful," I said. "I couldn't believe that was happening. Right in the middle of firing the poor guy. Oh, God."

"How do you feel?" Connie asked.

I sighed. "Scared. Adrenaline overload. Sad. So many things."

"What about Vito?" she asked.

"He'll be on the job tomorrow," I said. "Bob can take care of anything that comes up today. I want to tell the staff about Doug myself and prepare them for Vito before he just shows up."

We walked out of the building onto bustling Connecticut Avenue. An early winter chill was in the air. It was blustery. The holiday season would begin soon. I buttoned my coat and put on my gloves. "I can't believe I fired someone—and just before Thanksgiving, too."

"You did what you had to do. And you did well. You did it right." Connie paused and looked directly at me. "If the tables were turned he would have done it to you months ago."

I HAD ONE more trip to New York before Thanksgiving. Spencer came with me to take in the holiday sights and smells. For better or worse it was a chance for me to spoil him a little. He celebrated his sixth birthday in Washington with a party at Nathans and now we had several days just for us. For all the good times I had in New York with friends, colleagues, or Paolo, the best times were with Spencer. Publicist Jeffrey Schneider, someone I'd met through work but who had become a friend, met up with us to watch the Macy's Thanksgiving Day Parade. Afterward, Spencer and I got together with Martha, Vijay, and cousin Zal at the home of family friends who lived on Gramercy Park. We enjoyed the Thanksgiving feast with a warm crowd of people. We caught a Broadway musical, studied the amazing holiday windows along Madison and Fifth avenues, wandered in and out of grand hotel lobbies such as the Plaza and the Waldorf, and stood beside the pushcarts to smell the sweet scent of roasting chestnuts. One new Lego set from FAO Schwarz could keep Spencer entertained through lunch or dinner in a new restaurant I was eager to check out—just the two of us. I was grateful to the Carlyle. After all the money Howard and I had funneled their way for years, and now on my own through CNN and *Larry King Live,* they gave me a sharply discounted rate and upgraded us to a suite. Spencer loved running from room to room, almost as much as he loved exploring every square inch of the Museum of Natural History.

Could I spoil him too much? I didn't think so. I was going with my gut on parenting a fatherless child. The idea that a woman alone couldn't raise a son got my attention but I didn't let it consume me. I believed if I gave him time, love, guidance, and confidence I could fill up the empty spaces caused by the painful loss. What I didn't know, and couldn't know for a while, was whether he would develop a personality more like mine—comfortable, even eager to share feelings with friends—or more like his father's, with the hurting parts hidden deep inside, gnawing away, coming out in random fits of rage. I would understand if it was somewhere in the middle.

But we had New York. It was a joy we shared, and in the sharing we formed a strong bond.

"Can we live here?" he asked.

If only.

ONE NIGHT WHEN Spencer was asleep in the bedroom, Paolo came by the hotel after his dinner service. He brought a very cold bottle of champagne and some of my favorite cookies made fresh that evening by his incredible pastry chef. We kissed at the door. I put Harry Connick, Jr., on the CD player and turned it down low. The lights were low, too. We sat in the living room on the stuffed silk sofa, facing each other, our feet up and legs entwined, sipping champagne. We were both in jeans. We just looked at each other, not saying much, listening to the music. He was so handsome with his dark, tousled hair, sexy stubble, brown eyes, and soft lips. How did this wonderful man come into my life? I asked myself. It was November and we'd been flirting, kissing, holding hands, and talking, talking, talking since June, but I knew this was the end of the road. He did, too. Our crazy love affair had nowhere to go except, if we were lucky, back to friendship. He was married and would stay married, and I didn't want him to change that. Sometimes he would say to me, "If you were still married, making us both married, this would be different." Well, I felt like I was still married and it didn't make it any different. Married or not married, it couldn't go on.

I had to focus on Washington, home, the reality that the IRS would be issuing their verdict soon. But not tonight, not this sweet and sentimental night. Champagne glasses in hand, we danced a slow dance. Our kisses reminded me of our first kiss. Our stolen hours had been lovely—this evening, too—but when Paolo walked out of my room that night it ended my charged and wild ride of romance and pretend. I got up the next morning, packed our bags, boarded the train with my darling boy, and returned home to the life I needed to be living. I had scattered myself all over the place, hoping to find an emotional rescue that was not going to come, at least not from New York or Paolo. Any rescue had to come from me.

The closer my IRS case moved toward a decision, the further I moved away from fantasy. It was as if gravity was pulling me back to earth, to reality, to a place where I could settle in, get grounded, and begin to build some kind of future. As much as I loved being the New York Carol, I knew I was actually the Widow Joynt, who had to finish cleaning up the tangled mess my husband had left behind. Running away to New York felt good, and the person I was in New York was exciting and glamorous, but in truth it was as unreal as the life I had lived with Howard. My job was to make peace with the real world, where I had to be a mother, a homemaker, and a breadwinner while I waited for the IRS to come to a decision.

MY PSYCHIATRIST LET me off the hook a bit when he said, "So much got in the way of your being able to simply be a widow. You've never really been able to be just that." He was right. With the IRS and everything else, it had been a nightmare on top of a nightmare. Double horror. Huge chunks of my life as I'd known it simply vanished. All my support was kicked out from under me. To fill the void, to get strong again, I danced with my girlfriends and escaped to New York. Finally I got strong enough to face the facts.

I talked to the psychiatrist about Paolo and what I considered to be the end of our love affair. We didn't have a physical affair, but we did have love. The doctor reminded me that the relationship never had a future, anyway. "You needed to feel some control in your life and you could go to New York and control him," he said. "It was the one part of your life where you had some power. Now that you're beginning to feel more control—firing Doug, for example—you need Paolo less."

It made sense to me, sort of. "The thing is," I said, "when he kissed me under that streetlight on Central Park West and brought passion back into my life—I couldn't just walk away. That kiss relit my pilot light. That was real. To give that moment its true value he had to be part of my life. I'm not sorry. It may have been a folly, but I'd do it again." I looked at the doctor. "Maybe everybody needs a dose of unreality in their lives. It was pretty good medicine for me."

Spencer was waiting excitedly for an after-school visit from his grief therapist, Ellen Sanford. He always said her visits were his favorite day of the week. He wanted to show her some video of himself as a baby. "Can I do that, Mommy?" He helped me look through the tapes and we found one labeled "1995." While he was in the kitchen having his snack, I slipped it in the player to have it ready to go before the therapist arrived. I had no recollection of what was on it. I pushed the "play" button. Suddenly, there was Howard, all of him, filling the screen and very much alive. He was on the sofa with Spencer, who was crawling over him, squealing. They were laughing, obviously having fun together. Spencer drooled on him and got a giant kick out of Howard's goofy reactions.

I stood in the den alone, transfixed by the sheer normality of what I was seeing, something that once was such an ordinary part of our family's life and that I had simply taken for granted would always be there. I stared at Howard and saw not the liar or tax cheat but the man I loved and who—regardless of dismaying revelations and genuine anger—I missed. The yearning was tangible, a pressure in my chest. I quickly pushed "stop" and left the machine as it was. When Ellen arrived I told her about the tape. "It is cued up. You know what to do." Then I looked at Spencer and said, "Watch as much as you want, but when you don't want to watch anymore you can just turn it off." I kissed the top of his head, left the apartment, and walked to the elevators. Waiting for the lift to come, I burst into tears.

Chapter 30

LAWYERS HAD BECOME routine in my life. In less than a year I went from never having had a lawyer to having enough to fill a small bus. I also went from not knowing how to handle lawyers, behave around them, or maximize the costly time with them, to being able to teach a course on dealing with lawyers. There were many lawyers in my normal week but the two I talked to most often were Sheldon Cohen and Miriam Fisher. Miriam and I talked as often as close sisters.

There were long conversations and short ones, simple conversations and others that were painfully complex. We talked when I was in the middle of a child's birthday party or a kindergarten field trip to the zoo, and when we were both feeding our children or trying to get them to bed. More often I was in Nathans or my cubicle at *Larry King Live.* The lawyers' calls took priority over everything but Spencer. There were no two adults whose words meant more to me than Sheldon's and Miriam's. What they said would affect my day, my week, and ultimately my life. Their calls left me encouraged, discouraged, anxious, or occasionally in tears.

One December morning, at my basement desk at Nathans, I got a call from Miriam. "I've heard from Deborah Martin." The world collapsed and became only the receiver in my hand. No nation, no city, no building, no office, no people. Only Miriam's voice, the phone, my ear. I tried to inhale but it was tough. I braced myself. "Deborah said that if we accept certain of her judgments on other aspects of the case, and we settle, she will accept the innocent spouse defense because she believes you have a reasonable case." Just like that. Miriam talked on with a lot of complicated legal terms, but I knew what they meant: not guilty. We won. I was free.

For a moment I was speechless. My eyes moistened, my breath caught, my emotions were in gridlock.

"Carol, this is huge," Miriam said. "And it is the right decision. The IRS did the right thing."

Finally I mumbled something utterly prosaic: "I can't believe it. It actually happened." Inside, though, it was the Fourth of July. My mind flashed back to almost a year earlier, in the dour gray offices of Caplin and Drysdale, the law firm I inherited, and the moment when the lawyers there told me I didn't stand a chance of winning innocent spouse. And here it was. We'd won. I was the innocent spouse. The federal government said so. Deborah Martin had granted me a new beginning. She wanted us to settle on a dollar amount and not appeal the verdict. Miriam reminded me that with innocent spouse I could keep anything that was in my name or our names jointly—my income, my savings, our homes and furniture—but the estate, which was anything that was in Howard's name alone—chiefly stocks, bonds, and bank accounts, and possibly Nathans—became the property of the federal government. While Howard left me Nathans in his will, if the IRS wasn't satisfied with the estate alone, they could take the business from me and sell it. To my advantage, Miriam said, was Nathans' low value because it did not have a lease, and the fact that the IRS prefers not to be in the real estate business. The government prefers cash.

"Look at it this way," Miriam said. "Without this verdict you would have had nothing, possibly not even your income. You would have been cleaned out, down to zero, or making payments for a lifetime. This way you are protected; you get something. You will be able to afford your new house, and the government can't take it away from you." It also meant that if I kept Nathans, got a new lease, and then sold it, the money would be Spencer's and mine alone—after taxes, of course.

I wanted to jump through the phone line and hug her and Sheldon. I was relieved, happy, excited, and, for the first time in ages, optimistic. I knew we still had to deal with the IRS on some other issues, and the future of Nathans, but at that moment, on that day in the early winter, I had sunlight and possibility and permission to dream again. Spencer and I would have a roof over our heads in the neighborhood we called home. He could continue in his beloved school. I could pay my bills. I could sell Nathans and jump back into my career. All this because Miriam and Sheldon had believed in me and my case.

As a lawyer, Miriam was now focused on what next and how to proceed. There needed to be approval at several higher levels of the IRS, and whoever was making the call at those levels had to agree with Deborah's verdict. We still had battles to fight, but we had won the first and most important of them.

When I got off the phone with Miriam, I looked around the office. Vito was upstairs on the floor. Paul Wahlberg was busy in the kitchen. The busboys had done their daily cleanup and moved on to another task. I was alone. I pulled on my winter coat, shut and locked the office door, walked up the metal stairs, and headed out through the kitchen door into the cold air. I always thought if this moment happened I would cry, but I didn't. I walked down the hill toward the waterfront. When I reached the Potomac I kept walking. I walked and walked and walked beside the cold river to absorb the news alone.

THAT NIGHT I reached out to a dear friend. Jeannie Perin came to the apartment for dinner. She was Spencer's godmother and the kind of friend we all need at least one of. You call her, she appears. The first night I was alone in the apartment after Howard died and having a hard time of it, Jeannie had phoned from her home in Virginia.

"I'll be right there," she said. Jeannie lived fifty miles away, many of those miles on two-lane roads. Still, she got in her car at nine in the evening, drove to Georgetown, sat with me in the apartment for the hour it took me to calm down, and then drove fifty miles back home. It seemed fitting that on this night of good news we should share it with her.

Jeannie, Spencer, and I sat in the kitchen, where we made toasts with California sparkling wine while digging into a random smorgasbord of cold cuts, salad and soup, goat cheese, fruit, bread, potato chips, and big, chewy chocolate chip cookies from the deli. Spencer tried to figure out what all the fuss was about, but he could see that I was happy and that made him happy. I hugged him a lot.

"We're going to be okay, kiddo," I said.

"But Mommy, why? What happened?"

"Because today the federal government let me off the hook and made me a free woman," I said. "You don't have to understand that, sweetie, but it's good news. Very good news for you and me." He made that *whatever* face kids make when a parent says something possibly important but also incomprehensible.

"Let me just say this." I raised my glass. "I can't believe this has happened, but I couldn't have done it without Sheldon and Miriam. I wish they were here." Our glasses clinked to that. "Also, Fred Thimm was right from the beginning: I had to be my own driver." We clinked glasses again. "And to all the friends who've been there, like you." I looked at Jeannie. Then I squeezed Spencer extra tight. "And you, too."

SHELDON AND MIRIAM took me to a celebratory lunch at an Italian restaurant on the ground floor of their offices downtown. Connie joined us. Sheldon and Miriam sat on one side of the booth; Connie and I on the other. It wasn't all celebration.

"What do you want to do about the business?" Sheldon asked.

"I think I should keep it and sell it," I said, as if there were any doubt.

"Do you want to know what I think?" Sheldon asked.

"Yes, of course," I said.

"If you want to, right now, you can give the government the keys and walk away. Your lease is up, you're on a month-to-month with the landlords, you have innocent spouse, a clean slate. None of Nathans' debt attaches to you. You're free to go," he said. "You can leave the whole mess in the hands of the landlords and just get on with your life." He was right. I'd never be freer of Nathans than I was at that moment. There was nothing legally binding me to it: no lease or debt in my name, and the IRS had given me a pass. Still, I believed it had value and could easily be sold. Washington was full of wide-eyed dreamers who wanted to be in business at the corner of Wisconsin and M. At that moment I, too, was a wide-eyed dreamer, woefully ignorant, ignoring Sheldon's sound advice and blissfully believing my rusty bucket could have a shiny future.

"It's a gamble, I know, but still I think it's worth fighting for," I said. "If I can get a new lease and buff it up, I can still sell it."

Sheldon nodded but looked skeptical.

"Spencer and I need the money. If I could sell it at top price we would be in good shape. A new owner would keep the place going and people employed."

Miriam and Connie listened. Neither interrupted my back-and-forth with Sheldon. His question cut to the chase. I thought I was making the right decision; it didn't occur to me that it wasn't a wise one. I would stop to eat a forkful of pasta, and then I would talk again. I should have kept my mouth shut and listened.

"It's all I have, Sheldon. My job at *Larry King Live* is on the rocks, and even if I stayed there we couldn't survive on my CNN income. I get a part-timer's salary. Nathans has to be worth something. With the new lease I could sell it. That's what I would like to do. Keep it and sell it. I can't imagine there not being a Nathans at that corner."

The lawyers were more realistic. They could see a world without Nathans even if I could not. But they would do what I asked them to do, even though they had serious doubts about the wisdom of my decision.

"What's it worth right now?" Miriam asked.

"Without a lease, not much," Connie said. "Nathans' kitchen equipment is mostly leased and what isn't leased is in terrible condition. Carol's main asset is the liquor license."

"What's that worth?" I asked.

Connie shrugged and made a guess. "Probably $100,000."

Sheldon looked at me with an almost grandfatherly regard and gave it one more try. "Are you sure you want to be in the restaurant business? It's a terrible business."

"Only for as long as it takes to pull it officially out of the jaws of the IRS. When the case is finally closed, I'll sell it."

I HAD REASONS to be optimistic. The Doug Moran era was over. His lawyer wrote demanding a bigger severance package—six months' pay rather than one—but I held my ground. I said no.

Vito Zappala was firmly in place as Nathans' general manager, with chef Paul Wahlberg running a good kitchen and creating interesting and delicious food. They had shaken up the place in the best possible way, and the staff responded with enthusiasm. Vito brought with him management skills previously unheard of at Nathans. Schedules and systems and accountability were put into place. He stepped up the training program for the waitstaff. He delegated more authority to Bob Walker, the night manager, and monitored his intake of Grand Marnier shooters. Vito also showed up for work on time, stayed late, and worked weekends.

Life at Nathans began to feel like the best part of the television business: that we were all in this together and playing on the same team. I had an early season holiday party for the staff at a club nearby and raised my glass to the group. "I couldn't do it without you," I said.

A publicist friend in New York leaked to the *Washington Post* that Mark Wahlberg's brother was the new chef at Nathans. I was thrilled that they wanted to do a story. Paul was thrilled, too. The story appeared the next day with a picture of Paul in the kitchen. It was Nathans' second piece of publicity on my watch—the first was when Mayor Marion Barry had come to dinner—and the result both times was a discernible spike in business.

Nathans was in decline when Howard died. My goal was to put the place back on the map, to give it buzz, to get people to talk about it again and want to come in to drink and dine. I had had lunch with Phyllis Richman, the *Washington Post*'s restaurant critic, and was haunted by her remark: "No one ever mentions Nathans anymore." I couldn't live with that. I wanted everyone to talk about Nathans. My task was to give it the verve customers expected from a legendary restaurant at the best corner in the most powerful city in the world. And then sell it.

A regular stopped me at the bar one night. "Nathans feels like it's coming to life again. It feels warmer."

THERE MAY HAVE been warmth at Nathans but there was a definite chill at CNN. Becky seemed ready to hang me and I gave her the rope. My presence at the show became more unpredictable. Preoccupied with the demands of the IRS, Nathans, and trying to raise some cash by selling everything that was superfluous to my life, I was late for meetings or had to leave early. Wendy, my lifeline, had an erratic schedule, too, and it seemed to be the opposite of mine. We saw less and less of each other. The guests assigned to me for booking were moving down the ranks. I may have been the show's nominal big-game hunter, but I was bagging game from the B and C list. I sat at my cubicle, watching everyone else work. Sometimes whole shows were produced without my involvement. I was beginning to feel like a visitor.

As we sailed into the choppy waters of the Christmas holiday season, I kept my focus on the year ahead. I knew Christmas would be rough for Spencer and me, but I had to get us through it.

As we did in all the years before, we went to Bob's Trees to pick out a Christmas tree. While I got it secured in its stand in the living room, we listened to Christmas music and watched a Christmas movie. Spencer helped me hang a few ornaments but was more interested in the movie. "Does this make you sad?" I asked, referring to the tree decorating.

"Yeah. A little bit," he said.

"Well, it's a lovely, sweet tree. Our first tree on our own. Maybe we should get some special ornaments to mark the occasion." He liked that idea.

"We can get an angel for the top of the tree that looks like Daddy," he said.

I had a little laugh, doubting whether Martha, Sheldon, Miriam, or Deborah Martin at the IRS would appreciate the image of Howard as an angel.

In the car on the way to the store we talked about what Spencer wanted Santa to bring him on Christmas morning. I fished around, hoping to get clues on toys that would make his wish list. From the backseat came, "Mom, if I could have a dad for Christmas I wouldn't want anything else. Not even a computer."

One night I went through his backpack to look for any school newsletters that might be inside. I found some crumpled papers on which he'd practiced writing words such as "egg" and "dog" and drawings of squid, aliens, and laser blasters. There was his "magic pen," which was really a wooden stick. At the bottom, folded and clearly much fondled, was a picture of Howard.

Spencer came with me to CNN to pose, along with the staff, for the *Larry King Live* holiday card. We all dressed like Larry, in white shirts, ties, and suspenders. Spencer, very much the mini Larry King, stood beside me as we smiled for the camera. In the picture we were a big happy family.

Holiday parties were not high on my list. We did only a very few. There was something wrenching about exposure to too much family happiness. The best event was the Christmas pageant Spencer's school presented at the Washington Cathedral. His school made him happy. As his teachers worked with him and as he slowly adjusted to being the boy without a father, school bolstered his confidence and helped him be part of a community. I watched misty eyed as he paraded with his classmates down the center aisle of the huge cathedral and took his place at the foot of the altar.

Another holiday ritual was a visit to the national Christmas tree on the Ellipse south of the White House. I fondly remembered annual visits with my family after we moved to the Washington suburbs when I was eleven. The tree towers over the fifty smaller trees surrounding it that represent each of the states. It is the centerpiece of a spectacle called "The Pageant of Peace." While not striking during the day, the tree is magical in the evening when its thousands of colored lights fill the darkness. I suggested an after-dinner visit. Remarkably, considering the crush of people, I found a parking space near the White House. Hand in hand, Spencer and I walked alongside the state trees. The colored lights were cheerful, the carolers sang with gusto, and Spencer was thrilled by the miniature train that chugged around the base of the big tree. It was cold and our breath made mist that caught the lights from the tree. Every now and then we heard a child shouting out "Dad!" or "Daddy!" or a mother saying, "Go ask your father," or "Have you seen your father?"

I didn't anticipate this reminder of our lives without a father and a husband. It came as a sudden stab of pain, but there was nothing to be done. We had to push on. Spencer held my hand tighter. I tried to direct his attention to different ornaments or to the carolers. He was such a handsome little boy in his puffy brown jacket and the dark green hat that made his blue eyes look green—he looked so cuddly. We stood and watched, then began to sing along with the carolers on the stage. The more we sang the more our mood lightened. Spencer pulled me down to tell me, "I think our tree at home is the prettiest tree, because it has our own ornaments on it."

When Christmas morning arrived my spirits were up. Spencer had slept in my bed in his Santa and reindeer pajamas, and at dawn he jostled me. "Mom, Mom, wake up! Santa's been here!"

He jumped like a kangaroo as he made his way to the living room and then stopped and took it all in before making a lunge at the pile of presents. I sat on the floor beside him and tried to keep order and an eye on the dog, who kept disappearing in the discarded paper and ribbon. I noticed Spencer put a package under the tree. On the card he had written in his childhood scrawl, "Mom. Love Mom. I love you Mom. Spencer." Inside was a plaster cast of his tiny hand, glazed in deep blue.

For a while the Christmas presents thrilled him and made him happy. After that he lost interest. He pushed the presents away, got up, and walked past me down the hall to his bedroom. I followed. He was on his bed, holding his cuddle toy Baby very close, with his thumb in his mouth. I eased him over and stretched out beside him, wrapping my arm around him. He put his head under my chin. He spoke but his thumb was in his mouth and his words came out in mumbles. I pulled out his thumb with a pop like a cork from a bottle.

"I wished Santa would bring me Daddy. That was what I wanted most for Christmas."

At bedtime I said he could take a present to bed with him. He picked only one, a needlepoint pillow that said I BELIEVE IN ANGELS.

With Spencer now soundly asleep I filled the bathtub with water and submerged myself so that only my nose was above the surface. I stayed like that for maybe fifteen minutes, shutting out the world. The silence was a sweet present I could give myself.

I TOLD MY friend Randy Parks that there was only one thing I wanted to do on New Year's Eve. At midnight we stood in the middle of Key Bridge watching the twinkling lights of Washington, from the Kennedy Center to the Washington Monument and the Jefferson Memorial. The cold and glistening Potomac flowed beneath us. When the clock struck twelve I screamed at the tops of my lungs. I wanted to shake the city with my howl. That was my way of saying good-bye to 1997—certain it was the worst year of my life.

Chapter 31

IT WAS JANUARY 1998, a New Year and twelve harrowing months since I'd taken Howard to the hospital. Whoever I'd been before Howard died, I wasn't her anymore. A little late maybe, but I was becoming self-sufficient. I didn't want ever again to be the sheltered, pampered, and indulged woman who didn't know what a mortgage was or what *escrow* meant or whether her husband paid taxes. That woman was gone. Now I paid the bills, I decided where and how the money would go, I did the driving, and I paid the taxes. I wanted another man in my life at some point, and he would love *this* Carol, not *that* Carol: not perfect, by any stretch, but able to stand on her own two feet.

Early on Martha had said, "You'll make mistakes but you'll survive them." She was right. I did make mistakes, and I would make many more. But they were my mistakes.

It's a time of reckoning when what you had isn't what you have anymore. Money bought ease; less money meant much less ease and less generosity, too. Paying the electric bill was more important than sending off a check to the National Gallery of Art. I had to watch every dime, every dollar. I became a Scrooge in a lot of situations where I used to be first to open my checkbook. It's called adapting, and I adapted and learned to accept the new reality. Only I didn't want my friends to see me sweat.

Some moved on. Only a few rejected me outright. It was inevitable. I wasn't in their club anymore. Also, without a man I was the odd number and hard to place at dinners where everyone else was part of a pair. I was still included, but not as often and rarely on weekends. Weekends were the weirdest time, when the aberrant nature of my new life was underscored by the quiet of no calls and no invitations. I had Spencer, and we had fun, but he wasn't another adult. I have an enduring image of myself. It's a weekend evening. I'm dressed casually in jeans, no makeup, hair in a knot, walking the dog. I'm at a stop sign and a car pulls up. Inside are a man and a woman, dressed for a cocktail party or dinner out, talking to each other in that casual, familiar way married people do. I'm staring at them from the outside, they're on the inside, and I'm thinking, "I used to be them." That moment happened many times, and for me it told the whole story.

When I was included in the grown-up fun it felt like winning the lottery. At big formal dinners—galas and charity events, the few where I still had a little mileage from earlier giving—I was invariably seated between the priest and the gay man. At one, the men on either side of me were each almost one hundred, and neither could hear very well. A Washington social secretary volunteered that there was too much risk seating "even remotely attractive" unmarried women next to middle-aged married men. "The wives won't have it," she said. I wanted to suggest that maybe having a separate table for "remotely attractive" unmarried women would solve the problem. Instead I sucked it up and went along with the rules, making my way through dinner parties by shouting into hearing aids, talking about Jesus, or trading tips on lipsticks and hairdressers.

There is a myth that widows are looked out for and that people, especially men, feel sorry for them. That's true up to a point, and that point is reached rather quickly. Women simply have it harder, even the toughest and smartest ones. There always seems to be room and need for an extra man but not an extra woman. Why? Because there are more of us. Men die sooner and younger.

Widows also seem to be hung with a neon sign that shouts EASY TARGET. The two-legged sharks find their way to a widow as easily as their brothers in the sea spot chum. They know a husband is not going to step up and call them on their behavior or pop them one. In the course of that first year, I had to fight hard to win battles on many fronts that had to do with just getting through the day—the credit card companies, the utilities, the banks. It was a trial to have a plumber do what needed to be done without trying to sell me an unnecessary bill of goods. Initially I played the widow card, thinking that would inspire compassion and perhaps going the extra yard. Eventually I didn't reveal whether there was a man of the house, one way or the other, and asked lots and lots of questions.

The Halkias family, my elderly landlords at Nathans, even though there were three women to two men in the group, seemed to doubt my ability—as a woman—to run the business successfully. Dimitri Mallios told me that for the longest time the men received the rent money and then doled out the women's share. "That's why you now have to write five separate checks," he said. "The girls don't trust the boys."

The January anniversaries got to my heart, but my attention had to be focused on other events that happily had to do with moving forward. The closing on our new home was less than a month away. After I sorted and packed what we needed, everything else was up for grabs. I had an open house for friends to come get what they wanted of Howard's. My brother wanted some of his tools. A sailing friend took his foul-weather gear. Other friends claimed a mirror. Someone else bought the rubber dinghy. A local auction house took worthy items I could no longer use or have room for; the Salvation Army got the surplus of whatever we had in multiples: mattresses and beds, children's clothing and toys and furniture, kitchen utensils and appliances, towels, blankets, rugs, lamps, odds and ends. At first I was relieved to be lightening our load. We had so much. I couldn't keep it all. Things had to go. Later I would have little fits of remorse, wondering why I gave a particular item away, but then I got over it. I had to learn that they were material possessions, even the most sentimental. They were totems of the good life, but not necessarily what made life good. Over the years I became very clinical about what we had. If a precious item could go to auction and help pay school tuition, bring down the mortgage, or cover a Nathans debt that attached to me personally, it went to auction. If I worried about these decisions at all it was the effect they had on Spencer. In time, most of our furniture went out the door to auction.

I worked during the day and packed at night. It was the small things that made me cry, like a cowrie shell Howard had found in Florida, or a random anniversary or birthday card he'd given me, or his reading glasses. Most of his clothing went to the church to distribute to the homeless, but I saved some of his fine tailored suits and sport jackets for Spencer. It's not that I thought Spencer would one day wear them as much as I wanted him to have them to touch and to get a sense of his father's style.

One January morning en route to CNN, I was stopped at a light. While I sat there I looked up the street toward the Washington Hospital Center. It was only about ten blocks beyond my turn for work. When the light changed, rather than make my turn to CNN, I drove toward the hospital. It's a big hulking building. It's the best hospital in Washington for critical care, but there's nothing to distinguish its appearance. I drove around back, near the helipad and the entrance to the emergency MedSTAR unit. I stopped the car and sat with my foot on the brake. I leaned against the wheel and looked through the windshield until my eyes caught the big glass window at the end of the hall that I used to call my wailing wall. I looked up and imagined myself standing there, weeping. It seemed both like a decade ago and only yesterday. Then my eyes scanned to the right until I found the sliver of glass that had been Howard's window. I could see myself at his bedside, overcome with fear, fighting to be strong, begging God to intervene. I stared at the window wondering what poor individual was in there now, fighting for life.

At *Larry King Live* there were a few interviews for me to set up before the end of the month and my move. Paul Newman mattered the most. Newman was private and elusive. He was one of my most challenging pursuits, but eventually he relented. I was proud of that. This was no bizarre pop idol. He was a remarkable person and talent. I'd met him once, in the early 1970s, at a wedding in Connecticut. He was, of course, friendly, approachable, and gorgeous. After the wedding ceremony everyone settled on the lawn for a concert by a string quartet. Over to my right I saw Newman and his wife, Joanne Woodward. She sat on the grass and leaned against a tree. He was on his back, his head in her lap. He looked up at her and she looked down at him, fiddling with his hair. I thought, "Wow! That's beautiful. That's the marriage I want."

From my cubicle at *Larry King Live* I dialed Paul Newman's number to go over the interview. The voice that answered the phone was immediately familiar and transformed me into the fifteen-year-old girl in the tenth row at the Virginia Theater, watching Hitchcock's *Torn Curtain* as Newman pulled Julie Andrews behind a curtain to give her a kiss that gave me goose bumps. If only I could pull him through the phone line. Instead, I shook off my fantasy and we talked about the interview.

"Please tell Larry I'm not a naturally funny guy," he said.

That was endearing. "Of course you are," I said.

"I don't have any jokes."

"You don't have to have jokes."

"I hope not. I don't do that kind of thing very well."

"All you'll have to do is sit and be yourself and answer his questions, have a conversation with him. You'll be fine." When we finished talking, and the phone was back in the receiver, I savored the moment. My career of talk-show gets included presidents and vice presidents, world and national leaders, captains of industry; pioneers of medicine, science, art, and music; great writers and innovators; movie stars, rock stars, Broadway stars, comedians, scoundrels, and the people whose roof was torn off by last night's tornado. Paul Newman was the candle on that cake.

I sent a memo to Becky requesting two weeks of stored up personal time for my move. She scrawled across it "No! Personal time cannot be used for a move. You will have to use vacation time." Apparently Paul Newman didn't count for much.

I showed the memo to the unit manager. "Carol, when are you going to get the message?"

The pressure of the move got to me. As the date drew near I was up before dawn to make lists of all the things that still needed to be done. One morning as Spencer was getting ready for school, my thoughts were elsewhere. When he didn't hustle to get dressed I raised my voice. He sat on his bed, dressed for school, and said his sock hurt. I took off his shoe, took off the sock, and put on a new sock. I put the shoe back on. He said the sock still hurt. "You should put on your own socks and shoes," I said, "then you can get it right." He was in tears. I said, "You're going to miss the bus, you're going to miss the bus!"

He threw himself on the bed sobbing. "But Mommy, my sock hurts me."

"Well, go to school with no socks, then. Wear your Uggs. He followed me down the hall, still crying.

"But I have to go to the bathroom."

"Haven't you gone already?" I asked.

"No, Mom. I have to go."

"You better hurry," I said. "You've got to make that bus. We've wasted too much time already. I'm getting your jacket right now." I pulled his jacket from the closet. "Where are your gloves and hat?"

He stood in the bathroom, crying. "I don't know," he said.

"Hurry. Hurry!" I yelled.

He ran out, pulled on his jacket, grabbed his backpack, and raced with me to the street to wait for the bus. He stood there, looking pitiful. I felt horrible. "I have to go to the bathroom really bad," he said, grimacing.

"Didn't you go inside?" I asked.

"No. You were rushing me," he said.

"Can you hold it until you get to school?"

"No." He pressed his legs together.

"Well, go in the corner there," I said, gesturing toward a big bush in the corner of the building.

"No, Mom," he said.

He stood, eyes red-rimmed from crying, knees locked together, a little kid whose mom had started his day with a stressed-out fit. I sagged. "Oh, honey, I'm sorry. I hope you know that I don't mean to start your day this way. I have too much to do. It's not your fault. I'm so sorry." He dashed into my arms. "Do you understand?" I asked, as I held the back of his head with my hand.

"Yeah," he said, but he looked miserable.

"Run back inside real quick and use the lobby bathroom," I said. "Okay?"

"But what about the bus?"

"Well, be quick and I'll ask Fred to wait."

Two days before the closing on the new house, we both got sick with stuffed-up noses and fevers. We stayed in my bed together for a whole day. We were side by side, sharing the Kleenex, the thermometer, the orange juice, and the television remote. The dog flopped on the bed between us. We were Mutt and Jeff in pajamas. We wrestled with the covers and argued about which movies to watch. *Crocodile Dundee* came out on top. The next morning we were both better, and I treated him to a drive to school. I stopped the car in front of the school, we kissed good-bye, and he got out. But then he stopped at the school door and deliberately leaned over and untied his shoes.

"Why did you do that?" I called out. "Now I have to get out and retie them."

"I know," he said. "That's why I did it, to be with you longer."

Moments like that helped carry me through each day.

FEBRUARY 1, 1998, the anniversary of Howard's death, was a Sunday. Spencer, Martha, and I went to Christ Episcopal Church, where the rector, Stuart Kenworthy, mentioned Howard's name in the prayers and where the altar flowers were dedicated to his memory. I felt serene and peaceful. After services we walked to Oak Hill Cemetery to put flowers on Howard's grave. Apart from that, it was a Sunday like any other. The next day, after school, Spencer rode with me to Capitol Hill to the offices of the title agency where I signed the papers and closed on our new home. I paid attention to every one of the many documents that required my signature. I may not have understood every word, but I read through page after page. The settlement lawyer handed me the keys, shook my hand and Spencer's hand, and said, "Congratulations. Good luck in your new home."

It was late afternoon as we drove down Independence Avenue toward Georgetown, passing the Capitol, the Mall, and the Jefferson and Lincoln memorials. The lights of the city glowed golden against the backdrop of a sky streaked with lavender, pink, and orange clouds. "Well, it will be a few days before we move in," I said to Spencer. "But do you want to go see the new house?"

"Yes," he said, excited. "I want to see Teddy's room that's going to be my room."

Before unlocking the door we stood on the sidewalk and admired our new yellow brick home. It was not the biggest or most impressive on the block, but it was ours. It looked just right for a mom and a boy. It was dim inside but there was enough twilight for Spencer to scramble about. I wandered behind him, enjoying his joy. The pride and happiness that filled my heart supplanted the agony and loss of one year earlier and the fear and anxiety that had followed. I opened my heart to everything that was possible and new and just around the corner. This house would get us started.

In the bare living room, I got down on the floor and stretched out on my back. I gestured for Spencer to do the same. We looked up at the high ceiling. The empty socket for a chandelier stared back at us, wires dangling. My eyes scanned the pale yellow walls, the empty bookcases, the fireplace and mantel, and the big bay window that captured the deepening twilight. We held hands. We were silent, each lost in our own thoughts. This was our starting point, the first leg of a fresh voyage. We lay there on the floor of our new home, and when we rolled our heads to the side to look at each other, we smiled. I pulled him close, wrapped my arms around him, and put his head on my shoulder. Yes, this was a beginning. And so far it was good.

Chapter 32

BEYOND FREEDOM, I don't know what I expected of my life after the IRS had finished with me. Looking back, my naïveté was alarming. With the money the settlement left in my pocket—maybe half a million—I paid the IRS $118,000 to "buy" Nathans back from them, and I paid off more than $150,000 of various Nathans' debts, including taxes owed to the District of Columbia. The vendor debt that sat on Nathans' books was still more than a quarter of a million. Connie said such debt was "routine" in the restaurant business. That kind of routine required the guts of a riverboat gambler. Clearly, once again, this was not the business for me, but for now I was stuck with it—and partly by my own doing.

Howard's corporation was dissolved and Miriam set up my own limited liability corporation, or LLC, which I optimistically named "New Day." The rest of the money I put into the house, a tuition fund for Spencer, and some savings for me. We were luckier than many. We had a roof over our heads and food on the table. I thought my challenges were behind me.

That turned out to be a delusion. The problems kept coming, like tornadoes on an open plain. Not all of them had to do with Nathans, but most of them did. There was the lease and rent and an unexpected fight for my liquor license, but some of the challenges came from outside any rational expectation: exploding manhole covers in the streets and terrorists in planes in the skies. Call these developments what you will, tornadoes, avalanches, horror, but they never took a break, and each made Nathans less appealing to a buyer.

THE FIRST ORDER of business was a new lease. Out from under the IRS, we no longer needed to go month-to-month. Now, I needed a good long lease to boost the value of the business to its highest possible level so I could sell it for top dollar. I'd been told by successful local developers and commercial property professionals that $2 million was not an unreasonable expectation. From what I'd been learning about Nathans, that tantalizing figure seemed too good to be true, but who was I to argue with the "experts"?

What I did know was that once the general lease terms were agreed upon, the rent would have to be reduced for Nathans to survive. The landlords didn't agree. For them, it worked well as it was. Just as Mr. Joynt had spoiled Howard by subsidizing him for years, Howard had spoiled the Halkias family by honoring an old-school lease that had been written in 1969, essentially the dark ages, in which he agreed to pay a record-high rent, property taxes, insurance, and all upkeep for the whole building. That was a big nut for a small business. If I heard one thing routinely from other Georgetown restaurant owners and landlords, it was that Nathans' lease was, in a word, outrageous, particularly the amount of the rent. I didn't need to hear that. I was living it.

A new ten-year lease with the landlords happened at long last after a final bout of back-and-forth between Jake Stein and Dimitri Mallios, but I achieved no breakthroughs. If I wanted a new lease I would have to accept the challenging terms of the old lease. End of discussion. I tried to be positive. While a ten-year lease was less than I wanted, it would have to be enough for me to find a buyer. Most commercial tenants want a lease with a minimum of fifteen to twenty years. A longer lease justifies the capital expense, and the Nathans' building demanded a lot of expense. If the buyer kept Nathans as Nathans, a renovation was essential. If the buyer were a retail operation, the building would need even more costly work. Regardless, the Halkias family wouldn't budge beyond ten years.

The day I went to Jake's office to sign the lease his attitude was that if the old lease was good enough for Howard it ought to be good enough for me. But the truth was the old lease took me like a lamb to slaughter. I stood at Jake's desk, looking at the one-page "personal guaranty" that he eased toward me. It had a few paragraphs of legalese and a line for my signature. "What's this?" I asked.

"A personal guaranty. It's the only way you'll get this lease," he said.

"Did Howard sign a guaranty?"

"Yes."

So I signed it. If I could take back one moment of one day in my ownership of Nathans, this would be the day and the moment. It was dumb of me to sign the guaranty and it showed how I had not learned my lesson; I signed the guaranty the way I had signed our tax returns. I should have asked Jake for a full tutorial on the implications of the document, and asked questions: What does it mean? What are my options? What if I don't sign? It was a standard component of some leases, and I probably would have had to sign it anyway, but if I'd balked at signing I could have perhaps won some better terms from the landlords. The new lease, of course, meant the same high rent. The landlords were adamant on that score, and I was too naïve at the time to understand words like *leverage* and whether I had any. I did, but I learned of it far too late and by then I'd lost it.

We went back a couple of times to the landlords on the rent matter, but it was like hitting a brick wall. What my lawyers did have me do was to arbitrarily commence a de facto rent decrease. Ironically, it was the landlords' lawyer, Dimitri Mallios, who suggested I start "shorting" the rent by 30 percent. "They'll either kick her out or live with it," he told one of my lawyers in conveying the idea. Though not what I wanted, I could live with eviction, because it would at least be a decisive action. Instead, they didn't do anything. They lived with it. They cashed the rent checks. However, they also put the 30 percent of rent I didn't pay into a debt column with my name on it. The reduced rent kept the business alive and viable, but it created a debt pool that dogged and haunted me as it grew month after month, year after year.

BECAUSE OF AN arcane Georgetown ordinance, Nathans' liquor license didn't automatically transfer from Howard's name and corporation to mine. The IRS wouldn't close the deal until the liquor license was in my name. Just as important, I needed the license to stay open.

The campaign to keep the liquor license took all my time and fell mostly on my shoulders. Something in my life had to give and it was *LKL.* I took a long-term leave of absence from CNN. For a Washington journalist like me, my departure came at the worst possible time. The Monica Lewinsky–President Clinton scandal was breaking. The whole office dived into the story. I could easily have played a part in it. I'd even gotten close to Monica and had dinner with her and her first lawyer, William Ginsburg, at Nathans. While we ate pasta and chatted I talked Ginsburg into making a live on-air call to Larry, which he did—from my desk in Nathans' basement. While Ginsburg talked to Larry, Monica looked at my pictures of Spencer and asked if she could write him a letter. On a piece of Nathans stationery she wrote him a note about how cute he was. She dotted the *i* in Monica with a heart.

The quest to get Howard's liquor license transferred to me was essentially a political campaign, and I enlisted my closest ally, my son, to work it with me. Spencer and I went door to door, asking for signatures from as many Georgetown residents as we could find at home. I did most of the talking, but sometimes he'd just get to the point. "Would you please sign this piece of paper so we can keep my mom's restaurant?" I appeared before the various neighborhood civic boards to win their support, which wasn't a given. The board of the old-guard Citizens Association of Georgetown flat-out opposed the license transfer because they felt it would be wrong to allow any loophole in Georgetown's rigid alcohol law. When I appeared before them, and actually broke down in tears during my plea, one of the male board members said, "If we bend to you what do we do the next time some widow comes in here with a sob story?" Fortunately, that was a minority point of view. The elected members of the Advisory Neighborhood Commission, by contrast, voted unanimous support for the transfer. I was there for the vote and thanked each commissioner personally. When the day came for me to testify at the District Building before a critical D.C. city council subcommittee, I was determined to keep my composure. I had to be a warrior and warriors don't cry. There were no tears.

The lobbying campaign ended up before the full city council, which had to pass special legislation allowing me to have the liquor license. They passed it. The July day the bill was supposed to be signed by the mayor also happened to be the last day of the legislative calendar. If he didn't sign it that day it might sit there until fall. Miriam said the IRS wouldn't wait. We risked losing the whole deal if I didn't get that liquor license transferred now. I jumped in the car and headed for city hall, found the office where the bill sat in a stack of other bills, and with the clerk's permission removed it from the stack and walked it to the mayor's office. I lurked in the waiting room for more than an hour, trying not to pace too much, until his secretary called me in and said, "It's done. He just signed it."

I danced a happy dance as I skipped out of city hall, eager to call Miriam with the news.

SOMEONE ELSE WAITED for the news, too. Megan Rosenfeld, a reporter for the *Washington Post,* had spent several months working on a profile about me, the IRS, and the liquor license fight. The *Post* didn't want to run it until the mayor signed the legislation. Nobody had ever written a profile about me. I went along with the idea because I hoped it might help business. I knew the risks. The night the story went to press I was ebullient from getting the mayor's signature on the bill. A good friend and neighbor, Chris de Paola, stayed up with me to wait for the first edition of the *Post.* We drove across town to the newspaper's offices and bought a copy so fresh it was still warm. I was too scared to read it. I kept it folded up till we got home and then handed it to Chris. "Here, you read it and let me know." I watched his face as he read. Finally, he smiled and handed it to me. "It's safe to read. You'll be okay."

WITHOUT RESERVATIONS was the headline. The story—with a large photo—topped the front page of the Style section. The photo was taken in natural light, with me leaning against a column in the dining room, empty between shifts. I appeared somewhere between forlorn and lost in my dreams. There was a smaller photo, too, of me with Howard in foul-weather gear, snuggling on the deck of a sailboat. The piece dramatically detailed the battle with the IRS, Howard's shenanigans with taxes, and my struggle to save Nathans. Megan painted me as both dunce and heroine, and Nathans as one of the great Washington saloons. I was relieved the story was sympathetic. She wrote, "It is hard for Carol Ross Joynt to decide which was the worst day of the last 2½ years. There are so many to choose from." On that, I agreed with her wholeheartedly. It was only the first step in my becoming the public face of Nathans, an unexpected and initially awkward role reversal. I'd always been on the other side, the reporter not the subject. But Nathans had no money for advertising, and even though it was "legendary," a "Washington institution," and one of the city's "great" saloons, it needed to get back on the radar. Being the brand, being out in the public eye, would be integral to saving the business. Somehow, I would have to be the brand.

MY DREAM WAS to get out of the saloon business. The fact is, however, every battle I won for Nathans more tightly bound me to the place and pushed me further from my goal. After the yearlong ordeal to get the liquor license transferred, Jack Evans, my ward's city council representative, met me at Nathans for a drink. He was in a celebratory mood, which made sense. Together we'd gone up against the Georgetown old guard and won. But he also had a message. "The community really came out for you, supported you, and that means you can't just turn around and sell the place. You need to run it, revive it, and make it into the moneymaker you know it can be. I see great things in Nathans' future." He was right. A lot of people had got my back because of their love for a rusty old corner pub. Maybe I didn't want to be in the saloon business, but the community wanted Nathans to be in business. People who were strangers to me were strangers no more. I was beginning to put names to faces, and as I walked around Georgetown I got waves, high fives, and thumbs-up from neighbors, other merchants, and even members of the Citizens Association of Georgetown, who privately told me they never wanted to see Nathans close. This was an awful lot of pressure. I didn't want to be where I was, but I felt a new sense of gratitude and obligation to my community. Civic affection and support was not something I'd known in journalism, where the job is observation, not participation.

My emotions were in heated conflict, but there was no denying that the campaign to win the liquor license had connected me to Georgetown as never before, and it mattered. I couldn't tell these people that I wanted to cut and run. I didn't give up on my quest to unload the business, but I did my best to tamp it down—for a while.

THE *WASHINGTON POST*'s restaurant critic, Phyllis Richman, reviewed us in her Sunday column on April 26, 1998. It wasn't a great review but it was okay. What was most important to me was that Phyllis Richman had walked in the door in the first place. Simply to be reviewed was a sign we were inching back into the game. The review appeared Sunday, and on Monday we expected a boost in reservations. But the phones broke down and stayed down for three days. Vito Zappala and I were frantic.

"Didn't we pay the bill or is it really busted?" I asked.

"It's really busted," he said.

The minor calamity with the telephones reminded me why I wanted to get out from under Nathans and as soon as possible. In the meantime, I would focus on the business side and get a handle on Nathans' relative health, free now of the IRS, the D.C. tax office, and lawyers' fees. Connie crunched numbers. Vito assessed volume, staffing, payroll, maintenance, and managing the five upstairs tenants. Paul Wahlberg evaluated food costs. When that was done, Vito came to me with one message: Nathans could not afford itself.

"You're behind from the starting gun," Vito said, "unless you don't want to pay yourself."

Chapter 33

SPENCER AND I celebrated the turn of the millennium next to a raging bonfire in the middle of a vast wintry field at the foot of the Blue Ridge Mountains. A few dozen of us—all good friends—were gathered at our host's farm to watch the last seconds of 1999 tick down and the new century begin. It was a gorgeous night—not too cold. Eight-year-old Spencer ran with the other children around the crackling fire, elves silhouetted against the golden flames, while their parents danced to the greatest hits of the last century. I danced for hours. I was in seventh heaven.

I felt free, and I needed that feeling. I'd learned, in three years of widowhood, bar and restaurant ownership, and solo parenting, that opportunities for joy and laughter didn't come around every day. It was important to welcome them when they did. In the real world, the fulfillment of my goals always seemed to be out there on the far horizon, just out of reach. I'd march toward them but it was as if I were marching toward a shimmering mirage that dissolved as I drew closer. I felt I'd fulfilled my commitment to the community by keeping Nathans open after the liquor license drama, but now my community spirit had expired.

I was propping up the business with my own limited nest egg, just as Howard's father had done for him. The difference was, Mr. Joynt had millions. I had only thousands, and they were going fast. Eventually the nest egg was gone—poof! Just like that. Whatever other savings I had evaporated, too. I got paid, but Spencer and I were living paycheck to paycheck. I'd sell what I could to make ends meet. We could live with a blank spot on the wall or one fewer table if it meant we could keep our heads above water. Inevitably, though, some of the money would get sucked up by Nathans as a "loan." Vito regularly assured me, "We'll get you paid back next month," but it never happened. I could pay myself back or pay the rent. The rent always won.

I went back to work, this time as a producer for Chris Matthews on *Hardball* at MSNBC. Chris's executive producer took me to dinner and made it simple: "I'd like you to do for Chris what you did for Larry King. Go after the big game." He upped the pay considerably and said I could do it part-time, which allowed me to return to my old routine of driving from Georgetown to work on the other side of town and then back to Nathans and finally home. Spencer was in elementary school and his day pretty much matched my work day. Extra pay also meant money to take holidays. Holidays were important. I wanted Spencer to have time with me away from Washington, work, drama, and one calamity or another at Nathans. He needed to see a side of me that was not stressed out but happy and relaxed, and the best way to achieve relaxation was to be far away from Georgetown. Too often, meaning maybe once a month, he would see me at home in tears. Whenever I finished a phone call with Vito he'd say, "You're going to be in a bad mood now, aren't you? You're going to cry."

The school Spencer had been in since kindergarten ended at third grade, and then typically the boys went on to an adjacent boys' private school and the girls went to the adjacent girls' private school, where they would stay through twelfth grade. The progression from one school to the next was assumed, but still the children had to endure an application process that included a family interview with an admissions officer. The day of Spencer's interview I could tell he was tense. He would have to pass muster with a grown-up who was a stranger, and how many eight-year-olds are prepared for that? Even I was nervous as we met the man, "Mr. Smith," who happened to also be the lower school head, a dour individual in pinstripes, crew cut, and polished Weejuns, with all the charm of an undertaker. His reputation preceded him. He was known to call parents at home if he didn't approve of a television show a student reported being permitted to watch. Some parents adored him, some didn't, but most feared him. This much I could tell: He didn't warm to us.

The tour included a visit to a classroom that was empty except for a math teacher, who asked Spencer to answer some questions on the blackboard. As with his mother, math was his worst subject. He spoke up clearly and got it right, but he struggled a little. The interview in Mr. Smith's austere office didn't go a whole lot better. For one thing, the man didn't smile once! While I answered his questions about our family background and my line of work—"Ah, I own a bar"—Spencer sat at the round wooden table with us, swinging his feet and chewing on a Styrofoam cup. I gently kicked him under the table, but that only prompted, "Mom! Why are you kicking me?"

Spencer didn't get admitted to the school, one of only two boys in his class of forty who were rejected. Since he had the grades and the skills, I was alarmed that a child, a third grader, would be rejected on the basis of an office interview. Later a friend who had three sons at the school gave me a more enlightened explanation. "Mr. Smith prefers intact families," she said. "He doesn't like it when there's not a father in the picture." I wanted to punch him, but I had a more immediate problem: a heartbroken boy who sobbed for three days after he learned he would not be moving on to the same school with all his friends. Still, he was intent on attending a boys' school, and we applied to another, just as well regarded. For this family interview, the lower school head took us to the handsome library, where the librarian asked Spencer if he was a fan of Harry Potter. Yes, of course. She asked a follow-up that had to do with a certain detail of the elaborate story. "It depends which version you read," Spencer said. "It's one way in the American version and another in the British." The lower school head and the librarian looked at him more closely. "You've read both?" she asked. Spencer nodded. I beamed. He got accepted.

I BELIEVE WITH near certainty that Howard would have opposed the boys' school idea from the get-go, both the first one that rejected Spencer and the second one that accepted him. Howard had attended single-sex prep schools and was unhappy, and often got in trouble, and who knows what role the restrictive culture may have played in his general alienation and dysfunction. There's no question they aren't for everyone. But Howard was gone. Having not attended a boys' school—or a private school, for that matter—I assumed the general macho environment would be the ideal counterbalance to life with Mom. The private school part was appealing, again, because the D.C. public schools, at the time, had such dismal reviews and ratings. Too many people warned me away from them and, for a variety of reasons, I acquiesced to my son's wishes to attend a boys' school because it seemed like the right thing to do. After the rejection from the school he had his heart set upon, the letter of acceptance from the other made him smile, and I wanted him to smile.

OWNING A BUSINESS that was open 365 days of the year, from morning to late night, was something only a masochist could love. I was not a masochist. Every minute I was afraid of something going wrong, because something usually did go wrong. The building was old; the electrical system and plumbing were from the 1950s, if not earlier. Some of the pipes were held in place with ropes and rags. The rats had an assumption of residency. I imagined they thought *we* were the pests. The roof was in questionable shape. When it rained outdoors it rained indoors, too, usually onto the teak floors in the dining room and the toilets in the ladies' room. I never figured out how the rain made it from the roof to the ground floor of a three-story building, but it did. The basement flooded regularly. The kitchen floor sagged. At one point we had to close (the kitchen, not the bar; we never closed the bar) for a full week to bolster the floor to keep it from falling into the basement.

These were my problems, not the landlords'. Under the lease, the entire building was my problem, leaky roof and all. The means to do repairs came out of the bar, not the dining room. All the money was made in the bar. In a good year we grossed about $1.7 million. Approximately $300,000 of that went to rent, another $50,000 to insurance, and about the same amount to property tax, before the inevitable penalties and interest. Then payroll, repairs, utilities, goods, equipment rental, and so on. The tenants upstairs were a tailor, a tuxedo rental operation, and an expanding family of fortune-tellers, and their rent helped defray some costs, but they didn't pay utilities, and any time they needed a new air conditioner, a new toilet, or a door repaired, those obligations belonged to Nathans. I understood why Howard had kept two large toolboxes under his desk.

The upstairs tenants weren't without value. From time to time, usually after a few cocktails in the bar, friends and I would climb the two flights up to visit one of the fortune-tellers. The apartment was bloodred—rugs, chairs, walls, lamp shades. The gypsy would take my palm, scrutinize it, and always give me the same reading: "You've suffered a big loss, had unexpected burdens, but good things are just around the corner." My friends would be impressed. "Guys, she knows I'm the landlord. She'll tell me anything that softens me up for a late rent check."

I WISH SHE could have predicted the coming staff changes. Nathans' front doors should have been changed from swinging to revolving. Connie, the bookkeeper who got me through so much, moved on to other, better-paying jobs. Vito Zappala got burned out and resigned. It was tough to replace him. Vito not only understood the front of the house; he knew how to fix the sinks and patch up the rat holes. I relied on him. Managers like him weren't falling off the trees. The first person I tried disappeared on weekends and didn't answer his phone. It wasn't a whole lot better when he was there. The other managers and staff complained, and I was relieved when he resigned. A succession of general managers followed. Paul Wahlberg left when his wife was transferred back to Boston. I promoted Paul's sous-chef, Jamie Blankenship, but when Jamie moved on I pulled from the past and gave the chef's job to Loredonna Luhrs, the daughter of Nathans' original and longtime chef, Giuseppina. Lore had basically grown up there, working as a line cook, and made delicious food.

Then the management at *Hardball* changed and my job ended. I was back to the saloon full-time and one paycheck.

IT WAS A beautiful March morning in 2001. Sunny and pleasant, almost like spring. Spencer was at the table eating breakfast; I was at my computer reading the news. For a moment the lights dimmed, then bounced back. A second later they dimmed again. We heard a loud noise outside, sudden and short. The lights dimmed again. I went outside to check, saw nothing, and walked a few doors up to the corner.

Up the street, flames were shooting ten feet into the air—a monster blowtorch. It was impossible to know what had happened, but whatever it was, it had happened between two parked cars. Had either car been parked four feet farther either way it would have been a much bigger explosion. Neighbors were running from their homes, some in bed clothing or bathrobes. One man ran down the street screaming, "Evacuate!" In minutes the area was swarming with police, fire trucks, and, soon enough, media satellite trucks. Traffic was backed up for blocks.

When I returned, a neighbor said, "It was a manhole cover. An exploding manhole cover!" Our intersection made the news that night. I did, too, with reporters asking me for an eyewitness account. All I asked is that under my name they put "Owner, Nathans Restaurant." To me it was free advertising.

Georgetowners assumed it was a one-time event, but a week later the same thing happened a block down the street. This time at night. Again, flames shot up like a blowtorch, lighting up the sky. The fire trucks and police appeared, as well as the media satellite truck. Our power went out and didn't come back on for a few hours. Fortunately no one was hurt; no cars blew up. Again, I gave an eyewitness report on local TV. Again, I asked they identify me as the owner of Nathans.

Days later, while driving toward downtown in the early afternoon, I got a panicked call from a member of Nathans' staff. "Carol, you've got to get here! Manhole covers are exploding up and down M Street! They've shut us down. There are fire engines and cops everywhere."

I made an abrupt U-turn and sped back to Georgetown, parked, and started running toward Nathans. Wisconsin Avenue looked like a war zone. Police cars, cops, and yellow tape blocked the streets. I could see Nathans in the distance, surrounded by fire engines. Breathless, I said to one of the officers, "That's my business down there at the corner. I've got to get there." He let me through. As I neared Nathans, smoke poured from the holes in the sidewalks where heavy manhole covers used to rest. One storefront had its window smashed by one of the flying metal disks. Elsewhere, the sidewalk had buckled.

A group of police officers stood in the middle of the intersection outside Nathans' front doors. Their shirts and hats carried a lot of gold braid. They had to be the brass, and I headed their way. The man in charge was a tall, handsome, dark-haired officer named Peter Newsham, the commander for the Second District, a region that included the White House, Georgetown, and parts of upper northwest D.C. "You can't be here," he said. "We're closing down the whole block. Your staff has been evacuated. You've got to go."

I sputtered, "But, but, I need . . ."

He'd have none of it. "You've got to go. You cannot be here. It's not safe." He pointed to a restaurant a few hundred yards away. "You'll find your staff there."

I started stammering again, "But, but . . ."

He pointed and said, "Go!"

Later that day the police let us back into the building, but it didn't do us much good. Power was out up and down M Street, and the area was cordoned off. The electricity was off in chunks of the adjacent residential area, too, including our home, where Spencer and I resorted to camping lights and candlelight and an ice chest for refrigeration. This was not the last manhole-cover incident in Georgetown, only the most sensational. It became a chronic problem, due to old power lines, which was bad news for Nathans. Again I was interviewed on local news, but it wasn't the kind of advertising we needed. No one wanted to come to Georgetown and risk getting blown into the air by a manhole cover.

Desperate to get some attention and therefore customers, I created a drink called "The Exploding Manhole Cover." Actually, I created the name before I created the drink. When I mentioned it to my friend Lloyd Grove, who wrote the *Washington Post*'s popular "Reliable Source" column, he wanted to do an item with a photo for the next day's paper.

"Oh my God," I groaned to one of the bartenders. "We've got to come up with a drink and the *Post* wants a photo of it!" Together we concocted a root beer float in a champagne glass with half an Oreo cookie as the manhole cover. I hoped it wouldn't be as revolting as it sounded. What alcoholic beverage could possibly work in a root beer float with a cookie on top? The bartender and I tried several recipes—most of them undrinkable—before we settled on Old Dominion Root Beer, a splash of vodka, a touch of chocolate liqueur, a puff of whipped cream, half an Oreo and—for special effect—a few sparklers. At least it was photogenic.

The photo appeared in the *Post* the next day. Business picked up a little, a few people actually ordered them, and when former Clinton adviser Paul Begala came to Nathans to celebrate his birthday, I sent his group a tray of our joke drink, sparklers sparkling. CNN's Bill Schneider asked to interview me about the drink for a story about the explosions scaring away customers. Between Lloyd's item and CNN's piece, Nathans scored a share of media buzz and a few more customers.

The manhole explosions exposed a critical problem under Georgetown's quaint streets: The infrastructure was rotted. That's why the power lines ruptured into flames. Some of the utilities, like water lines, were a hundred years old. The mayor announced a major public-works program—"The Georgetown Project"—a three-year repair job that required pulling up the sidewalks and most of the major streets, but when it was finished everything would be up to code.

I looked at the plans for the "big dig" and slumped. It was broken into quadrants, and each of the quadrants met at the intersection outside Nathans' front door. There was no day of the entire project when Nathans wouldn't be compromised, either with torn-up sidewalks and streets or heavy equipment out front making a horrid racket—not exactly the background music diners want with their steaks and wine. The work would be at night and they would tow all parked cars at nine p.m. It would start in October 2001.

Chapter 34

SPENCER STARTED FOURTH grade at his new, all-boys' school in the fall of 2001. I thought this school would be good for him, particularly because it had seventy-two acres of sprawling green lawns. He was growing fast. He needed room to move around. The school was a half hour from home, which gave us precious time together in the car. We talked, we joked, we listened to the radio. Howard Stern was a family favorite, though sometimes when the guests were strippers I changed to another station. "Mom," Spencer would admonish me, "do you think I'm a baby?"

It was a routine Tuesday morning. I dropped Spencer off at school and then headed back to town for an appointment with Jake Stein at his office on Connecticut Avenue, only three blocks from the White House. It was an especially beautiful September day—dry, seventy degrees, an incredible cerulean sky—and I drove with the windows open and Diana Krall on the CD player. When I arrived a few minutes early and got parked, I switched over to the all-news station for the headlines on the hour. "A plane has crashed into the World Trade Center. . . ." I got out of the car and headed to the meeting, concerned but not frightened.

In Jake's reception room, a woman who'd been waiting near me snapped her cell phone shut and said, "A plane has hit the Pentagon." She got up and left. I didn't know, but I assumed terrorism. Within a minute a coterie of lawyers, briefcases in hand, rushed through the lobby to the elevators. One of them said, "B'nai B'rith is one floor above us. We should all get out of here."

I said to the receptionist, "Tell Jake I'll call him from home," and I joined the procession.

Back out on Connecticut Avenue, it was still that gorgeous day, and the street bustled with the vehicle and pedestrian traffic of a typical workday morning. I could tell from their faces who else knew, and who didn't know. A group of construction workers stood laughing over a joke. A businessman anxiously flagged a cab. A woman on her cell phone demanded, "Where's Mom?" A few blocks away the White House was being evacuated. The vice president had been squirreled away in a secret bunker. In a few minutes the broad avenue would transform as workers streamed from their offices. I got home and called Spencer's school.

"We're not changing the routine as yet," the operator said. "We'll notify all parents if there's a change of plan." School was sixteen miles from the White House. He was safe out there. I turned on the TV and saw black smoke pouring from the two towers. I watched and watched. When the first tower fell I ran outside to find someone, anyone, human company. When the second tower fell I picked up the dog, packed him and some food into the car, and headed to Spencer's school. Traffic had begun to build. No panic, no rage as each car inched along, headed away from the city. On the radio they reported a hijacked plane that might be heading toward Washington. I scanned the blue sky. By the time I parked at the school the radio reported United Flight 93 had crashed somewhere in Pennsylvania.

The school called an assembly to attempt to explain the events to the students. With the dog in my arms I waited outside Spencer's class, and as the children filed out his teacher's eyes caught mine and for the first time I got emotional. Tears welled in my eyes. Maybe it was because I felt safe and knew my son was safe. Spencer saw me and looked alarmed. It was hard to tell how much he or his classmates knew. Their expressions were worried, confused, but not frightened. They were fourth graders. Could nine-year-old boys comprehend what was happening? Spencer was happy to see the dog. I bucked up, gave him a hug, and walked with him to the assembly.

The school's outdoor amphitheater was filled with students and parents, who were arriving by the minute. I looked up at the tall green trees and the bright yellow sun and tried to reconcile the beauty and the horror. It was not possible. I held the dog in my lap and wrapped an arm around Spencer. The principal gave an eloquent talk about the terrible things that had happened, the lives lost, the fear and uncertainty that still gripped us, and how the students needed to know they were safe. "You are safe here and you will be safe when you go home. If your parents aren't here yet, we will stay here with you until they arrive. We'll have lunch, and classes will go on as long as you are here."

I looked at the crowd and thought, With one of the doomed planes out of Washington, it's possible some people here will be personally affected by this nightmare. We later learned that a classmate's father was on American Airlines Flight 11, which crashed into the Pentagon.

Driving home, Spencer and I were struck by how the lanes of Massachusetts Avenue headed out of the city were jammed with cars, and the only vehicle going in our direction was ours. The sidewalks, even as far as five miles out, were packed with pedestrians walking away from the city.

"Will we be okay?" Spencer asked, holding the dog in his lap. I assured him we would be okay. We heard the occasional fighter jet streak overhead. By evening there were tanks parked at intersections throughout our neighborhood. Smoke was still rising from the Pentagon across the river. Neighbors came over, I made pasta, and we ate and watched the television coverage together. That night, in bed, I listened into the wee hours to the jets patrolling overhead.

I did not call Jake Stein that day, nor did I think of Nathans.

Chapter 35

Before I ever fell in love with a man, I fell in love with *Two for the Road,* a movie starring Audrey Hepburn and Albert Finney. It follows the romance and complicated marriage of a smart and stylish couple who have one child. I was drawn to their nomadic, freewheeling existence and especially to Finney's bad-boy persona. I'm one of those women who have a weakness for brains but also for mischief. I didn't know it then, but as I look back over my life it's fairly plain. Even before Howard, I was involved with men who were very good at what they did, but who also made their own rules, for better or worse. Good-looking, smart, successful, and just scoundrelly enough to attract and keep my interest, the kind of characters screenwriters transform into heartthrobs.

Howard was the quintessential irresistible rascal. He seduced me that way, and I succumbed willingly. It was—more often than not—a great ride. Roller coasters are thrilling, until they go off the rails. Ours went off the rails. It's bittersweet that the best years were the last years, after therapy and Prozac helped to tame the beast within him. Once I returned to work, and began to assert myself in our relationship, he never got aggressive with me again, and the marriage was solid. Still, I had my eyes clamped shut. Looking back was like recalling the most thrilling ride and wondering if either I had been too ignorant, or too caught up in the thrill, to notice we were riding on thin air, destined for peril. It never occurred to me then, but there were so many signs of trouble: his offhand mention of an "audit," his frequent appointments with lawyers, and his more-than-occasional fitful nights. Howard made it so easy to live in an ignorant bliss, though, because he always had a comforting answer. If something struck me as odd, and I asked, he'd tell me "Everything will be okay," and I'd close my eyes once more.

Another movie I loved was Martin Scorsese's *Alice Doesn't Live Here*

Anymore with Ellen Burstyn and Kris Kristofferson. It begins with the sudden death of her husband, upending her life and the life of her young son. They are left with not much more than each other, the proceeds of a yard sale, a station wagon, and the grit needed to survive. Like *Two for the Road,* there's a lot of road-tripping as mother and son try to find a safe haven and start over. I was only twenty-four years old when I first saw it—long before a husband, widowhood, and road-tripping with my own son. The bonding moments of my relationship with Spencer have often been in the car, whether it was driving him to and from school or the many road trips we took together, up and down the East Coast and one adventurous three-week cross-country drive from Washington, D.C. to Oregon to California and back. When he was little—and not so little—if he wanted to have a serious talk with me, he would ask, "Can we go for a drive?" On the road we didn't have to stare at each other, allowing both intimacy and space, or maybe it was because the open road is about moving on.

After Howard died I discovered a "widow" movie that I liked because it had some truths in it and a great line. The film is *Bounce.* Ben Affleck is talking to Gwyneth Paltrow about wanting her to be happy. She replies, "If you grade on a curve I'm happy. I may be widow happy, but I'm happy." I've used that phrase dozens of times. I'm a widow. It can't be erased or taken back or revised. It changes everything.

Often someone would pull me aside and ask, "How are you *really* doing?" as if they could see through my "I'm fine" mask. What I learned was that unless the questioner was also a widow or widower it was impossible to tell them how I was *really* doing. Details of being utterly alone, of raising a child by myself, of debt and business woes, of sharks in the water, of loneliness and grief—they were a lot more than most people could grasp. I learned to keep it simple. "I'm fine. Really, I'm fine." When the Tom Hanks film *Cast Away* arrived in theaters in 2000 I went to see it as soon as I could. The story aside, I looked forward to two hours of looking at a tropical sea. But it was the story that got to me. A person otherwise enjoying the routine of life crash-lands on a deserted island in the middle of the sea. He's trapped, stuck, torn away from everything he takes for granted. All he wants is to build his life raft and get back to civilization, and when he does return to the world he discovers how much he's changed. That was me, only minus the soccer ball named Wilson. I had a child to keep me sane as I tried to build the life raft and get us to dry land.

SIX YEARS INTO owning Nathans, and with six years still to go on the lease, my corner bar still confounded me, scared me, and caused me to feel very alone, especially in the middle of the night—worrying, tossing, thinking, worrying some more, tossing some more. I was only a little smarter. I learned to understand "tolerable" theft, that it was an expected part of the business. I learned that in a bar nothing much good happened after midnight. And I now knew the legal drinking age was twenty-one. I learned this lesson in an embarrassing way when one lunchtime I stood in the middle of the bar and joyfully asked a bartender to send a glass of champagne to a friend's daughter who was celebrating her eighteenth birthday. The bartender froze, the room fell silent, and the birthday girl said, "But, Mrs. Joynt, I'm not twenty-one." Yes, I learned everything on the job, and too often in public.

Then there was the daily task of staying in business. The roadwork, combined with the recession that hit all of Washington after 9/11, caused our gross to drop by as much as 30 to 40 percent, but our costs stayed the same or climbed. At one point, after churning through general managers, I hired a management company to run the place. They lasted a year. A very bumpy year. They had me take out bank loans that put me deeper in debt—"If you don't get $75,000 right now you'll have to close"—and when an employee filed suit against them they packed up and left, leaving behind the lawsuit and a more than $100,000 bill for their services. Fortunately for me, Vito Zappala, who had resigned, exhausted, a few years earlier, was "tan, rested, and ready," and agreed to come back and take the reins. I warned him, "We have work to do. The mismanagers I brought in from the outside did a lot of damage. They scared away loyal customers and vendors. We have to mend fences. The debt, of course, is monstrous. And me? Well, I'm still as useless as before."

"Actually, Carol, you shouldn't say that. What you should realize is that, whether you like it or not, you know what you're doing. Pat yourself on the back. You're better for Nathans than that outside management company ever was."

Pat myself on the back? Nice thought, but no, I didn't think so. Maybe when I was rid of Nathans.

AT LEAST I could talk to Vito, confide my doubts to him and share my ideas, which I couldn't do with the management company, who didn't want to hear my thoughts about my own business. Nathans was a part of my life that was tough to ignore and tough to discuss honestly with others. I tried not to take it home, because it was impossible to discuss with a young son. I tried not to take it to cocktail parties, either, or out to dinner with men. When a man did innocently ask, "How's Nathans?" and I answered honestly, he would soon be crawling toward the exit, or at least eager to get me home to my front door. I was happiest when the subject didn't come up at all. Sometimes at parties where people didn't know me I would make up a fake job or say I was still a journalist. Then, just my luck, someone would walk up and go, "Oh, do you know Carol? She owns the best bar in town." For me, at that point, the party was over.

The cemetery where Howard was buried is on Oak Hill, Georgetown's highest point. Spencer and I would visit occasionally and leave flowers and plant kisses on Howard's white marble bench-shaped gravestone. When I had a really bad day, when I felt the walls and sky were falling on me, when I felt my most alone or was my most depressed, I'd go to his grave, not knowing when I got there whether I wanted to scream at it or to cry. Most often I'd cry for a while, dry my eyes, and then carry on.

SINCE THE EARLY years of owning Nathans I had used every opportunity for free publicity to help the place get its buzz back. At this I was a natural. I would talk to a reporter about anything—and I mean anything—if it meant getting the word *Nathans* in print or on television. In addition to my own drama, the exploding manhole covers, and routine Georgetown crime stories, I was quoted in the *Washington Post* on how to make the perfect cosmopolitan; the *New York Times* asked me to comment on the Barbara Walters interview with Monica Lewinsky; another *Washington Post* reporter included me in a story on mothers who sleep while waiting in the carpool line (I was an expert); local TV always liked an on-camera comment about Halloween escapades in Georgetown; a restaurant writer wanted to know what the cleanup crew finds on the bar floor after a big night ("wedding rings"); various media asked about the impact of the (good or bad) economy on a small business; and *Newsweek* wanted to know whether Washington was hip. I said yes, "Sex, drugs, and rock 'n' roll do exist in Washington." Whatever the subject, I did my best to utter the perfect sound-bite, to have a quotable opinion—for one reason and one reason only: It got my saloon's name out there.

In October 2001, I created something that got attention for Nathans but also suited me to a T. I hosted a talk show right there in Nathans' back dining room. I called it *The Q&A Café,* and it quickly became popular and, best of all, satisfying for me. Essentially it was the Charlie Rose show in Nathans at lunchtime with me as Charlie. I created it as a response to the terrorist attacks, when so many people seemed desperate for information. Week after week, my gets were experts on terrorism and Islam and Osama bin Laden. For almost an hour I interviewed one guest—the two of us sitting across from each other on barstools—while around us the patrons enjoyed lunch. From the aftermath of 9/11, the subject matter expanded to every topic under the sun. I liked the challenge of booking interesting guests, loved the research in preparation for them, and was increasingly comfortable with the onstage interviews. After all, I had trained with the masters. Each week I looked forward to my moment with the audience and guest. It was doubly exciting when a comment made by a notable guest landed in a newspaper column with the attribution, "said at *The Q&A Café* at Nathans." I no longer had to give a clever quote to market my business. My interviews made news. It was gratifying to see the pile of clippings grow, and even more gratifying when the show was videotaped and began to appear on two local cable channels. If my talk show in a restaurant could be called restaurant work then this was the restaurant work I was made for.

With each show the audience of men and women filed in, paid the fee at the bar, and dashed into the back dining room to snag good seats. Some people came to every show. We served house-made potato chips before the program began and a warm meal as the interview started.

Since there were no reserved seats, late arrivals were blended into other tables. Strangers met and became friends. Some ordered beer and wine, and the camaraderie was strong. I called them *The Q&A Café* "lunch bunch." I welcomed each person. Those were the only times I felt comfortable greeting guests in the restaurant.

The Q&A Café made national news when Maury Povich and Connie Chung appeared only two days after a member of his staff hit him with sexual harassment charges. They wouldn't talk about the suit, but that didn't matter. The audience included plenty of reporters. We made news again when Deborah Jeane Palfrey, "the D.C. Madam," in a rare interview, said Washington was a good market for her line of work. Dan Rather appeared soon after filing suit against CBS News and got a tear in his eye when talking about the suit's stress on his family. That got me on morning network television, with a clip of Dan. When Joe Wilson, the former ambassador who publicly questioned the rationale behind the Iraq War, appeared for an interview he gladly posed for me afterward for a photo for the Nathans website. Smiling in the picture with him was his previously unphotographed wife, former CIA operative Valerie Plame, whose cover the Bush administration had blown in an attempt to discredit Wilson. The photo went viral and global.

My favorite interviews, however, were with people such as Dr. Anthony Fauci, director of the National Institute of Allergy and Infectious Diseases and famous for his work with the HIV/AIDS virus. He talked about bioterrorism and the vulnerability of the nation's subway systems to a deadly attack. Fred Smith, the founder of FedEx, was fascinating in the plainspoken way he told his story of global business success. Another favorite was Kenneth Feinberg, special master of the U.S. government's September 11th Victim Compensation Fund, who put human faces to the thousands of family members who were left behind to cope with their losses.

Nathans brought a lot of anxiety and pain to my life, but the success of *The Q&A Café* made up for scraping to pay the plumber. It was my success, something I created all on my own and that I understood and could do well.

Nathans gave me another pleasure, too, and it can't be discounted. It gave me time to spend with my son that might not have come with other jobs. I was my own boss, and because of that it was easier to slip away as needed. As Spencer grew from little giggle-puss to teenage boy, I cherished and embraced the role of parent and all its rewarding and sometimes tedious parts. I liked driving him to and from school each day, to athletic practices and games, and to guitar practice; I tagged along on field trips, showed up for school assemblies, and made all the parent-teacher conferences. For a while he was a skateboard fiend, and I became versed in Washington's best "spots," could talk half-pipes with the best, and sat in one arena or another, biting my nails, as he thrilled to the harrowing performances of superstar Tony Hawk. When his passion turned to lacrosse, Spencer played year-round, in school and in leagues. Game after game, I arrived with my trusty folding chair. I learned the sport, knew the names of the plays and gear, and could debate the merits of the top teams in the NCAA rankings; together we traveled to many college games and tournaments. I could do these "guy" things with him because, like some of the dads, I had the time because I was fortunate to own my own business.

In the afternoons when I waited in the carpool line, however, I became a "normal" mother. He wasn't crazy about me catching a quick nap—"Mom, people see you sleeping and they think you're passed out!"—but I told him if I didn't catch a snooze I'd probably drive off the side of the road on the way home. He cared how I appeared. It was especially important that I look young, to match the younger mothers. When gray hairs started to show he would say, "It's time to get your roots done." Comments like that made me laugh, and I loved when he made me laugh. But time moves inexorably on, as parents well know. The boy becomes a young man. One day Spencer was a five-year-old with his hand in mine, and the next his draft card arrived in the mail.

When he was in elementary school, especially through first and second grades, his teachers and I knew Spencer needed special consideration. He was fragile, and we watched closely for ways he might act out because of his father's death. Through guidance from his grief therapist, Ellen Sanford, and my own psychiatrist, I learned important lessons about how to raise a child who had lost a parent. The first thing Ellen said was "Too many families try to shield a child from a parent's death. Don't do that, because you can't." She continued, "If you want him to grow up healthy, don't act like it didn't happen. He'll begin to think Howard never existed, or that perhaps it was his fault his father died."

"Ask Spencer about his father," I would suggest to his teachers. "Its okay, even good, to encourage him to talk." We were at a meal with friends when their daughter, who was Spencer's age, blurted out, "Spencer, you don't have a father. Your father is dead!" Her parents were mortified and started to scold her and apologize to me. But I told them it was okay and meant it. Spencer said, "Yes. My dad died from pneumonia but we have his picture everywhere and he's alive in our hearts." When his first-grade class had the children talk about their parents, I urged the teacher to let Spencer make a presentation about his father. This particular teacher, Dan Specter, was remarkable. He gave Spencer his time, even if it meant sitting out in the hall for private chats. Occasionally, the three of us would take weekend walks or go to the movies. Dan wrote a letter to Howard, and Spencer brought it home and cherished it.

As Spencer got older, into fourth, fifth, and sixth grades, and especially in middle school, I told his teachers it was time to treat him like any other boy. At that moment between adolescence and becoming a young man, he was tall for his age, good-looking, lean, athletic, smart, well mannered, and popular. At school he did well academically but had brushes with upper management caused by the bad decisions boys can sometimes make. I didn't like his acting out, but I tried to understand and face it head-on. I worried about how it related to Howard. Was it genetically hardwired or was it insecurity? On occasion as he aged, I would dole out more truthful bits of background on his father, filling in the gray areas of the legacy that had landed on us, helping him to see a bigger and more focused picture. I measured what I told him based on what I thought he could accept and understand. I always made clear that Howard loved us, and loved him most of all.

Mischief would happen. Transgressions would happen. Unfortunately, too many times what I'd hear from school officials, and sometimes other parents, was "I know this happened because he doesn't have a father." Excuse me? He has a parent! Whatever he'd done was because he was a teenage boy who occasionally used bad judgment, not because he didn't have a father or because his mother owned a saloon. Or was it? I did my best, but was it enough?

I was home almost every night. If I went out with friends, I had a trusty sitter and was home well before midnight. If he had a friend sleep over, I was on duty, not out partying. Most nights I was in bed by ten, not hosting after-hours parties at Nathans. I was defensive, I know. What I wanted was for these well-meaning but hurtful people to give me some credit. As for my son, when male teachers offered to "father" him, I would say, "Thank you for volunteering, but he doesn't need you to be his father. He needs you to be his friend." I wished his uncles, my brothers David and Robert, could have been more involved in his growing up, and also his aunt, Martha, but David was in Seattle and Robert lived out in Virginia, and they had busy lives. Martha and her husband, Vijay, moved to Washington and lived near us, and we did see them from time to time, but for whatever reason she did not have a pronounced role in Spencer's life. I wondered if it was just too hard; Spencer and I, and the challenges that had landed on us, were perhaps too painful a reminder of what her brother had done.

What I thought was best for my son and what *was* best for my son were not always the same thing, and the learning curves were sometimes steep and painful. My greatest blunders involved the schools I chose for him. I was so hell-bent on making sure his educational environment was traditional and what I mistakenly viewed as "normal" that I simply missed seeing who he was. After trying it for grades four through eight, I was not happy with the coat-and-tie boys'-school choice, believing the single-sex setup may have been a factor in his occasional run-ins with school authorities. Mentioning this to one of his former teachers, she said, "You know, he'd do well at Georgetown Day School." It was not the first time this coed school had been recommended, but I had a bigger idea. He would be in ninth grade and entering puberty, and I thought he would benefit from some distance from me, some independence, and that a coed boarding school made sense. We applied to only one, and he was accepted. I called it Hogwarts. It was an old and respected school in New Jersey, where we knew some families. We liked the fact that it was not too big. It was close enough but not too close. I was positive this separation from me would be good for him, and that he'd thrive. Wrong.

From practically day one he was in hot water for one stupid act or another. It seemed to me he had more weekend detentions than he had weekends in which to serve them. Talking back to his dorm supervisor, talking back to a senior, not being prepared for a class, needling a classmate. When I talked to him on the phone or drove up for a visit, he'd assure me "It's all good. I've got it under control. Don't worry. I'll stay out of trouble." His offenses, while disturbing to me, at least did not count as "strikes." This was a two-strike school, meaning just that: Two strikes and you're out.

One weekday morning, as I walked along the C&O Canal from a breakfast meeting to Nathans, my cell phone rang. It was Spencer. I could tell from the tone of his voice that I should brace myself. "Mom, I'm in big trouble. Some of us were caught smoking dope." My heart sank. This was a definite strike. I called the school. The boys were caught smoking marijuana in a dorm room and had been suspended. Spencer would be sent home immediately. He returned home to a very grumpy mother. I gave him a strong lecture about his crime and why it was wrong and not okay with me, and I handed out his punishment—a week of helping out at Nathans and at a friend's lunch shop downtown. I couldn't help but point out that most kids, when they smoke dope, don't do it in a dorm room. "Most kids go into the woods, and you guys decide to do it in the dorm! Were you out of your minds?"

"We had a vaporizer," he said, as if that made any sense.

"You realize you are a freshman and you already have one strike?"

"I do, Mom, I do. I've learned my lesson." I told him about his father's experience at Choate: He got kicked out for drinking, and that was that. "You don't want to lose this opportunity," I said.

"I know, Mom. I won't."

The next school year started well, and when he returned to Hogwarts after the winter break I eased up on the worrying. Boarding school was working out. His grades were good, his teachers were pleased, he was maturing. I'd made the right decision, after all. It was time for me to stop focusing so much on him and begin to focus on myself, perhaps test the waters out there. Gosh, maybe even get involved with a man. The house seemed bigger and emptier without Spencer there. I missed him every day, but I also enjoyed being on my own for the first time since I met Howard.

Spencer was back at school only a few days into the second semester when I got the call. It was Friday afternoon. I was working at my desk at home. "Mom, I've been kicked out of school. I copied from Wikipedia. Two strikes. I have to leave the campus now." I saw no point in yelling into the phone. His shaky voice made clear he was scared. The next voice on the line was his housemaster, who was kind but said there was nothing that could be done. Two strikes meant two strikes and no reconsidering. I asked the housemaster if he could please help get him to the train station.

"Of course," he said.

It was late at night when Spencer walked out of Union Station to the car. He got in, kissed me, and said nothing during the fifteen-minute drive to the house. He quickly ran upstairs to his room, threw himself on his bed, and cried for a very long time. Finally, I knocked, stepped in, and sat on the edge of his bed. "I know it hurts," I said, rubbing his back. "It hurts a lot. Some things are just not meant to be, and I guess boarding school was one of them."

The following Monday we returned to New Jersey to clean out his room. As we departed through the gates of the school I called the admissions office of Georgetown Day School. If I had to beg on my knees, if I had to grovel, I would, because I planned—finally—to follow the recommendations I'd ignored before, that GDS was the right school for him. There was a long admissions process. Not knowing if he would get in, I took him to the public school to try it out. That was a wake-up call. Before I left, the head of the school said, "You should give your mother your jacket and untuck your shirt," which Spencer did. Then the man said, "Here are the rules: No drugs, no guns, no knives, no other weapons, no leaving the school grounds between classes. Otherwise, you're on your own." He was a long, long way from Hogwarts. Dealing with me was no walk in the park, but he realized he'd done it to himself, and that I could help him only so much. That was ultimately a good thing.

When the good news came from GDS, we were elated. GDS is a famously down-to-earth school, open-minded, progressive, geared toward letting young men and women be responsible and accountable for their behavior. It was the first private school in Washington to integrate, in the 1940s; it celebrated diversity and emphasized academics over athletics while still promoting a good sports program. Spencer was like a duck finding water. In the spring I popped my head in the office of principal Kevin Barr. "I haven't heard from you," I said. "I'm not used to going through a week without getting some kind of troubling report about my darling boy, and here it's been a few months. What gives?"

He looked up with a smile. "There's nothing to report. If there were anything we would call you. He's doing great."

ONE THING I'VE learned through life is the amazing ability of human beings to transfer to one object, animate or inanimate, the emotions felt for another. What I had to face eventually, especially as Spencer became a teenager and young man, was that sometimes my anger toward him was actually the anger I felt toward his father. That came out especially when Spencer lied. It's understandable for a parent to get upset when teenagers fudge the truth, but my anger was grounded in fear that Howard had somehow genetically transferred his lying to his son. When the cheating incident happened at Hogwarts, I forgave him, but my gut ached with fear. Another time, when he told me he'd spent the night at one friend's but I later learned he was at another friend's, I threw the book at him. "Don't come home," I told him. "I can't live with a liar." I had a revelation at that moment: This is my anger, transferred from my dead husband to our son. I felt terrible. Spencer was a normal teenage boy, telling the normal fibs that teenagers tell their parents. I was the woman, the mother, at the end of her rope, who had her own unresolved issues. When I recognized what I was doing, it was as if I'd released the last pressure point, and I began the journey toward closure.

I did want him to learn to see his behavior through the eyes of others. Fair or not, he had to understand how he might be perceived if he lied, or misbehaved in the extreme. "You know, you have to deal with this," I told him. "Because people are going to judge you differently. Heck, they judge me differently. With you, if you lie, they are going to think, 'Well, his father lied to his mother about taxes and so, you know, like father like son.' You can't play to that. You *cannot* let that happen."

"Mom," he said, "I know I lie sometimes, and I'm working on it. I don't like it, but I do it because I think sometimes that if I tell you the truth you will get mad at me and I don't want to get in trouble." These were the same words I had heard from his father after so many little stupid lies over the years—fibs that were so minor I can't recall even one, except my response would always be the same, and it was exactly what I'd say to Spencer: "Maybe the truth would make me mad, but the lie makes me furious."

EVERYTHING ABOUT RAISING a child alone requires creative thinking. I found my surrogate "co-parent" in many forms. *Sex and the City* would be my teacher's aid on the matter of male-female relations. Mother and son, side by side on the sofa, watched every episode. The plots and characters gave us a way to talk about sex in a less threatening, more comfortable way, whether the subject was condoms, multiple partners, or STDs. We'd be in the car on the way to school and I'd ask, "What do you think of the women on the show? Who would you date?"

"Well, Carrie's okay. Miranda is gay and Samantha is a slut. I think I'd date Charlotte."

We shared *The Sopranos,* too. It was a tutorial in business. "In a way, this is like Mommy's business but without the guns."

Without our shared sense of humor, Spencer and I wouldn't have survived. A good laugh was what got us through just about every adversity, and we laughed about some of the darkest parts of our life together, especially when I'd get frustrated with some of his behavior and demand, "Stop channeling your father!" Or I'd look to the heavens: "Howard, leave his body, *now*!" Usually Howard would. It was the least he could do. Quite often Spencer asked me to back off, to trust him more, to give him space. Fair enough. Just as trying as it was for me to have to be both good cop and bad cop, I know for him, as for all children with only one parent, it had to be equally tough to have no court of appeals, no other parent to run to for understanding when one parent was laying down the law. There's a reason for the cliché "Life's not fair." It's not, and solo parents and children with only one parent know this lesson better than most.

When Spencer hit bumps in the road, I wanted to be a fair guide, adviser, and advocate, and not an out-and-out paranoid, wagging my finger while snarling, "You're just like your father." The similar patterns were eerie, though. Both were smart and talented but capable of pulling a stunt or telling a fib that sabotaged what was precious to him.

Is Spencer his father? *No.* He's entirely his own person. But during those teenage years, when he got in trouble for seriously bad decisions, I worried that the apple had fallen too close to the tree.

Most of the time, however, he was *not* in trouble; he did well—sometimes very well—impressed teachers and others, and even had an eighteen-month devoted high school relationship with one girlfriend, which I thought showed stability and maturity. Invariably, adults who met him pulled me aside to talk about his smarts, humor, and good manners. They'd say, "You've done such a good job." I was grateful, but I didn't take it for granted. Honestly, a mother's work is never done.

WHEN I REFLECT on my career in journalism it becomes apparent that I was a skyrocket. It wasn't clear to me then, but most young people aren't reporting for a national news organization at age eighteen or writing the network news at twenty-two. It made sense to me. It was logical. I was determined, driven, and capable. It didn't occur to me that I might be young for my line of work. Journalism was a cause as much as a profession. While I was honored to be in their company, or on their staffs, it never struck me as odd that I would be working alongside journalists of such note as Walter Cronkite, Merriman Smith, Helen Thomas, Hugh Sidey, David Brinkley, Dan Rather, Ted Koppel, Charlie Rose, and Larry King. Yes, mostly men, but that's the way it was.

Of them all, Walter was the one who was both mentor and friend, and his death in July 2009 was a painful loss for Spencer and me. Walter and I had an easy, comfortable, and appropriate way with each other that endured for forty years, starting with the day we met in 1970 at the *Apollo 13* launch and he bought me a Coke. I was there to write a story for UPI on the network-news coverage of the launch. Before heading to the Cape, I'd sent Cronkite a fan letter, mentioning that, like him, I was starting my career at UPI. Remarkably, he answered and said, "If we're ever in the same place at the same time, let me know."

When I mentioned this to the CBS News publicist at the launch he thought I was out of my mind, but when that same publicist told Walter I was outside the CBS launch-pad facility, Cronkite put down what he was doing and asked, "Where is she?"

We met, we had that Coke, and we became friends, kept in touch, and eventually he hired me to write for him. Working with Walter was the best of what popular culture now calls *broadcast news.* CBS was the Tiffany network when I was there—the news division was the network's jewel in the crown—and Walter Cronkite was a living, breathing, walking legend. He was my journalism hero.

Being in the top tier of Walter Cronkite's staff in the mid-'70s was not unlike being an associate of God. I took a holiday in the Outer Banks of North Carolina and the local paper put my picture on the front page with the headline WALTER CRONKITE'S WRITER VACATIONS IN NAGS HEAD. When I needed to catch a flight back to Washington for President Richard Nixon's resignation, the airline held a passenger jet for me. Not because of me, but because I was Walter Cronkite's writer. One day, walking with Walter back from lunch, a school bus stopped beside us on 57th Street. Suddenly, all the windows came down and dozens of young heads popped out. "Look, it's Walter Cronkite!" they shouted. "Walter! Hi, Walter! Walter!" He stopped, smiled, waved and then we walked on.

Walter Cronkite's role in journalism and American cultural history has been and will be written about and analyzed for years. He is a legend, but he wasn't a God, and he'd be the first to say so. Like most talented and successful humans, he had a complicated personality with a fierce ambition. Most people liked him. Some didn't, and some feared him. I can write only about my own experience with him, and it was good. There were many aspects to our friendship. Journalism, of course. But we shared a love of sailing, too. We could sit and talk about boats, charts, sails, and anchorages for hours.

Over the years, and especially after I left the show, I worked to maintain my friendship with Walter and his wife, Betsy, and the Cronkites became friends with Howard. The four of us met socially in New York or Washington. We attended their annual Christmas parties. In Annapolis they took us sailing. Howard and I were in the studio for one of Walter's last *CBS Evening News* broadcasts.

After Howard died, each Christmas morning—no matter where he was or where we were—Walter would phone to check on Spencer and me, to make sure we weren't alone, that we had plans, that Christmas would be good for us. Walter and Betsy, or Walter alone, would meet us for lunch whenever we were in New York. It was a delight to introduce Walter to my other good friends and Spencer's godparents, Harry Shearer and his wife, Judith Owen. Walter was amused by Harry's very good impression of him and other news notables, particularly those of whom Walter was not particularly fond.

It was after Betsy died that Harry and Judith invited Walter, Spencer, and me to a Museum of Modern Art event that honored Spinal Tap, the mock-rock band in which Harry performed as bassist Derek Smalls. At the loud, crowded dinner afterward, Walter, sitting beside me, leaned in close. "Now listen, this is what I want to do," he said above the din. "I want to marry you. I want you to marry me, if you will, and I want to adopt Spencer and take care of you two." I didn't know what to say. I looked closely to see whether there was a twinkle in his eye, or if a punch line was coming, like a "gotcha." But, no. He was serious, and he hadn't been drinking anything more than a glass of wine.

"You can unload the bar and move to New York," he said in my ear. "You like it here, anyway."

I didn't know what to say. No matter our friendship, he was still Walter Cronkite and this was a vulnerable, sensitive moment, and we were at a crowded table in the noisy back room of a busy restaurant. It was hard to hear and he couldn't hear very well even when there wasn't lots of noise. For me, the room disappeared around the two of us. Instinctively I sensed his "proposal," if it was a proposal, was probably an emotional whim, not something borne from love or need or desire. If anything, he was still tender after Betsy's death, and his grief surely enhanced his view of Spencer's and my aloneness and vulnerability. I think he wanted to do something for us, and this made sense. He had his hand on my hand. It was a touching but also awkward moment. He'd never before been this intimate with me. I had to say something, and the words had to be sincere and gentle.

"That's such a loving suggestion and I'm deeply touched," I shouted so he could hear me clearly. "I know you want to help us, and just having you in our lives helps so much. But Walter, I have a mess on my hands in Washington and I wouldn't want to involve anyone I care about in that, and getting involved with me would force you to be involved. And I care about you too much to do that to you." I tried to explain that Nathans wasn't a situation I could simply walk away from; the legalities would follow me. I wasn't a free woman under the terms of Nathans lease. I couldn't give it away. What I didn't say—couldn't say—was that no matter how much it moved me, I couldn't be married to Walter. It would be like marrying my father.

"Would you think about it?" he said. "Because I'm serious. We don't have to say another word about it, but the offer stands."

It was neither warmly romantic nor coldly businesslike. If anything, it felt like a friend throwing a life ring, as much as or more than anyone had offered us.

"I know you care, Walter. That's always with me."

Funny, but we both continued on to other subjects and the evening rolled along. The marriage proposal never came up again. Walter found warm companionship with a widow, Joanna Simon, who was good for him. She was patient and loving, especially as his hearing went from little to zero. I don't know why he didn't marry *her.* That would have made sense to me.

Spencer and I had dinner with Walter and Joanna, visited them at Walter's New York apartment and, memorably, spent time with them one July on Martha's Vineyard, where Walter had a second home. The evening of our arrival, the group of us, plus Walter's daughter, Kathy, had dinner at the Edgartown Yacht Club. By now, Spencer towered over Walter and doted on him, taking his arm as he walked. The next day, Walter and Joanna took Spencer and me out for a sail. It was sunny with a good breeze. Walter steered his handsome Hinckley off the dock and out of the harbor, only then handing the helm over to the captain.

When he wasn't resting on Joanna's lap or contentedly whistling, Walter put Spencer at the helm and showed him how to read the wind and the sails. I have a picture of Walter next to Spencer, the two of them looking toward the horizon. It was a happy day and a happy memory; it was also the last time I saw Walter. The first Christmas after he died I kept expecting—and missing—his call.

Chapter 36

VISITS TO THE psychiatrist were not a luxury for me but a necessity. It was like going to a brain-spa where I could let down, be brutally honest, and vent my frustrations. I went in the door a mess and came out a little less of a mess. In the beginning I had a session every week, later they were down to once or twice a month. "Fine-tuning," I called it. Sometimes I sat through a session feeling on top of the world, like I was getting control, learning my business, making my way. Other times, not.

That's where and how I was when I walked into my psychiatrist's familiar office in the late summer of 2005, almost nine years after Howard died, a period of time I was beginning to view as my lost decade. So much water was under the bridge. I had changed so much, but I was still stuck in a place I didn't want to be. When I sat down in my usual chair I was calm, but when we shifted gears from my private life to Nathans, I choked up. "I'm out of options," I lamented, recounting how high the debt had grown—close to three quarters of a million dollars—that the landlords were silent to my requests to renegotiate or to take back the keys, that I couldn't afford to keep paying lawyers to beat their heads against a stone wall, that I could see my sixtieth birthday on the horizon, and, worst of all, that my son saw his mother in a constant state of stress. "Yes, there's *The Q&A Café* but it's a hit show on the *Titanic.* No matter what I do, we're still going down. If not today, then when the lease is up and the landlords ask for the excess rent they claim I owe them. By that time it will equal the value of my house."

"I still don't understand why you can't just declare bankruptcy and walk away," he said.

"Because I signed that personal guaranty on the lease. I didn't know what it was all those years ago, but what it means is that even if I close or go bankrupt I personally still have to meet the rent. Nathans could be zapped by Martians and the rent would have to be paid. I'm cooked."

"Why did you sign that?" he asked as he had several times before. "It made you an indentured slave."

"I know, I know," I said. "Who the hell knows why, but I signed it. It's done."

His words prompted a moment of reflection and then tears, a flood of tears. They welled up from that pool of frustration that sloshed around somewhere deep inside me. Words stumbled out between snuffles and nose wiping. "All because of what Howard did . . . and because I tried to run a business I didn't want. Did I kill babies in an earlier life?" I stopped to take a tissue. "I'm exhausted. I don't sleep at night. I stare at the ceiling and worry. I just want options, but I don't see any. I don't know what to do. I can't think anymore . . . and . . . and . . . you know . . . I do this all alone. . . . Yeah, I see lots of lawyers, I get sound advice, but there's no one in it with me. It's . . . it's . . . just me . . . at the end of the day. . . . It's just me alone at home with a child . . . trying to figure it out . . . do the right thing."

The office was quiet, except for my tears, which slowly subsided to a whimper. "You are in it alone," he said, "but you are very strong. You fall down, you get back up. It's been one avalanche after another, and it takes a toll."

"You have no idea," I said.

Actually he did have an idea. He'd listened to the saga from the beginning. "It's good I'm not an alcoholic because I'd be off the deep end. As it is, I do drink too much, take too many drugs, eat too much. I take it all out on my body. Every time I go to the doctor with an ailment he says it is stress related. My lower back is like a brick, my shoulders are locked in high gear, and I have TMJ disorder in my jaw. I used to be the most supple and relaxed person, ages ago. Now, I'm a tightly wound wreck."

"No one can cope indefinitely with heavy stress," he warned me. "It does take a toll on overall health. You need a break."

There was a pause, then he asked me, "Have you thought of going to Brendan Sullivan?"

My look was incredulous. "Brendan Sullivan? Well, sure, in my fantasies." Brendan Sullivan, the lawyer to go to when all the options have evaporated. Of course I'd thought of Brendan Sullivan. Anyone in Washington—and beyond—who really needed a defender in court would think of Brendan V. Sullivan, Jr. He was senior partner at the world-class firm of Williams and Connolly, protégé of the late Edward Bennett Williams, and one of the nation's top trial lawyers. He'd tried a lot of famous cases. He was known for dogged preparation, self-confidence, toughness, and winning. "Brendan Sullivan isn't gonna give the time of day to a saloon owner on the ropes."

My psychiatrist looked across the desk. "He's a friend of mine," he said. "Would you mind if I called him on your behalf? Perhaps he'd give you a consultation. That's what you need. You have nothing to lose."

"Oh, God, *yes.* Just to hear his take on this mess."

Not only did Brendan Sullivan see me, but he agreed to take me on as a pro bono client. His first words to me were, "You must have a sense of humor, because I read what you've been through and in my entire career I've never seen or heard of anything like this. It's bizarre. You've got to be able to laugh."

"Yes, I know. Yes, I do laugh," I said. "That's my only relief."

"You've really had it all. Your husband dies, the IRS, the city, the lease, bad management, exploding manhole covers, a huge public works project outside your door, and the landlords—round after round after round."

His voice was warm and reassuring, approachable, with an "I'm in your corner" quality. I could easily imagine him wooing a jury with that voice. When we met for the first time, I thought that if anyone ever makes a movie called *The Brendan Sullivan Story,* John Slattery has the part. The lean build, the silver hair, the entirely fair Irish face—and there's no doubt Slattery could harness the voice, with its shades of Rhode Island. They could be twins, though Brendan would be the older brother and would have an amused but skeptical attitude about his sibling's career in the entertainment business—not that arguing a case before judge and jury doesn't require performance skills. Brendan was one for the history books. He may have had his suit jacket off and his shirtsleeves up, and asked kindly at the outset of every meeting, "How's Spencer?," but there was an inner toughness that made me think I could sail across storm-tossed oceans with the man.

When it came to getting my neck out of the noose that was the

Nathans lease, Brendan Sullivan changed the game. It's not that a slew of other good lawyers hadn't tried, but there'd been no progress, and the inertia only pushed me deeper into debt—to the landlords and everyone else. With a big gun like Brendan in the picture, the Halkias family would have to realize I was dead serious about wanting them to take back the keys: to let me out of the lease, to take the business for themselves, or to renegotiate our agreement with an eventual exit strategy. Certainly on the bad days, but even on the good days, all I wanted was out. I just wanted out, without having to give up my house to pay added rent they claimed they were owed. I'd already had to give up one house in this saga, our home on the Bay, and I didn't want to lose another. To get out from under Nathans was to regain my freedom, all kinds of freedom: most of all to rebuild my life and my career, and for Spencer and me to move on from the detritus left by Howard. Since he was five years old my son had known me only as a woman at war. While he was still sharing the same home with me I wanted him to know me as a woman at peace.

From the outset, Brendan said "no" to paying any rent claim. The landlords, in his view, had agreed to the rent I did pay because they had cashed the checks. He based this on the likelihood a court could say that by their actions the landlords had, in fact, agreed to the reduced rent. Brendan's theory, which he was willing to argue in a courtroom, was simply that "the landlords had repeatedly accepted the reduced rent, without complaint, every month for more than sixty months. In essence the landlords had acknowledged for years that the rent stated in the lease was unable to be sustained by the business. The landlords knew it and accepted it." It was "nonnegotiable," he said. "Off the table." Period.

Brendan took the reins and I left the matter to him. If he needed to talk to me, he would let me know. It was the first time I'd felt a semblance of peace since before Howard died. But, of course, back at Nathans, like clockwork, Murphy's Law was reliably in play.

NATHANS' NEW CRISIS was a conflagration that demanded the small-business equivalent of a four-alarm emergency response. This time it was Vito. He disappeared—just like that. We couldn't find him and no one knew what was up. For several days he didn't call, which was unheard-of for him, and there was no answer when we called his home or cell phone. Eventually his sister let us know he was in the hospital with a failing heart. This time he'd burned out seriously. My God, I wondered, did Nathans have the power to kill? First Howard. Then one of the landlords had died after breaking his neck in a household fall. His son swore to my face: "Nathans killed him." Vito's sister appeared to feel the same way about her brother.

Nobody but Vito knew how Nathans got through a day. Our accounts were built on so many promises to so many vendors—and so much bank float—and only he knew the formula that kept it all working. But Vito was unconscious in a hospital bed. From the moment Vito disappeared there were unhappy people on the phone demanding money, and we were perilously on the verge of losing the power, water, and phones. The only person in the office who could help me was the brand-new administrative assistant, a recent graduate of Colby College and completely wet behind the ears. Jon Moss had never before worked at a restaurant. He'd been at Nathans all of two weeks. He barely knew where to find the paper clips and now he had to help me prevent what could be a disaster.

In Nathans' cramped, cluttered office, with the rattraps on standby and the fans stirring a feeble breeze, Jon and I went into battle mode, largely unaware of the last days of summer playing out in the sunny world above. We worked from morning into evening. With the dogged help of our friendly local banker, Joseph Reamer, we tracked checks as they went through the system, trying to catch them just before they exploded. I drove Jon to the offices of various utility companies and idled the car outside while he ran in with cashier's checks that spared Nathans for another month. We did the same with weekly tax payments. We sweated. We paced. But we made it through the storm. When the ordeal was over, I made Jon Moss the new general manager.

We were the oddest of odd couples—an accidental restaurateur who'd had a dysfunctional business thrust upon her and a manager half her age who'd also never worked at a restaurant—but somehow we were a good fit. Jon brought aboard a twenty-first-century business paradigm, to the extent that was possible at Nathans. He also put Spencer's and my survival into the equation and tried to protect me from mounting debt. He learned to deal with the landlords, especially family liaison George Halkias, who called often, always worried I was about to go AWOL. As I did at home with my son, I shared a dark sense of humor with Jon that carried us through the highs and lows. I thought, "We can make it. We can get through this." As we sailed into 2006 and 2007, Jon managed to show me some genuine profit. In 2007 we grossed just under $2 million, a high-water mark. Bills got paid, rent got paid, taxes got paid, and I got paid. Jon chipped away at the monstrous debt. We had fewer angry vendors, and the landlords seemed more accepting of reality. *The Q&A Café* continued as a success, attracting more notable individuals to sit with me for an interview. Our heyday didn't last. It was just a year or two, but it was my only happy and contented stretch as owner.

IT'S GOOD I was content because the negotiations for my freedom that Brendan Sullivan thought we could wrap up in a matter of months ended up lasting a few years, until the very moment the lease expired in April 2009. Now he understood intimately the frustration and angst I'd lived with for so long. He didn't disparage the Halkias family, but he said, "They're like nothing I've ever dealt with in my entire career." That's a career that included his single-handedly taking on the U.S. Congress in the sensational Ollie North hearings, which ran for seven days on all the networks in 1987, when Brendan famously said to Senator Daniel Inouye, "Sir, I'm not a potted plant. I'm here as the lawyer."

The drama of our dispute got in the way of my being able to tell the landlords that I wasn't blind to their point of view. I did understand them and I did care. I just needed them to understand what I was trying to tell them as well: that the business was sinking, and it was a business we all relied upon for income. Early on we probably needed relationship counseling more than lots of lawyers. It would have saved us heartache and money. Howard left them holding the bag, too. He'd spoiled them by seeming to effortlessly meet their lease demands, and they were content with the way things were, but he was lying to them as much as he was lying to the IRS and to me. It was simple: Once his father died, Howard couldn't afford the place, and when Howard died,

I couldn't afford the place, either. That simple fact got lost in so much dust and dustups: The landlords did not trust me and I did not trust them, either. The Halkias family—the principal landlords and their several children—were like many families in that everybody had a different opinion and they disagreed with one another much of the time. When they couldn't reach a consensus it was easier to shut down rather than continue the debate. That would cause the long and frustrating stretches of silence between my shouts of "Mayday."

With the lease up I was technically free to close up and go, except I wasn't entirely free: There was still the claim by the landlords that I owed them back rent. The lease had expired, but as we negotiated our differences Nathans remained open on a month-to-month agreement based on the terms of the expired lease, including the personal guaranty that made me liable for just about everything. Brendan remained adamant that the issue of back rent was off the table, but the landlords did not concur. Since the day in 2001 when their lawyer had first suggested I decrease the monthly rent by 30 percent, and my lawyers at the time directed me to do so, the amount of so-called debt had reached about $800,000. I did not have that kind of money. I owned my home, free and clear, and a few last antiques that didn't amount to much in value, but that was it. There was no other money. All savings, CDs, and stocks were gone.

Brendan, Jon Moss, and I had several meetings in which we agreed that the most critical issue before us was resolving any debt that attached to me under the personal guaranty, chiefly rent and taxes. Only then could I walk away a free woman. If the Halkias family didn't accept an agreement on the contested debt, and we went to court and I lost, then the only option would be a new lease that would enable me to operate the business and pay the debt over the years. Neither side wanted that. They wanted me out so they could sell their building. I envisioned a new lease as a prison sentence. While the negotiations went on, the Halkias family officially put the building on the market. Every commercial real estate broker in the city, or so it seemed, brought a client through to kick the tires: banks, retailers, phone stores. They sent surveyors and measured every square inch, but none made an offer the family would accept. Publicly I had to pretend we were staying open, but privately I knew the end was only a matter of time.

I SAID TO Jon, "You know we're going to close. We don't know exactly when but it will happen." He nodded. "We should have a party," I said. "I don't want it to be viewed as a closing party. In fact, I'm not keen on an official closing party. If we close—*when* we close—that party will be open to everyone, we'll just go until we turn the lights out. But for now, since it's 2009 and officially Nathans fortieth birthday year, let's have a smaller party to mark that milestone. It can be a happy occasion." He agreed. We posted it on the website and it sold out. The room filled with a mix of regulars, friends and family, including Martha, Vijay, and Spencer with his girlfriend, Courtney Prillaman.

In 2007 we'd had a similar party to celebrate the tenth anniversary of my ownership. On that occasion, too, it sold out. We set it up like *The Q&A Café,* but the tables were turned: A local television personality, Dave Statter, interviewed me. The guests included the city's popular new mayor, Adrian Fenty, who said nice words about Nathans and its legend in Washington. While dinner was served I sat on a barstool in the middle of the dining room and answered Dave's questions. Toward the end he asked if I missed Howard.

"Oh, every day."

What else could I say? The truth? Oh, God, no. A roomful of paying customers, drinking and making merry, who wanted to laugh and who certainly didn't want to hear the truth, not my truth. Who could handle that?

But had I been interviewed in 2009, at the party celebrating Nathans fortieth year, my answers might have surprised the customers.

I would have said, to even my own surprise, I missed Howard less and less. I could no longer instantly recall the sound of his voice. I visited his grave less often. Spencer and I talked about him, of course, but whole weeks would pass without mention of his name. The twelfth anniversary of his death arrived and we remembered it only late that evening. Along with missing him less, I was processing the anger more, but it was muddled up with regret, remorse, and disappointment. Publicly, I made excuses for him. He never meant to leave Spencer and me with a life of turmoil, debt, and uncertainty, but regardless, that's exactly what he did do.

The closer it came to Nathans' end the more clearly I saw the emotional landscape around me, especially what was behind; the widow's fog from the beginning of this journey had started to lift. I'd like to ask generals who have been to war if, as the end draws near, they start to reflect on past battles with new eyes. In making peace with the so-called "enemy," do they make peace with themselves, too? That's what was happening to me. My enemies weren't so much people as the questions I didn't want to answer and the anger I'd kept tamped down inside for too long.

Whether they were posed to me in front of an audience, or from a friend, or even inwardly from myself, there were important questions to answer. My friend Rachel Pearson asked, "Aren't you mad at Howard forever for hitting you?" Well, I was, but I made peace with that before he died. I mean, I fell apart at the time, but then with the help of therapy I put myself back together, and actually better than before. Howard never acted aggressively toward me again. I became whole and strong. When he died, though, he submitted me to a whole new type of abuse with his legacy of lies, the IRS, an endless stream of lawyers, and—worst of all—Nathans, the restaurant equivalent of a failed state.

I was asked if I was angry at the IRS. No, I could have been their poster child. I don't think of the IRS as warm and cuddly, but they didn't do wrong by me. Howard did wrong by them (and me), and they did right by me. I paid—and pay—my taxes. Was I mad at the landlords? Yes and no. Honestly, I was more frustrated. They didn't want me, trust me, understand me, or appreciate me, and they shut down every avenue I pursued to try to save Nathans, which was counterproductive because I had to save Nathans for all of us. With the crazy lease Howard had signed, and that the Halkias family held me to, I couldn't sell it. I had to keep it going, bailing it out, because it was all Spencer and I had. In their defense, the Halkias family didn't ask to be stuck with me, either. Howard had made that happen.

Anger is real, and it serves a purpose. It needs to be put out there and dealt with, because just like stress it can chip away at well-being. There was no bottom to my anger toward Howard, but just as it was time to cut Nathans loose to regain my freedom, it was time to cut the cord with Howard and my anger toward him. I did not want to carry it around. I was a sailor, I'd always been a sailor, and sailors know that an anchor slows and even stops the forward motion of the boat. I had two big anchors on me—Nathans and Howard—and they had to be let go if I was to find my wind and move forward toward whatever the future had in store. That, with considerable help from Brendan Sullivan, was the goal as we steered Nathans toward closing day.

UNBEKNOWNST TO ALL but a few people, for a couple of years I had been writing a column about Washington under a pseudonym. It was called "This Town"—it appeared in the monthly *Washington Life* magazine—and the name I used was "Michael Strange." The style of it was commentary, woven from my experiences and imagination, but while part of it was fiction, many of the tales I told were true. It was fun for me, a little bit of private literary michief as a distraction from the Nathans struggles. But it didn't pay and the anonymity began to be stifling. In fall 2007, a serendipitous event happened.

Two charming men from New York came to Washington and offered me a job. David Patrick Columbia and Jeff Hirsch owned a popular website called New York Social Diary, a compendium of the good life brilliantly varnished with David's perceptive, informed, and blunt view of the upper classes, present and past. David wrote a daily "Social Diary" column focused on New York, and Jeff put the site together, took photos, and collected columns from contributors that covered travel, food, home furnishings, real estate, art, openings, and shopping. I'd met David and Jeff earlier when David appeared for an interview at *The Q&A Café*. When they were back in town for a social event they stopped by Nathans to have lunch with me. Over dessert they made their pitch. "We'd like you to write a column about Washington for our site. You'd be perfect. Please do it." I hemmed and hawed. I was not a socialite, didn't have a whole lot of interest in social life, and was uncomfortable at parties.

"We'll pay you," David said.

"Okay, done," I replied.

In addition to the anonymous *Washington Life* column, I'd had my own personal blog for a few years. Swimming in Quicksand was a daily rant about my life, with occasional civic observations and thoughts on food, travel, and life in Washington. My readership was modest, maybe a thousand people on a good day. With New York Social Diary, I got a readership of six hundred thousand. My $250 a week salary was hardly a living wage, but my little column had a value greater than money: It was a chance to report and write and have a byline in the media—and in this case new media—which felt modern and forward. I was all about going forward.

Chapter 37

THE LAST DAYS of Nathans were chaotic but not a blur. My memories of them are indelible. I put away all the aggravations, frustrations, and anger, and instead focused on making the closure as special as possible for the bar's loving fans and loyal staff. In the end, as with all bars and restaurants, it was about the customers. They had made it, they had loved it, and they deserved the opportunity to say good-bye. That's what guided Jon and me as we made our decisions about when and how to close and when we'd make the fact public.

Even though Nathans' problems were long-term and complicated, its fate was in sync with the times. In spring 2009, Wall Street was on the ropes and the national economy was in turmoil. Home foreclosures and the closing of small businesses were becoming routine news. While Brendan and his law partner Stephen Sorensen were in the last stages of peaceably negotiating me out of any liabilities to the landlords, the Halkias family had their new real estate lawyer file an eviction action. It was exasperating. I mean, why? We were so close. For a week I dodged the process server, literally—sometimes in disguises, sometimes with him pounding on my front door—but he finally gave up and delivered the papers to Williams and Connolly. Brendan and Stephen were able to head off the eviction and finish the settlement, in which I agreed to pay a load of back property taxes—tens of thousands of dollars—and an assortment of debts that attached to me personally. I never paid any of the $800,000 back-rent claim, however. Brendan was good for his word on that. Getting out of Nathans cost me about $250,000, which I covered with a mortgage on my home. Thank God I owned it free and clear; using a mortgage made sense.

Typically when restaurants close, it's at midnight and a surprise to everyone: customers, staff, vendors, the bank. Again, because of the history of the place, and the customers and the staff, I didn't want to go out that way. It didn't feel right. Jon warned me there were risks in announcing in advance that we would close. "Everybody we owe money to will be pounding on the door." So what's new? We put the word out on Nathans' website two weeks before the scheduled closing date. Fortunately it got picked up quickly by the media, and word spread far and wide. That was important. I wanted everyone in the Washington area to know that now was the time to come in for that last beer, shot, plate of fresh fettuccine Alfredo, or basket of the great house-made potato chips—all those folks who had met at the bar, had their first date over a burger, or got engaged in the dining room. Or, for that matter, partied after hours till the sun came up.

What Jon had feared came true. Our bold public announcement got the attention of the District of Columbia's tax and revenue office. Did they freak out? Yes, they did. Nathans had an outstanding sales tax debt of $26,000, which we planned to pay promptly after closing with the enhanced profits we expected from the last two weeks. The tax office would not wait. They wanted the money, or they would close us down immediately. My mortgage had not gone through yet and there was no way to get our hands on that much money. When I mentioned the crisis in my daily blog, a reader suggested I ask for contributions of $100. "If 260 people each give you $100, which is not outlandish, you will have the money." I posted his message on the website and, in a scenario out of *It's a Wonderful Life,* customers began to pour through the front door with checks for $100. They even stopped Jon or me on the street to hand us checks. They mailed them from distant cities, sometimes with little notes mentioning how much Nathans had meant to them "back in the day." One very generous customer sent a check for $5,000, another sent one for $3,000, several others sent checks for $1,000, and quite a few contributed $500. The money came in so fast it was all Jon could do to get it across the street and into the bank account. The tax office granted us a brief stay of execution to see what we could raise. Within a few days we'd raised the $26,000, paid the tax, and got the reprieve that would keep the place open till its last "last call."

The final day and night, Sunday, July 12, 2009, Nathans was packed like it was New Year's Eve. Earlier that morning, in the wee hours, someone had driven a Ducati motorcycle into the bar, parked it, posed on it, and put the pictures on Facebook. Many of the barstools had walked out in the hands of souvenir hunters, along with all the menus. It was that kind of last day. Local television crews and newspaper and Web reporters were part of the throng that filled the bar. Spencer and I sat at the round table in the back dining room with his girlfriend, Courtney Prillaman, her parents, Martha, and a dear old friend and fellow widow, Sally Hosta. We sipped martinis and dug into our last baskets of chips and plates of pasta. I turned the music up loud, like the old days, when Howard would be the life of the after-hours party, whirling around with his sleeves rolled up, a mischievous grin lighting up his face. His was only one of the ghosts dancing in the back room that night, preparing to say good-bye.

Jon Moss and his girlfriend kept an eye on everyone, though not without savoring the moment. Jon and I were the only ones there who knew the remarkable series of events—and the hurdles crossed—that had got us to this night. I could see the relief in his eyes, too. The police came by but not to bother us. They presented me with an honorary Metropolitan Police badge. They looked at the crowd and said, "Have at it." Three bartenders hustled to slap fresh cocktails into the many outstretched hands, pouring down the inventory, eventually making drinks out of whatever was left on the shelves. For old times' sake, a few men defied the no-smoking law and lit up cigars. The jukebox was up as loud as it could go, but its hours were numbered. The rental company arrived before closing and pulled it off the wall. With and without music, couples danced in the middle of the barroom, at least as best they could in the crush. Several members of the staff circled around me with a tray of drinks and asked me to do a shot with them. "C'mon, Carol." It would be my last drink at Nathans. On its final night, Nathans was as it had been on its best nights—the most crowded, loudest, and wildest party in town.

Nathans wouldn't close until two o'clock Monday morning, but at midnight, like Cinderella, I headed for the door. With a few friends in tow, I walked from Nathans' front door out into the pleasant summer night. When the light turned green I crossed the iconic Washington intersection of Wisconsin and M, looked back, then turned and walked up the hill toward home.

Chapter 38

THE NATHANS BUILDING remained for sale but empty throughout the summer, fall, and winter of 2009 and into the spring of 2010. It wasn't a good time to put the building on the market. With the country suffering under the worst recession since the Great Depression, commercial real estate prices were following the economy down. The Halkias family kept dropping the price until finally they took it off the market altogether and looked for a new rental tenant. It was still empty in early 2011 but the spot was leased to reopen as an ice cream parlor franchise from New York.

Over lunch one day I said to Brendan Sullivan, "I need that building to reopen as something new. I'm eager for it. When I walk by now all I see is the wounded ruin that was Nathans. I want something in there that wipes out that memory." He understood. That's why soon after closing, when the city rudely took my only asset, the valuable liquor license, and arbitrarily gave it to the landlords, without even allowing us a hearing, we opted not to pursue it in court. Enough. It was the equivalent of having $100,000 pulled from my hands, but that's a measure of how much I wanted to move on. Debt was awful, but it was better than going back into the muck. The landlords wanted the license as a means to lure an occupant for the building.

"We'll go to court if you want," Brendan said. "We'll go with guns drawn and we'll win." Any court action would tie up the building for months, maybe years. He knew that and I knew that, but we also knew that any kind of court case would involve months of filings and motions and depositions. I didn't want that. For me or for anyone. I wanted Nathans to slip quietly beneath the waves and to rest in peace at the bottom of the sea.

For the first time that I could remember, I was utterly without a safety net. No job, no paycheck, no health insurance, and with a $500,000 mortgage on our house. Most of the mortgage money went to getting me out of Nathans, and the rest was used to pay tuition, buy food, and keep the lights on while I figured out the future. *The Q&A Café* relocated to the Georgetown Ritz Carlton Hotel, where I cut back to a once-a-month schedule. The new venue was a pleasure, and the loyal "lunch bunch," at least most of them, followed me there. The show continued to air every Friday evening on D.C. cable. The guests in my first year included the comedian and actress Alexandra Wentworth, journalist Gwen Ifill, director Oliver Stone, and the notorious White House gate-crashers Michaele and Tareq Salahi.

My New York Social Diary column got me out of the house to all kinds of events, small and large, exclusive or not, rubbing elbows with the power elite or the "drones" who really run the capital. I had one black cocktail dress and one black evening dress. I wore one or the other to every opening, dinner, or event I covered. No one noticed. I knew they wouldn't. My editors let me write about Washington as I saw it: how it really works, who the people are, and what goes on behind the headlines and the network news. It warmed my heart the first time I was introduced to someone as "Carol, who writes a column about Washington," and not as "the owner of Nathans."

Spencer and I settled into a new routine. He liked having Nathans out of our daily lives, even if it meant living on a very strict budget. We had the mortgage money and my income from the New York Social Diary and *The Q&A Café,* which meant not much. Like a married couple we squabbled about finances, but he got a job and worked every weekend and on days when he didn't have school. He got accepted at the college of his choice, which made us both proud. When he and Courtney broke up it made me sad, but there was nothing I could do. I thought, Well, I guess I'm going to have to get used to this. He's his own man with his own life.

My stress level dropped dramatically. I felt vaguely similar to what I imagined a person who'd come out of prison would feel like. Even my shrink noticed: how eagerly I needed to reconnect with simple pleasures; how I learned it was possible to have a completely good day, with no bad news; that I didn't need to be afraid. At first I felt I still had to stop at Nathans every day, or go to the bank, or call Jon Moss, but that faded. With each day I moved away from the nightmare and opened my mind and spirit to what might come next. I yearned for a job where I would be in charge and able to work hard, but also see tangible, positive results.

In the end, I knew that Sheldon Cohen had been totally right when he told me, over lunch after winning innocent spouse, that I should just give the government the keys and walk away from Nathans for good. I still rue that I ignored his advice, and it's why I never argued with Brendan Sullivan.

SEVERAL MONTHS AFTER Nathans closed I took down and opened the box of photos I'd packed up and sealed soon after Howard died. At first I slowly pulled out one picture at a time, examining each one quite closely, but after an hour I had dozens of them spread all over a large table, and eventually I was surrounded by a near mountain of photos that spanned twenty years of my life. There Howard was, frozen in time, and there I was, a relic of another era, riding on her magic carpet. The photos show me as cute, pretty, sometimes glamorous; always smartly dressed; laughing, smiling, in love. What they don't show is how clueless I was, which I see now quite clearly but thankfully without rancor or sadness. I thought to myself, Well, ignorance is bliss. I'd rather have knowledge and power.

In photo after photo, Spencer is the happiest little boy, having a good time with his happy parents. I look at him and see huge reserves of joy and wonder if that's what carried him through our bumpy journey, hoping the supply hasn't been run dry. Peccadilloes aside, he has a strong center. He's out of the nest now and will have to fly on his own.

And Howard? I look at the photos, and I don't see the man I thought I knew, but I also don't see a stranger. I've cut through the lies, and I know the man now. I know the real person. He's not a mystery to me. I see the truth behind the façade.

Add to this batch of photos all the family pictures from the last many years since Howard died, and it adds up to more than three decades of my life. They say pictures don't lie, but I wonder. These pictures don't tell the whole story. What they can't show, but what I know as sure as I know the ground I stand on, is that for twenty years I lived in a dream, followed by another ten years of nightmare. But the dream gave me a son, and without him I couldn't have survived the nightmare. Thanks to each other and our friends, we got through it.

Dear Readers

THE HARDCOVER OF this book was published in May 2011. A few months earlier, at my annual mammogram, I was diagnosed with breast cancer. Because it was caught early it was literally microscopic, stage zero, non-invasive DCIS (ductal carcinoma in situ). I was scared to death but felt blessed that it was caught when it was. There were tears and optimism. After consultation with doctors at the Washington Hospital Center I opted for a lumpectomy, followed by radiation and Tamoxifen. My last radiation treatment was five days before the book arrived in stores, five days before an appearance on the *Today* show. When my friends and I discussed this latest turn in my life, we decided that if I had coped with everything the last decade had handed me, I could cope with breast cancer. So far, I have. My next challenge was to reenter the workforce. Professionally, I'd been out of my natural habitat for more than a decade. Even though I had a strong resume as a journalist, it was out of date. During the previous twelve years, even with *The Q&A Cafe* going strong, I was essentially as "saloon owner." Could a woman my age still find meaningful employment in the American job market, which was on the ropes of the Great Recession? Would there be opportunities in journalism, especially in television, which in most instances has an obsession with youth? I was skeptical. I bought a new suit and a new pair of shoes, which became the official "job-hunting uniform." My rule was that I would apply to five jobs every day. It didn't matter what they were. I had to push myself out there. I surfed job websites and met with a head hunter (dispiriting, to say the least). I heard back on maybe three percent of my applications. I was genuinely open-minded and wide-ranging. For example, I applied for head of National Public Radio, explored becoming a medical foundation fundraiser, but I also applied for the position as administrative assistant for a group that represented tugboat captains. For one reason or another, they didn't materialize. I aimed for a crisis communications consultant position. I would soar in that industry. But after five interviews with one top-flight company, which even brought me to New York to meet the brass, they made the painfully familiar decision to "go in a different direction."

In an almost random way, I reached out to an acquaintance, the editor of Washington's most enduring monthly magazine, the *Washingtonian*. My email to Garrett Graff asked if he was looking for freelance writers. He invited me to breakfast, to which I arrived in my job-hunting uniform. We had a good talk, and he asked me to consider joining them in a full-time staff position. As the Brits say, I was gobsmacked. I never told Garrett this, but I left that meeting full of joy. We had some negotiating to do, but the unbelievable had happened: I could return to my professional home, to journalism, my wheelhouse, to my natural habitat, to the career I'd had to abandon all those years ago. I began work in October 2011. I still have my job-hunting suit, but I haven't worn it since. I considered this the happy ending to my book.

What also brought me happiness was learning of Nathans employees who went on to other jobs, especially Jon Moss, the manager, who had stuck by me at the end. He became the operations manager for Georgetown Cupcake, the chain-cupcake phenomenon in the hit cable-television show *DC Cupcakes*. Jon and I remain friends. We get together for meals. We talk about the old days. We shake our heads. We laugh. Brendan Sullivan remains a friend and one of the nation's top defense attorneys. His most recent client is Rupert Murdoch. My sister-in-law, Martha Kumar, continues to go to the White House every day and pursue her scholarly observations of the presidency.

Spencer did his freshman year at Georgetown University, and then transferred to the University of Texas in Austin because he preferred to attend school in a town where he didn't grow up. He wanted a big state school and an environment that wasn't at all like Washington. He got that with UT. He's in their well-regarded advertising program. As for me, I'm happy about his new school. It gives me an excuse to visit Austin, an all-round excellent town. We've made some memorable road trips driving to and from Texas.

Since the publication of *Innocent Spouse,* I've heard from a lot of incredible people who've had their own hard roads to travel, many of them harder than mine. My message is always the same: You can get through it. Finding your way out of heartbreak, a financial morass, or a business nightmare won't necessarily be easy, but it can be done. And love will still be there, too.

Carol Ross Joynt
September 2012
Washington, D.C.

Acknowledgments

EVERY WRITER WITH a story to tell harbors the fantasy that an agent and publisher will feel the same way too. For me, that agent was Laney Katz Becker with the Markson Thoma Agency in New York. In more ways than can be adequately expressed, she made this book happen. I wish every author an advocate like Laney.

The dream was complete when Suzanne O'Neill at Crown picked up the book. It was a pleasure to work with Suzanne and the remarkable team at Crown. I'm especially grateful to the fine work of copy editor Michelle Daniel and the helpfulness and good eye of Anna Thompson.

Writing a memoir, by its nature, leads an author into the boggy turf of one's own life. By the third draft the story can get lost in a bit of a warren. At that point William McPherson, a writer's editor, helped me to see what did and didn't need to be there. Thank you, Bill, for your sharp eye. And to Aubrey Sarvis for all those La Chaumiere lunches, where he patiently listened to Bill and me.

What Spencer and I went through over thirteen years was often tough going. We survived because of each other, but also due to the care and attention of so many. Lawyers don't usually get thanked at the top, but special and enduring gratitude go to Sheldon Cohen and Miriam Fisher; Brendan Sullivan, Stephen Sorensen, Victoria Radd Rollins, and Bob Shuaghnessy—you got me freedom. You are why young people should want to be lawyers. Also at Williams and Connolly, thank you to the very able Rhonda Meadows. A special thank-you to Nelson Deckelbaum and David Deckelbaum, and to Gary Leiber, who also gave me important legal advice.

The doctors at the Washington Hospital Center, particularly Michael Hockstein and Peter Levit, are among my heroes. Even as Howard's luck ran out, Michael and Peter continued to try everything to save him.

Harry Shearer and Judith Owen—thank you for always being there. You are family.

I'm sorry Vito Zappala didn't live to see this book. He would have been pleased.

There's a special place in my heart for the dozens of people who listened to me, danced with me, dined with me, drank with me, counseled me, who gave me breaks, kept me in mind, who tossed me a bone, and gave me friendship. Survival wouldn't have been possible without them.

To the hundreds of people who worked at Nathans and its thousands upon thousands of customers, keep the happy memories; they are Nathans best legacy.

Jon Moss, thank you. I could not have made it to and through the end without you.

Howard, wherever you are, no one else may get this, but I know you understand.

Now, we move on.